THE MILLENNIUM TIME TAPESTRY

PINDAR PRESS

Millennium circle and all digital illustrations by Liz Bailey

Book design by Izabella A. Jaskierny
Produced by Pindar Press

Library of Congress Catalog Card Number: 99-75217
ISBN 0-918223-04-0

Lithography by Quad/Graphics, Inc.
Paper by Champion International
100 lb. Savvy Matte

Published in 1999 by Pindar Press, New York

First Edition

The dawn of a new millennium
is a time of unbridled imagination.
To have any hope of understanding what promises to be,
it is important to reflect upon the past.

The Millennium Time Tapestry™ commemorates history "in the round"
with an artfully layered tableau of 10 centuries.
This digital painting incorporates some 400 images of archival art,
each of which stands alone yet simultaneously fuses with all the others
to form a unique perspective of human endeavor
throughout the past millennium.

The book is designed to amplify these images with detailed explanations
of the people, places and events represented in the tapestry.
Schematic diagrams identify selected images.
An extensive timeline of significant events
provides sweeping coverage of 1,000 years.

In addition, "Day to Day" captures a "slice of life" from
each century, examining significant cultural or economic conditions,
while "Contemporary Philosophies" explores how thought was evolving
around the world and, to some extent, who we were and how each of us
in a global sense came to be what we are today.

CONTENTS

PREFACE

In truth, history writers create history as much as they record it. In a work that covers events throughout the world over a thousand years, it is clearly impossible to record every occurrence. In point of fact, it is impossible even to show all the important aspects of any single event. Not only must the author choose which events to write about, but also which aspects of those subjects to discuss. Through these choices of what will be remembered or forgotten, emphasized or repressed, the historian becomes as important a part of history as the events themselves. In the end, the writer is really telling a story from a particular point of view, one that, like any viewpoint, is only partially truthful.

This book is no different, and it is important for the reader to understand the perspective from which the text has been written. In some ways, I have depicted the second millennium as the gradual rise to prominence of the Western world. At the beginning of the millennium, Europe is somewhat of a chaotic backwater; by the end, its culture, technology, and politics have transformed the world. Consequently, as the centuries progress, the text gradually devotes more and more attention to Western events as their global repercussions become more significant. Other regions and cultures, discussed more extensively earlier in the book, are by necessity explored less fully in the later chapters.

While the overall structure of the text reflects this gradual shift in focus, the individual entries take on a particular point of view in describing events and persons. Considerable effort has been made to highlight aspects of important historical events often overlooked by popular opinion. Thus, I have not shied away from suggesting that, for all his heroism, Richard the Lionhearted was a bad monarch or that, for all his glory, Louis XIV was really a megalomaniac who set France on its inevitable course to revolution. Of course, adopting this myth-breaking attitude only tells part of the story. It is my hope that, by highlighting the untold part, I can help the reader construct a more complete framework in his or her own mind.

Matthew Hurff

Author

1 Handwritten manuscripts are decorated with elaborate illuminated letters *1000s*
2 Toltec sculptures are made in Mesoamerica *1000s*
3 Typical clothing of maidens in Europe features the kirtle *1000s*
4 The Temple Visvanatha is built in India *c. 1000*
5 Asian languages and literature flourish *1000s*
6 Danish Vikings land in Britain *1003*
7 Lady Godiva rides naked through her town *1040*
8 Venetian nobility popularize the fork *1050*
9 William the Conqueror invades England *1066*
10 Work begins on the Bayeux Tapestry *1067*
11 Construction begins on St. Etienne, the first Romanesque cathedral *1068*
12 China's Shen Kua invents the navigational compass *1086*
13 The University of Bologna becomes the first to confer degrees *1088*
14 Gondolas are mentioned for the first time in Venetian records *1094*
15 First Crusade sets forth for the Holy Land *1095-1096*
16 European dress is influenced by Eastern styles brought home by Crusaders *1097*

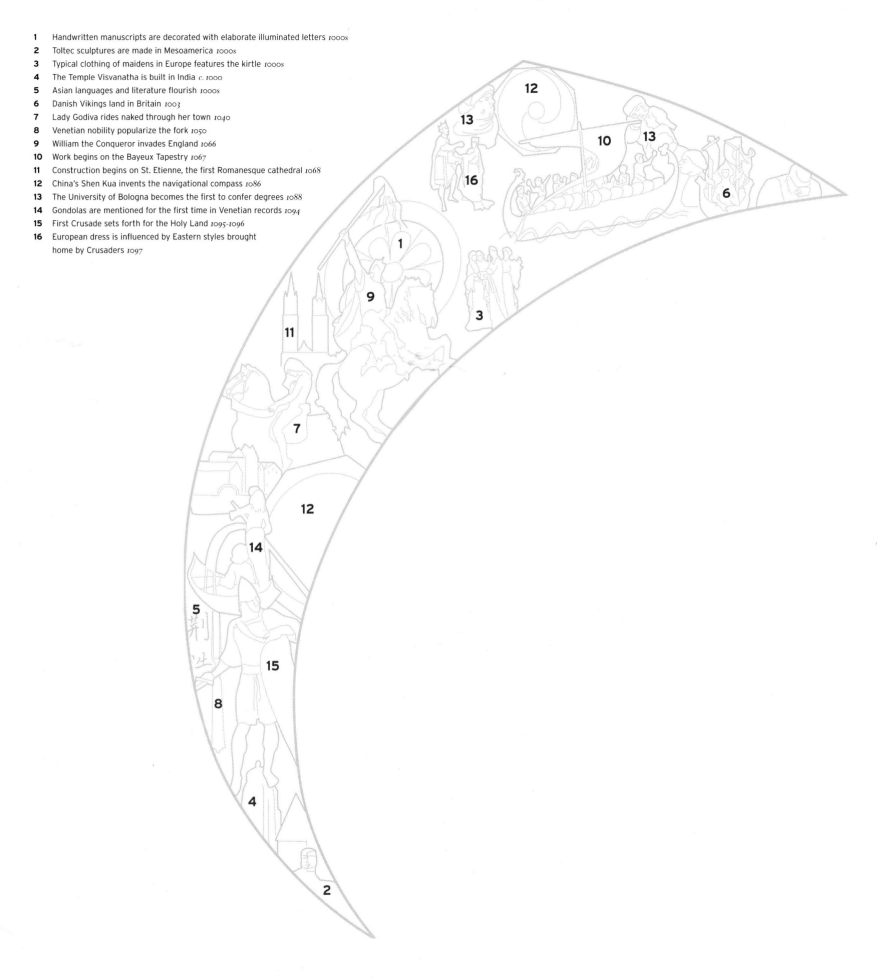

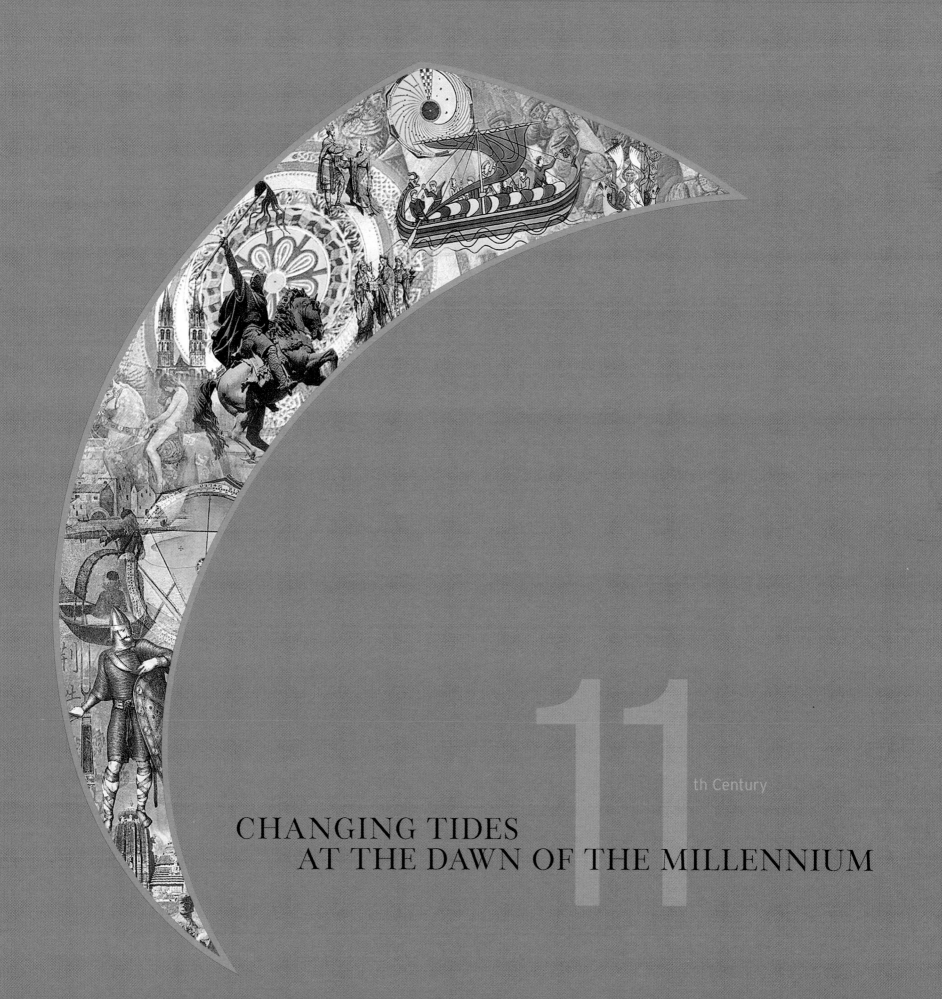

11
th Century

CHANGING TIDES
AT THE DAWN OF THE MILLENNIUM

CHANGING TIDES AT THE DAWN OF THE MILLENNIUM

Reversing fortune is the constant tale of the second millennium's first 100 years. Where political and social chaos had reigned unchecked in the 900s, as it had in China, lasting forms of government and culture suddenly emerged. Conversely, regions like Europe and Mesoamerica, which had experienced relative stability in the 10th century, now were faced with new realities of fluidity and change. Even within the externally stable Islamic world, new internal borders and political structures developed, with newcomers such as the Seljuk Turks taking away the power of older, more established peoples. In Central America, venerable civilizations like the Maya and the Moche were overrun or eclipsed by the rising Toltec and Chimu nations, who were in turn overcome by the Aztecs and the Incas.

Perhaps the trend is best exemplified in Europe and Eurasia, where a Viking civilization at the height of its expansion in 1000 had all but vanished by mid-century. At the turn of the millennium, Nordic tribes lived in locations as remote from one another as Newfoundland and Kiev. As traders and raiders, they plied their longboats on all the oceans and rivers between the Atlantic Ocean and the Caspian Sea. Scandinavian merchants could be found in Basra and Baghdad, even as their attacking cousins terrorized the coasts of England, France, Spain, Italy, and Africa. Viking soldiers and mercenaries served in the imperial guard of the Byzantine emperor, conquered parts of Ireland, and battled with the Eskimo natives of Greenland.

By 1050, however, the Vikings were gone, genetically absorbed by the indigenous people amongst whom they had settled. While they lived on as the Normans of France, the Russians of central Eurasia, or the blond-haired, blue-eyed inhabitants of northern Spain, their cultural and political ties to Scandinavia faded. In their wake, a new generation of warrior people arose, continuing the legacy of migrant invasion left behind by the suddenly absent Nordic tribes. In particular, the Normans, who would establish kingdoms of conquest in Italy, France, and England before 1100, made sure that, even if the Viking world was slipping away, the constant European fear of invasion by seaborne marauders was not.

1000S: **European, handwritten monastic manuscripts** are decorated with elaborate illuminated letters. (1)

1000: **Viking settlers, led by Thorvald Eriksson,** establish a settlement in Newfoundland. Branching out from colonies in Greenland, Eriksson's group is unable to establish themselves in America, and the new community lasts little more than a year. In time, the Greenland settlements will fail as well. The high watermark of Nordic expansion, manifested in Eriksson's Canadian village, passes quickly.

1000: **Iceland's parliament votes to adopt Christianity** as the state religion. The conversion of Nordic tribes to Christianity is one of the chief causes of their absorption into Latin European cultures.

1000: **Chinese inventors perfect gunpowder.** The Chinese will use the mix of sulfur, potassium nitrate, and charcoal for a variety of purposes, including fireworks, rockets, artillery, and general explosives.

c. 1000: **The folk epic "Beowulf"** becomes the first major piece of literature written in Old English. The development of written literary traditions in languages other than Latin will prove to be a driving force in the shaping of Western culture.

when they themselves are overshadowed by the growing power of the Incas.

c. 1000: **The Indian mathematician Sridhara** realizes the importance of zero, greatly expanding the scope and utility of mathematics.

c. 1000: **Typical clothing of maidens in Europe** features **the kirtle,** a long, loose-fitting dress that conceals the figure and has large sleeve openings. A tight undershirt prevents excess skin from being unduly exposed by the loose sleeves. (3)

c. 1000: **The Temple Visvanatha is built in Khajuraho, India.** The temple, composed of a long meeting hall for prayer and a tower to house its deity, is a beautiful example of Indian religious architecture. The carefully carved stone of the temple proper sits on a base or plinth of rough-cut stone, just as the refinement of the deity rests above the crudeness of corporeality. (4)

1000S: **Asian languages** and literature flourish. (5)

1000S: **Buddhism and Hinduism continue to spread** through Southeast Asia. Slowly expanding out from the

Klutans. The Sung dynasty returned order and stability to China by weakening the authority of local lords and high-ranking military officers. While weakening the army helped bring domestic order, it also reduced China's ability to defend itself against foreign aggression. Unable to repel the Klutan invaders, the Sung buy them off with an annual tribute of 100,000 ounces of silver and 200,000 rolls of silk.

1006: **The Islamic world continues to expand** as Muslim invaders push back indigenous cultures and settle in northwestern India.

1009: **In Jerusalem, the Church of the Holy Sepulcher is sacked by Muslim conquerors.** The collapse of small, independent Christian kingdoms in the Holy Land, combined with the continual erosion of Byzantine territory in Anatolia throughout the 11th century, establishes undisputed Islamic control in the Middle East. With the brief interruption of the First Crusade, Muslim hegemony in the region will remain intact for several centuries.

1009: **Arab astronomer Ibn Junis, author of the "Hakimite Tables," dies.** The tables, which chart star positions throughout the year, are of immense aid to Muslim sailors in calculating course and latitude. The sophistication of Ibn's work,

> "All goods are good through a single being,
> which is good through itself…"
>
> S T. A N S E L M

c. 1000: **Southern Spain becomes the spiritual center of Judaism.** The religious and social tolerance of Moorish culture provides a haven for Jewish settlers in a Western world that is becoming progressively more anti-Semitic.

c. 1000: **The Toltecs replace the Mayans as the dominant people of Mesoamerica.** In decline for more than 100 years, the Mayans slowly fade away as the center of power shifts northward to the Toltec capital at Tollan. Adopting Mayan religion and infusing it with their own traditions of secular culture and military aggression, the Toltecs build a powerful empire that will dominate Central America for the next 150 years. (2)

c. 1000: **The Chimu rise to power** in the western coastal regions of South America. Eclipsing the failing civilization of the Moche, Chimu society will control the region politically and economically until the 15th Century,

Indian subcontinent, Buddhism in particular, already introduced into China and Japan, also will become a dominant religion of Siam and Indonesia.

1002: **Almanzer, Caliph of Cordoba, dies.** With his death, Islamic presence in Spain slowly begins to wane. Over the next 500 years, Christian kingdoms will expand southward, driving the Moors completely out of Iberia in 1492.

1003: **Danish Vikings land in Britain, conquering most of England by 1013.** The kingdoms that remain under Saxon control do so only by agreeing to pay an annual tribute to the new settlers. By 1035, however, a confusing series of successions will return control of the island to a Saxon monarchy, and the Danes gradually are absorbed into the general population. (6)

1004: **Sung China becomes a tributary** to the Tungusic

which will not be matched in the West for centuries, demonstrates the current superiority of Islamic scientists and philosophers over their Latin contemporaries.

1010: **The Li dynasty finally brings order to the land of Annam in modern Vietnam.** After successfully expelling Chinese overlords in the 10th century, Annam's people fell into civil war while trying to determine who should lead the freed nation. With the rise of the Li to unchallenged power in Annam, roads and canals are built, a central government established, and agriculture improved. Like most nations in Southeast Asia, Li society is a balance of resistance to and adoption of Chinese culture. Chinese models of government, religion (Mahayana Buddhism), art, and architecture are modified to coexist with Annam customs, dress, and animistic beliefs.

c. 1015: **Japanese literature flourishes within the Heian Court.** Sei Shonagon completes her famous "Pillow Book," a

revealing diary of daily life in the Imperial precinct, just as fellow female courtier Murasaki Shikibu writes "The Tale of Genji." The first modern novel, "The Tale of Genji" skillfully portrays human character while symbolically exploring its deeper Buddhist themes.

1022: **The Synod of Pavia insists on the rigorous celibacy of priests.** Catholic priests who have been married are stripped of their religious offices. Along with the Pope's refusal to accept the religious authority of the Byzantine emperor, the Orthodox church's disagreement with the Catholic church over celibacy eventually becomes one of the major dividing forces of the Great Schism.

1031: **Ibn al-Bawwab,** great calligrapher and inventor of the cursive rayhani and muhaqqaq Arabic scripts, dies.

1032: **In Venice, Doge Dominico Flabanico** establishes a system of balanced oligarchy in the city's government. By preventing powerful individual families from abusing civil authority, the new system provides Venice with the internal stability it will need to become a great empire at the end of the century.

1033: **Turkish Sultan Mahmud of Ghazna dies.** The Persian ruler has led 17 invasions of northern India over the last 30 years. These campaigns, while collecting loot and firmly establishing Islamic presence in India, cement a relationship of hatred between invading Muslims and indigenous Hindus that has continued unabated for 975 years.

1040: **Duncan, king of Scotland, is assassinated by**

1042: **Edward the Confessor is crowned King of England.** More pious than regal, Edward's chief accomplishment will be overseeing the construction of Westminster Abbey, the site where all future English monarchs will be coronated. Unable to control his Saxon subjects in England and personally loyal to the Normandy in which he was raised, Edward leaves the balance of power in his kingdom uncertain when he dies childless in 1065. Although he will pass the throne to the Saxon Harold Godwin on his deathbed, Edward's earlier promises to make William the Conqueror king will open the door for the Norman invasion of 1066, spelling the end of Saxon rule in the British Isles.

1043-1070: **St. Mark's Cathedral is constructed in Venice** as a symbol of national pride and religious independence. The building's Byzantine style subtly reveals Venice's connection to the East and its complete unwillingness to take sides in the constant power struggles between the Papal States and the Holy Roman Empire. These qualities of religious neutrality and Eastern affiliation will help Venice develop into the greatest Mediterranean trade empire of the 11th and 12th centuries.

C. 1050: **The Hoodo Pavilion,** part of the Byodo-in Temple in Uji, Japan, is completed. The sweeping rooflines of the building, heavily influenced by Chinese architecture, earn it the nickname "Phoenix Hall." Dedicated to Amida Buddha, the hall points to the growing strength of Buddhist populist sects in Japan.

1050: **The astrolabe,** an Arab invention that greatly eases the calculation of latitude, is introduced to Europe. The abil-

complaints, the underlying cause of the division is one of political power and policy. Orthodox bishops refuse to acknowledge the Pope as anything more than a regular bishop, while the Pope declines to accept the authority of the Byzantine emperor over the Christian church.

1060: **Moses ibn Ezra,** one of the greatest Hebrew poets and critics, is born in Spain. Under Islamic rule, Jewish culture thrives in Iberia. Ezra's poems, some of which include the earliest examples of secular Hebrew poetry, reflect the sophistication and depth of the culture that later Christian monarchs will expel from Spain.

1061: **The Normans, a people of northern France descended from the Vikings,** overtake the Italian island of Messina. Inheritors of the Viking tradition, these adventuresome Norman lords and warriors will establish kingdoms in Sicily and southern Italy and conquer the last pockets of Byzantine territory in Italy by 1071.

1064: **The Seljuks conquer Armenia; the Magyars conquer Belgrade.** Facing stiffening resistance from the Holy Roman Empire in the West, Magyar nomads, long the terror of the Latin world, turn their attention to the Balkan possessions of a Byzantine Empire greatly weakened by Seljuk offensives.

1066: **William the Conqueror's Norman army defeats the**
⑨ **Saxons at the Battle of Hastings;** William is promptly crowned king of England. An invading Viking army from Denmark had failed to defeat the Saxons a few weeks earlier, but they did succeed in spreading English resources thin,

---

"Let those who have been accustomed unjustly to wage private warfare against the faithful now against the infidels …"
P O P E   U R B A N   I I ,   C A L L I N G   F O R   T H E   C R U S A D E S

Macbeth. The murderous lord rules Scotland until his own unnatural death in 1057 and becomes the inspiration for Shakespeare's Renaissance play of the same name. Macbeth eventually will be defeated by Malcolm at Dunsinane.

1040: **A reputedly naked Lady Godiva rides a horse**
⑦ **through her hometown.** Wife of the earl of Mercia, Godiva had asked her husband to lower the taxes levied on his vassals, which he consented to do on the condition that she streak on horseback. Apparently, she does so, but since the town's occupants remain indoors out of respect, no one can say for sure.

1042: **The Seljuk Turks become the dominant force in the Middle East.** Gaining control of the Holy Land and driving the Byzantine armies out of modern Turkey, the Seljuks eventually force the Byzantine emperor to beg Rome for assistance. In response, the Vatican will organize the First Crusade in 1095.

ity to determine latitude with accuracy is a boon to Western navigation, making more ambitious voyages of trade and exploration possible.

1050: **Polyphony begins to replace Gregorian chanting** as the standard in religious singing. The birth of polyphonic singing marks the beginning of distinctive Western music and composition.

1050: **The two-pronged fork** gradually evolves into the prin-
⑧ cipal eating utensil of Western Europeans. Invented by the Romans and used throughout the early Middle Ages as a serving utensil, the fork is popularized as tableware by the Venetian nobility. During the course of the century, it replaces the two pointing knives that had been the standard instruments of Europeans too refined to eat with their hands.

1054: **The Roman and Orthodox churches formally divide in what becomes known as the Great Schism.** Although disagreements over protocol and religious belief are cited as

leaving the kingdom weak and exhausted when William lands. While the Nordic failure to conquer England in 1066 signifies the end of Scandinavian dominance in northern Europe, Norman success in the same endeavor marks the ascendance of the Vikings' natural successors.

1067: **Norman artisans begin the Bayeux Tapestry in cel-**
⑩ **ebration of the conquest of England.** The 70 scenes of the narrative work, telling the story of William's just taking of his rightful crown from the wicked Saxon usurper Harold, reveal fairly intimate details of the distinctive dress, habits, and daily lives of 11th-century Normans and Saxons.

1067: **Shen Tsung, the new emperor of the Sung dynasty, institutes sweeping reform in China's government.** Perhaps one of the first modern "big governments," his administration grants low-interest loans to farmers, increases the supply of hard currency to acknowledge a developing money economy, introduces a graduated tax scale, and uses government trade in private markets to help stimulate economic growth.

CONTEMPORARY PHILOSOPHIES

CHRISTIAN PLATONISM

Christian theologians found an unlikely inspiration in the pagan philosophy of ancient Greece

The dramatic success of Christianity as a religion of conversion has rested in part on its ability to manipulate foreign cultural elements to its own purposes. It is no accident that Christmas is celebrated at the time of the winter solstice—the intentional confusion of the birth of Jesus with the return of the sun greatly aided Christian missionaries in converting the pagans of northern Europe.

Against the more urbane cultures of the Mediterranean, however, Christian missions found that they needed to bring more sophisticated intellectual weapons to bear on a highly educated populace. The indigenous belief they found most convenient to their purposes, the school of philosophy founded by the Greek thinker Plato, emerged as the primary template of Christian justification in the 2nd Century. Until the reintroduction of Aristotle to Europe in the 12th century, Christian Platonism served as the primary philosophical current of the Latin world.

Modified by theologians like Boethius and Augustine, Plato's separation of ideal form and its imperfect physical manifestation evolved into the division between the lower body and the higher soul. Christian Platonists believed that the human spirit, existing on a higher plane than the body, was above its influence.

This conclusion had two important consequences. First, if the body could not influence the soul, then sin stemmed solely from the soul's imperfection. Consequently, the soul was incapable of achieving its own salvation. Only the divine grace of God could redeem the inherently flawed spirit. Second, the senses, as an extension of the physical body, could provide no enlightenment to the soul. Showing only the superficial events of the physical world, sensory information could not offer the spirit any higher understanding.

Under such a belief system, scientific culture withered. Since synthetic revelation could not be garnered from the senses, scientific observation was pointless. In time, Plato's subjugation of the actual in favor of the ideal was blended by Christians with other, more actively anti-corporeal sources. Ultimately, this mixture generated an outright hostility toward the human body. Physical experience came to be seen only as a temptation of the imperfect soul, a distraction from the hope of receiving divine grace. To avoid the confusing pleasures of the physical world, many Latin Christians would punish their bodies, subjecting themselves to the discomfort of hair shirts, flogging, or, in extreme circumstances, self-mutilation. Even though Platonic theologians believed that the Earth, as a creation of God, was inherently good, the philosophical system ultimately encouraged a rejection of the material world.

Crusader

1068: **The beginning of construction on St. Etienne Cathedral in Caen** marks the birth of Romanesque architecture in Normandy. Based on better understandings of structural load and stone vaulting, the new construction methods allow not only buildings of unprecedented size, but also ceilings of stone, greatly reducing the risk of fire associated with wooden roof structures.

1071: **Constantine the African** brings ancient Greek medical knowledge to Europe after a 500-year exile. During the Middle Ages, Greek medicine was all but lost to the Latin world and was preserved only by the diligence of Byzantine and Islamic scholars.

1072: **The Chinese poet Ou Yang Hsiu dies.** One of the finest masters in the Chinese technique of mixing verse and prose, Ou particularly will be remembered for his stories about the Tang dynasty of the distant past. His creative exploration of history, used as a means to define and characterize contemporary society and culture, typifies much Chinese art and literature that will be produced throughout the millennium.

1073: **Hildebrand of Soana is declared Pope Gregory VII in Rome.** Although his papacy will be marred by political chaos as he struggles with the German Holy Roman Emperor, Gregory's religious tenure will be one of the most important and influential in the history of the church. Determined to restore spiritual authority and autonomy to the church, he will work with some success to extricate it from the control of secular feudalism. In 1074, he will enforce the Synod of Pavia by excommunicating married priests. In 1075, his "Dictatus papae" will declare the supreme sovereignty of the papacy over the entire world. While the immediate impact of these declarations will be restricted by military setbacks and the fallout of the Great Schism, Gregory's vision and ideals will help to define the goals and aspirations of the papacy throughout the rest of the millennium.

1077: **St. Anselm of Canterbury writes "Monologion,"** one of the first Latin texts to argue the existence of God through philosophical reason. Anselm's thesis, which contends that all goodness must come from a supreme goodness (God), is interesting in that it demonstrates the growing need of Western religion to justify itself in terms of the secular traditions of Western philosophy.

1082: **As a reward for helping to limit the expansion of Italian Norman kingdoms** into Byzantine territories, the Byzantine emperor grants an exclusive trading contract to the city-state of Venice. Although the two powers will experience a severe falling out at the end of the 12th century, by that time Venice will have established a vast trading empire in the Eastern Mediterranean, granting it a virtual monopoly on all European trade with the Eastern world.

1086: **Chinese inventor Shen Kua develops the navigational compass.** In conjunction with Arab inventions like the astrolabe, the compass enables navigators at sea to calculate their course with great accuracy. With the new confidence that precise information gives, sailors begin to chart routes farther and farther away from the coast and into the open ocean.

DAY TO DAY:
POETRY AND LIFE IN THE HEIAN COURT OF IMPERIAL JAPAN

For Japanese courtiers, poetry was an essential means of communication

'**M**ore than a cuckoo's song she went out to hear," wrote 24-year-old Sei Shonagon, 48 hours after she had taken an excursion outside the Imperial palace during the rainy fifth month of the Japanese year. Having been called on by the Empress Sakado to produce a poem reflecting upon the adventures she and the other ladies-in-waiting had sought, Sei had initially demurred, explaining that one must only write poetry when in the proper mood, and that such a mood escaped her.

Perhaps it was the day itself that sapped Sei's creative energy. The fifth day of the fifth month, the date in question was known as the Iris Festival, so described because iris was hung from the buildings, its mugwort decorating the rooftops. Iris also was woven into the hair and attached to swords, and throughout the day horse races and archery contests were held both inside and outside the palace. These traditional activities all were in an effort to ward off evil spirits believed to be active throughout the month. Furthermore, the fifth month was the anniversary of the suicide of Ch'u Yuan; evil spirits and suicidal poets seemed a poor backdrop against which to compose poetry.

Earlier in the day, a four-seat, ox-drawn carriage had pulled the female courtiers through the gates of the Imperial precinct and out into the city avenues, which neatly divided the city's population according to social rank. Passing a field where officers were playing archery, the ladies proceeded to the home of Sei's uncle, where they relished hearing the singing of some cuckoos and snacked on the rustic fare of husked corn freshly prepared by five servant girls.

Travelling on to the more prestigious fifth ward, the courtiers visited with Captain Funiwara, cousin to the Empress, but finally returned to the palace with no poetry to show. As the Empress continued to cajole the ladies for verse, a poem arrived, sent by Sei's cousin. "Would that of this journey I had heard. So had my heart been with you when you sought the cuckoo's song." Still uninspired to write, Sei was gently reassured by another courtier that an unaddressed poem required no response.

After two days, Sei finally wrote her brief poem, explaining to the Empress her resentment at being commanded to write at another's whim.

Poetry served as an underpinning to the daily rituals of the Heian courtiers, whose lives revolved around aesthetic accomplishment. Typical poetry used natural elements, such as the cuckoo, to describe human occurrences. As a social interaction, poetry was written much as a letter would be, with the expectation of a response. Many a love affair was kindled through poetry, for any woman worth loving was expected to write beautifully.

"Immerse your heart in pleasure and joy, and by the bank a bottle drink of wine"

MOSES IBN EZRA

1088: **The University of Bologna becomes the first educational institution to confer a degree.** Over the preceding 100 years, the school had developed from a collection of tutors and students into a genuine school of law with licensed professors, student housing, and tuition costs subsidized by the Holy Roman Emperor.

1090: **The first mechanical clock, driven by water power, is built in China.** Over the next 900 years, the clock will prove to be one of the dominant instruments in producing a global understanding of the world contrary to common experience. Local time will be replaced by time zones, days will begin and end at certain hours regardless of the sun, and the clock will turn time into a monolithic, objective experience for most of humanity.

1094: **Gondolas** are mentioned for the first time in Venetian records. The 32-foot-long, flat-bottomed boat, with its distinctive high prow, becomes an international symbol of the great maritime state.

1094: **Spanish knight Rodrigo Diaz de Vivar, known as "El Cid,"** successfully leads his troops in an assault on the city of Valencia. Strictly concerned with the accumulation of his own personal wealth and power, El Cid moves skillfully through the complex political world of Spain, smoothly changing his loyalties among the various Christian and Islamic rulers as the moment suits. When he finally finds himself alienated from all the competing factions, he storms Valencia and makes it the seat of his own private kingdom, which he rules until his death in 1099. A man of selfish interest, limited vision, and ultimately minimal influence on the development of Spain, Diaz nonetheless will become a national hero and a cult icon on the basis of his undisputed brilliance as a field general.

1095-1096: **The First Crusade sets forth for the Holy Land.** On the surface a simple religious war, the Crusades prove to be a complex political affair for all Christian powers involved. Desperate for help in fighting back the Seljuks, the Byzantine emperor had to swallow his pride and ask the Pope for help. Pope Urban II agrees to raise support, not so much for the weak promise of being recognized as the religious leader of the Orthodox church, but rather because he hopes to develop his international power in Europe by becoming the leader of a multinational movement. In turn, the kings and soldiers who do the actual fighting are inspired more by a hope for adventure and booty than a sense of religious duty. Despite the lack of sincere purpose, the First Crusade is temporarily successful in its nominal goal of driving the Turks out of Palestine. After defeating the Turks at the Battle of Antioch in 1098, the Crusaders advance on Jerusalem, which they recapture in 1099.

1097: **Patterns of dress in Europe are altered** by an influx of Eastern styles brought home by Crusaders returning from the Holy Land. Arriving with silk and damask in large volumes, the returning soldiers inspire new fashions. Wealthy men trade in course trousers and shirts for silk stockings, knee-length tunics, and heavy capes, often lined with fur. Both sexes add tight waist belts and sleeves to their outfits, giving their dress a more shaped look than previous fashion had proscribed.

1098: **A large population of Jews migrates from Western Europe to Poland,** forming the Ashkenazic branch of Judaism. In Poland, a territory beyond the reach of the Holy Roman Empire, the Jews find an environment of tolerance that does not exist in the Latin world. Although subjected to cyclical patterns of hardship and xenophobia, Polish Jews will flourish for more than 800 years, thriving until they are all but annihilated by the Nazis during World War II.

BIBLIOGRAPHY AND FURTHER READING:

Joel Colton and R.R. Palmer, A History of the Modern World, 5th ed., Alfred A. Knopf, New York, 1978, pp. 49-69.

Horst de la Croix and Richard Tansey, Gardener's Art Through the Ages, 8th ed., Harcourt Brace Jovanovich, New York, 1986, pp. 458-461, 470-471, 548-577.

Chandice L.Goucher, Charles A. LeGuin, and Linda Linda A. Walton. In the Balance: Themes in Global History, Vol. 2, McGraw-Hill, Boston, 1998, pp. 468-480, 528-536, 555-557, 562-570.

Goetz, Philip W., ed., The Encyclopedia Britannica 15th ed., Encyclopedia Britannica, Inc., Chicago, 1990. vol. 6 pp. 216-217, 222.

Grun, Bernard. The Timetables of History, Simon and Schuster, New York, 1979, pp. 198-220.

Hanes III, William Travis, editor. World History: Continuity and Change, Holt, Rinehart, and Winston, Austin, TX, 1997, pp. 330-339, 349-350, 360-379, 418-441.

Janson, H.W., History of Western Art, 3rd ed., Prentice Hall Abrams, Englewood Cliffs, NJ, 1986, pp. 391-463.

McGreal, Ian P., "St. Anselm of Canterbury," Great Thinkers of the Western World, HarperCollins Publishers, New York, 1992, pp. 81-86.

ON JAPANESE COURT LIFE
Morris, Ivan, The World of the Shining Prince: Court Life in Ancient Japan, Penguin, New York, 1979.

Waley, Arthur (trans.), The Pillow Book of Sei Shonagon, Unwin Brothers Ltd., London, 1957.

ON CHRISTIAN PLATONISM
Goetz, Philip W., ed., The Encyclopedia Britannica 15th ed., Encyclopedia Britannica, Inc., Chicago, 1990, vol. 25 pp. 880-892.

1 The reverence of Mary flourishes in Europe *1100s*

2 Hohokam pottery is made in Arizona *1100s*

3 Persian fiddles arrive in Europe *1100s*

4 Coins reappear with the growth of towns and trade routes in western Europe *1100s*

5 Illuminated manuscript depicts St. George and the dragon *1100s*

6 Theatrical sets enhance the first performances of the passion play *1110*

7 Flying buttresses characterize the new Gothic architecture seen in the Chartres Cathedral *1137*

8 Toltec civilization disappears as the Aztecs rise to power *1150*

9 Frederick I is crowned Holy Roman Emperor *1155*

10 Chrétien de Troyes invents the legend of Camelot *1170*

11 Construction begins on the Tower of Pisa *1174*

12 Knights of the Third Crusade fail to recapture Jerusalem *1189*

13 Richard the Lionhearted orders beheading of Saracens *1189*

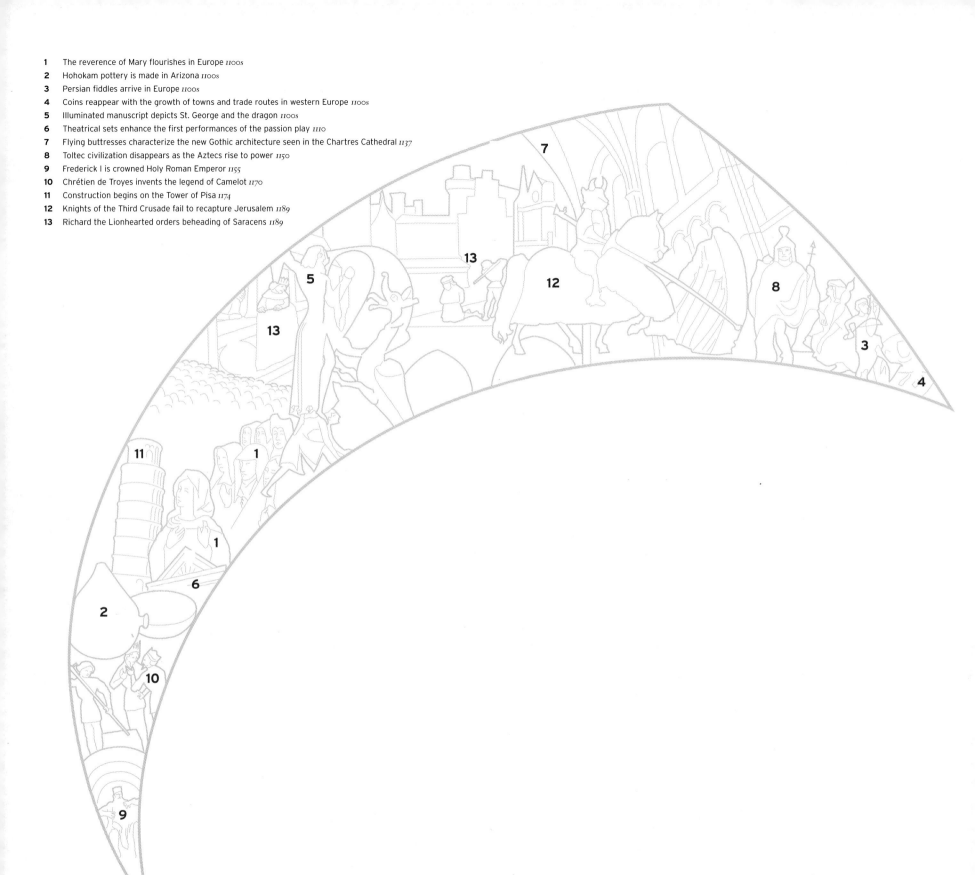

A BALANCE OF FAITH
& SCIENCE

12th Century

A BALANCE OF FAITH & SCIENCE

If the normal flow of history typically involves the simultaneous rise and fall of oppositional forces—the flowering of one people, ideology, or political system necessarily implying the decay or weakening of another—then 12th-century Europe is a great exception. While most of the world continued in predictable patterns of subsequent growth and decline, the Latin world experienced the concurrent intensifying of diametrically opposed religious and secular forces. European society became polarized by the conflict between church and state, religion and philosophy, faith and science, disputes that would characterize the development of Western culture for the next 500 years.

Elsewhere, the cycle of cultural life and death continued. In Japan, the puppet court of the Taira family was replaced by the openly militaristic government of the Minamoto shogunate. Northern China fell to Manchurian conquerors. Buddhism was all but erased from northern India by Islamic migrants, even as the Toltec civilization of Mesoamerica vanished before the invading forefathers of the Aztecs.

In Europe, however, the pattern types that had washed away the Vikings in favor of the Normans no longer held. While European scholars rediscovered Aristotle, and with him the independence of science from religion, the cult of the Virgin Mary flourished. As Innocent III brought the papacy to the apex of its influence and power, strong monarchies developed in France and England. With each trend gathering strength, neither one yielding to the other, there arose what might be termed a balance of conflict in Latin society.

Two characteristic developments of the 12th century, the Crusades and the evolution of Gothic architecture, demonstrate how this balance was forged into a singular culture. Gothic cathedrals were an intense expression of spirituality made possible by an extremely sophisticated knowledge of structure, which meant that a heightened spiritual experience was predicated on a passion for understanding the physical world. In a similar way, the Crusades united the factious knights of Europe in a common religious goal simply by giving them an outlet for the chivalric code's very un-Christian demand for war, blood, and adventure. By channeling barbaric, pagan impulses, the Crusades united Europeans as Christians.

Over the next few hundred years, the scientific, secular Christian would replace his mystic, religious counterpart, but in the 1100s the two stood fused together in complementary opposition, two halves of the same man.

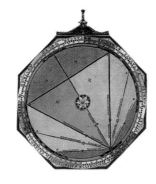
1100s: **The reverence of Mary gains special prominence in the religious life of Catholic Europe.** Intercession of a lesser divinity on the behalf of an earthly supplicant is to become a fundamental aspect of Catholicism, resulting in the development of an ever-expanding pantheon of saints and angels. (1)

1100s: **Hohokam culture thrives in the Arizona desert.** Highly developed irrigation systems allow the agricultural society to grow in a harsh, arid environment. No longer forced to live as nomads, the Hohokam develop an urbane culture in which the arts, particularly pottery, reach new heights of aesthetic accomplishment. (2)

1100s: **Stringed instruments,** in the form of the medieval fiddle, arrive in Europe. Originating in 9th-century Persia, stringed instrumentation will develop into one of the fundamental voices of Western music. (3)

1100s: **The growth of town centers and trade routes** in Western Europe stimulates the need for a money economy, resulting in the reappearance of coins. With the establishment of a merchant class, the old barter system of reciprocal feudal relationships is no longer sufficient for Europe's economic needs. The sudden materialization of specie is somewhat of a mystery, however, as it begins to appear in Europe before the first documented instances of modern minting. (4)

perceived by its audiences to be real, producing a genuine physical impact on their daily lives.

1115: **Arab, Greek, and Jewish copies and interpretations of Aristotle's major works** begin to filter into Christian Europe. Translated into Latin, the new texts introduce Europeans to the philosopher whom the eastern Mediterranean world has studied continuously for the last 1,500 years. Aristotle's writings will become the backbone of a new Latin intellectual movement, scholasticism, which slowly will disentangle Western philosophy from theology.

1126: **Northern China, including the capital city of Kaifeng, is invaded and conquered by Jin invaders** from Manchuria and Mongolia. The invaders push the Sung forces as far south as the Yangtze River, which becomes the new border between the Jin Empire and the remaining portion of Sung China. Undaunted, the Chinese establish a new capital at Hangzhou, marking the beginning of the prosperous and highly cultured southern Sung dynasty. Hangzhou becomes one of the great cosmopolitan trade and art centers of the world; its residents include Buddhists, Christians, Jews, and Muslims from origins as distant as Greece and Persia.

1137: **Gothic architecture is developed by the French Abbot Suger.** In cathedrals like the Chartres and St. Denis, the new architecture is a brilliant technological response to a (7)

from modern Panama to the Mississippi Delta, the Toltecs simply vanish as their cities are razed by the invaders, which include among their number the Aztec people. As the Aztecs rise to predominance in Mesoamerica, they will claim to be the legitimate heirs of the Toltecs, adopting the older nation's practices of military conquest and human sacrifice.

1151: **The Moors bring the Islamic development of the paper mill to Spain,** introducing the technology to continental Europe. By 1189, a paper mill is operating in Christian France, but similar facilities will not appear in countries like England until the 15th century.

1154: **Nicholas Breakspear becomes the first and only Englishman ever elected Pope,** taking the name Adrian IV. The principal act of his short tenure is to crown Frederick Barbarossa Holy Roman Emperor.

1155: **Frederick I is crowned Holy Roman Emperor.** Known in Italy as Barbarossa, Frederick I is a great proponent of the chivalric code, which blossoms during the 12th century. Like most German emperors before him, Frederick spends much of his reign openly fighting with the papacy for control of the German church. Through military diligence and political acumen, Frederick maintains the power of his office for his lifetime, but with his death German power begins to wane before the rising monarchies of France and England. (9)

"Now just as the moon derives its light from the sun and is indeed lower … so too the royal power derives the splendor of its dignity from the pontifical authority"

POPE INNOCENT III

1100s: **The fine art of manuscript illumination,** as exemplified by this decorative representation of St. George and the dragon, flourishes in Europe. (5)

1110: **The first dramatic enacting of the Passion of Christ** occurs in Dunstable, England. Theatre, lost to Europe since the fall of Rome, slowly will move out of churches and into the streets, developing into a rich tradition of medieval experience. With a sense of authenticity gradually lost in the 15th and 16th centuries, the events of medieval theatre are (6)

spiritual problem. Complex ceiling vaults and elaborate piers and buttresses relieve the walls from the responsibility of carrying the heavy roof, allowing for very large window openings. Sunlight, perceived by the faithful as the physical embodiment of God, floods through these larger windows, bringing a divine presence to church ritual and worship.

1150: **The Toltec civilization of Mesoamerica** disappears as it is overrun by nomadic tribes from the north. Rulers of central Mexico and the hub of a trade network that stretched (8)

1156: **The Taira and Minamoto families of Japan clash during the Hogen Disturbance.** Although the fighting is decided in a single night, the Hogen Disturbance underscores the fact that the real struggle for power in Japan is among members of the new samurai class, and not the imperial or noble authorities for whom they nominally work. In 1159, the Taira defeat the Minamoto and gain control of the imperial court, running it much as the Fujiwara did before them. The surviving Minamoto, however, slowly will begin to rebuild their strength in outlying provinces.

DAY TO DAY:
MARRIAGE & FAITH IN 12TH CENTURY EUROPE

For European women, marriage was not always a matter of choice

During her youth, Christina of Markyate went to the local monastery of St. Alban and knelt before the altar. With offertory penny in hand, she prayed, "Grant me, I beseech Thee, purity and inviolable virginity whereby Thou mayest renew in me the image of Thy Son, who lives and reigns with Thee in the unity of the Holy Spirit, God forever and ever, Amen." During an age in which marriage represented a division between secular and spiritual thought, Christina revolted against the notion of marriage for reproductive purposes.

Producing an heir to continue the family name was highly valued during the Middle Ages. The Christian church had devalued marriage as an accommodation to the flesh, but gradually began to accept it as a sacrament necessary for procreation. The average marriage age of most women was between 17 and 18, though in the high aristocracy, young girls sometimes married before puberty. Married women typically spent nine out of every 18 months pregnant. Following the birth of a child, a wealthy mother would give her infant to a wet nurse. If the child survived its second birthday, it was returned home. Nearly half of all children born to wealthy families died before age 20.

Despite Christina's wishes to remain chaste, her noble parents forced her to marry a young suitor. Amongst nobility, the desire to marry off daughters was keen in order to preserve inheritances for the male children. A dowry, usually consisting of the woman's personal property and some money, was offered to the groom, who was as interested in finance as in children. Once the marriage was consummated, it was customary for the man to offer a present to his wife as gratitude for the wealth she had brought him and the child she hopefully carried.

Married, Christina still refused to break her vow of abstinence, professing her desire to follow the chaste life of St. Alban. Frustrated and angry, Christina's father felt his daughter had scorned tradition and brought dishonor to his name. The Archbishop of Canterbury eventually absolved the woman of her marriage, saying, "Hence I now exhort her to persevere in her vow of virginity, and I pray God that He will bring to fulfillment that angelic desire which He Himself inspired in her." Later in the century, Church canon established that "it is not lawful for parents to hand over a betrothed girl to another man; but it is lawful for her to choose a monastery." A daughter's consent had become essential to a valid marriage.

1157: **The first self-proclaimed public house,** or "pub," opens outside London.

1159: **John of Salisbury writes "Policraticus,"** one of the first political critiques in Latin Europe since the fall of Rome. A man of the cloth, John criticizes the secular, administrative bureaucracy that is becoming the essential structure of modern government in European states.

1172: **Henry II, King of England, imprisons his French queen** for inciting rebellion in northern France. Established in England, the Norman kings find it difficult to retain control of their French homelands. Henry spends most of his reign beating rebellious Norman nobles into submission and resisting the growing power of the kings of France. For the next 300 years, English and French nobility will wage war to determine who will rule the hereditary Norman homelands.

"I am born of a rank which recognizes no superior but God"

RICHARD THE LIONHEARTED

1170: **English knights murder Thomas Becket, Archbishop of Canterbury.** Becket and King Henry II, old friends, had parted ways over conflicts of jurisdictional right between church and crown. Hoping to curry favor with the king, four minor nobles confront Becket in Canterbury Cathedral and stab him to death. In later English history, Becket will become a hero to Catholics and an arch villain to Anglicans.

1170: **Chrétien de Troyes invents the character Lancelot du Lac.** In his poem "Le Chevalier Á La Charette," de Troyes gives chivalry the permanence of literary form, allowing its influence to extend far beyond the 12th century.

1171: **All Venetians in Constantinople are ordered arrested by the Byzantine emperor.** The growing friction between Venice and Byzantium is in large part due to the continuously expanding power of Venetian merchants. Throughout the 1100s, Venice gains more and more control of trade in the eastern Mediterranean, establishing a virtual monopoly on commerce between the Far East and Europe.

1174: **Construction begins on what will become known as "The Leaning Tower of Pisa."** The campanile of the city's cathedral, the Byzantine-styled tower starts to rotate even before it is completed due to poor soil conditions and inadequately designed foundations.

1189: **German, French, and English troops embark on the Third Crusade,** an attempt to recapture Jerusalem from Islamic forces under Saladin. The German emperor drowns en route. In the Holy Land, French King Philip II and English King Richard I quarrel, and a pouting Philip takes his armies home. Richard's skill as a soldier leads the Crusaders to a brilliant victory at Arsuf, but without French support the capture of Jerusalem proves elusive. A truce is made, and the Europeans go home, leaving the city under Islamic control.

1189: **Richard I, King of England, orders the beheading of Saracen hostages in the Holy Land** and watches the massacre from a balcony. Richard's public life is the ultimate expression of the violent chivalric ideal. Ironically, Richard, the greatest living symbol of a social system partly based on the idolization of women, is gay. An excellent soldier but an irresponsible king, Richard abuses the wealth of England, using it to satisfy his need for adventure through warfare. In his 10 years as king, he spends less than 12 months in England. He dies fighting in France in 1199.

1192: **Minamoto Yoritomo forces the Japanese emperor to declare him shogun,** or supreme military ruler. By smashing the military power of the Taira family in a sea battle seven years earlier, Yoritomo had made the Minamoto clan the de facto rulers of Japan, a position acknowledged in his new title. Fully aware that his power is built on the allegiance of local lords in outlying provinces, Yoritomo establishes his seat of government in provincial Kamakura, isolating the imperial court from state matters for the next 650 years.

1198: **Innocent III is elected Pope, beginning one of the most powerful periods in papal history.** Through careful use of the church's economic power in European states, the skillful playing of one European prince off another, and a liberal use of excommunication, Innocent III becomes the most authoritative and influential Pope of Medieval times.

CONTEMPORARY PHILOSOPHIES

SCHOLASTIC ARISTOTELIANISM

Europe's rediscovery of Aristotle laid the foundations of modern science

The reintroduction of Aristotle to the Western world revolutionized European thinking. Reading Latin translations of Byzantine and Muslim writings, European intellectuals were inspired to create a new form of study and thought loosely known as scholasticism.

As cities continued to grow in the 12th century, the physical locus of Western thought shifted from rural monasteries to newly established universities in cities like Paris and Oxford. These somewhat secular institutions established a more intellectually flexible environment in which the "new" ideas of Aristotle could be compared with older Platonic traditions. The result was the development of scholasticism, a Western system of thought independent of church doctrines.

Latin interpretations of Plato had reduced his philosophy to a simplistic formula in which physical objects were poor facsimiles of the pure ideas or thoughts they represented. In this way, the pure, abstract idea of man was much more important and beautiful than its physical incarnation in an actual human being. This understanding was in good keeping with the Christian faith, which required its adherents to forsake the physical world for the ideal spiritual world of Heaven.

In contrast, Aristotelianism was much more concerned with systems of thought, with rules and orders that could be applied both to physical and abstract realities. Aristotle's writings explored a diverse range of topics—logic, grammar, the physical sciences, psychology, and politics—always with an eye to uncovering the underlying systems that ordered these fields. Although his ideas of scientific observation were much less developed than those that would be established by Descartes, Bacon, and Galileo in the 1600s, Aristotle's investigations were primarily about shedding light on the mysteries of the world. In this somewhat limited way, his thinking can be credited with triggering the development of the scientific method in Western thought.

As the scholastic tradition evolved, it found itself in deeper and deeper conflict with church doctrine. Even as the church began to accept many of Aristotle's individual conclusions, the philosopher's concern with finding structure behind the specific events of the world continued to establish a tradition of scientific and philosophical inquiry that challenged Catholic beliefs. By the 17th century, men like Descartes and Galileo, who were actually debunking Aristotle's particular theories even as they pushed his methods to their logical conclusion, would live in fear of being declared heretical by the Church. The decisively secular tradition of Western thinking had been born.

BIBLIOGRAPHY AND FURTHER READING:

Adams, Laurie Schneider. Art Across Time: Vol 1, McGraw-Hill College, Boston, 1999, pp. 389-395.

Ballantine, Betty and Ian, ed. The Native Americans: An Illustrated History, Turner Publishing, Inc., Atlanta, 1993, pp. 63-64.

Joel Colton and R.R. Palmer. A History of the Modern World, 5th ed., Alfred A. Knopf, New York, 1978, pp. 14-31.

Goetz, Philip W., ed. The Encyclopedia Britannica 15th ed., Encyclopedia Britannica, Inc., Chicago, 1990, vol. 7 p. 571, vol. 16 pp. 101-106, vol. 18 pp. 610-613, vol. 22, pp. 47-50, 309-310, vol. 24, pp. 651-652.

Horst de la Croix and Richard Tansey. Gardener's Art Through the Ages, 8th ed., Harcourt Brace Jovanovich, New York, 1986, pp. 372-382, 453-455, 468-470.

Chandice L.Goucher, Charles A. LeGuin, and Linda Linda A. Walton. In the Balance: Themes in Global History, McGraw-Hill, Boston, 1998, vol. 1 pp. 245-246, vol. 2 pp. 451-452.

Grun, Bernard. The Timetables of History, Simon and Schuster, New York, 1979, pp. 144-163.

Hanes III, William Travis, editor. World History: Continuity and Change, Holt, Rinehart, and Winston, Austin, TX, 1997, pp. 201-202, 290-298, 304-308, 313-314

Janson, H.W. History of Western Art, 3rd ed., Prentice Hall Abrams, Englewood Cliffs, NJ, 1986, pp. 301-316.

ON WOMEN AND MARRIAGE IN 12TH CENTURY EUROPE
Duby, Georges. Love and Marriage in the Middle Ages, Jane Dunnett, trans., Polity Press and the University of Chicago, Chicago, 1994.

Friedberg, E., ed. "Decretum Magistri Gratiana," The Middle Ages Vol. 1: Sources of Medieval History, 5th ed., Brian Tierney, editor, McGraw Hill Company, Boston, 1999, pp. 189-194.

Talbot, C.H., ed. "The Life of Christina of Markyate," The Middle Ages Vol. 2: Readings in Medieval History, 5th ed., Brian Tierney, editor, McGraw Hill Company, Boston, 1999, pp. 194-198.

Klapisch-Zuber, Christiane. "Women and Children" The Middle Ages Vol. 2: Readings in Medieval History, 5th ed., Brian Tierney, editor, McGraw Hill Company, Boston 1999, pp. 183-188.

Brian Tierney and Sidney Painter. Western Europe in the Middle Ages: 300-1475, 6th ed., McGraw Hill Company, Boston, 1999.

ON SCHOLASTIC ARISTOTELIANISM
Goetz, Philip W., ed.The Encyclopedia Britannica 15th ed., Encyclopedia Britannica, Inc., Chicago, 1990, vol. 4, pp. 59-71,vol. 25, pp. 751-755.

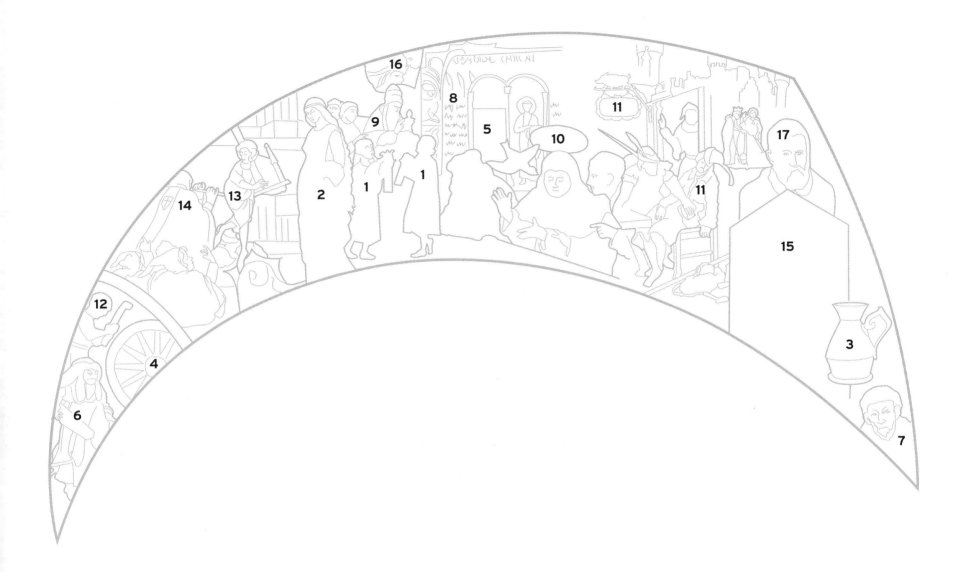

1 Jesters and musicians entertain in Europe's courts *1200s*

2 The standard dress of European women becomes more form-fitting *1200s*

3 Beer production in Western Europe grows into a large industry *1200s*

4 Stained-glass windows educate the illiterate *1200s*

5 European manuscripts and calendars are lovingly but tediously produced by hand *1200s*

6 Genghis Khan unites the Mongolian tribes *1206*

7 Francis of Assisi founds the Franciscan Order *1209*

8 The Magna Carta is drafted in England *1215*

9 Pope Gregory IX dies in Rome *1241*

10 Thomas Aquinas studies philosophy in Paris *1245*

11 The legendary career of Robin Hood ends *1247*

12 St. Chapelle is completed in Paris *1248*

13 Bagpipes and portable organs are used in royal court *1252-1284*

14 The Pied Piper reputedly steals the children of Hamelin *1284*

15 Florentine painter Cimabue paints "Madonna Enthroned" *1285*

16 Distinctive Venetian glass is Europe's finest *1291*

17 Marco Polo returns from his journey to the Far East *1295*

13_{th Century}

THE RISE
OF THE MONGOLS

THE RISE OF THE MONGOLS

The story of development in the 1200s is fundamentally the story of the Mongolian empire. While Europe remained stalled in 12th-century patterns of internal conflict, Mongol armies forged the largest empire in history. Great moments and individuals—a Magna Carta or a Roger Bacon—graced the Latin world of the 13th century, but their immediate impact on European society was minimal. On the whole, Europe's cultural accomplishments were fairly modest. Ultimately unsuccessful in their repeated attempts to wrest Jerusalem from Muslim control, the Crusaders turned to easier Latin and Byzantine targets to satisfy their need for loot and adventure.

Popes squabbled with Holy Roman Emperors; French and English monarchs waged inconclusive wars in northern France; scholars and clergy disputed Aristotle. The 13th century found European culture stalled in a state of political, military, and intellectual deadlock. Far to the east, however, Mongol civilization was sweeping across all of Asia.

The sudden and total conquest of the Earth's largest continent was achieved with a new kind of fighting force: light cavalry. Travelling light and living off the land, or even at times off the milk of their mares, mounted Mongol soldiers were able to move with unprecedented speed. Suddenly concentrating in large numbers on fields of their choosing, the great khans' armies easily destroyed their slow, unwieldy opponents. This ability to move and quickly field large numbers of adequately supplied men was to become a primary strategic objective of modern warfare—something later learned to great advantage by the generals of Napoleon and the architects of the German blitzkrieg.

More important than the military revolution, however, was the Mongols' ability to retain lasting control of the regions they conquered. Without the benefit of modern communication or transport, the governments of the great khans maintained administrative order in an empire that came to encompass almost all of modern China, Korea, Afghanistan, Persia, and the former Soviet Union. Brutal in conquest, Mongol lords were careful and tolerant rulers, allowing local talents and customs to shape regional policy. At the same time, an ambitious network of new roads kept central authorities in regular contact with outlying districts, facilitating the efficient movement of information, commerce, and soldiers. In time, the empire would inevitably break apart, but for most of the 13th and 14th centuries, Asia belonged to the khans.

1200s: **The Hanseatic League,** a loose confederation of northern German trading cities, forms a powerful trade network on the Baltic Sea. The various cities band together to protect their collective interests and provide for common needs. Under their direction, pirates are quelled, lighthouses are established, and training for pilots is provided. Technological improvements in ship design, including a rear-mounted rudder and a small bowsprit sail for better steering, also are shared.

1200s: **Jesters and musicians** become a commonplace amusement of European courts. (1)

1200s: **The loose-fitting kirtle,** still the standard dress of European women, gradually becomes more fitted and shaped during the 13th century. Men's late 12th-century fashion of stockings, long tunic, and cloak or cape continues to be the standard dress of the 1200s. (2)

1200s: **The dress of noble and royal women in Europe,** much like that of their less wealthy counterparts, became more fitted in the 1200s. Their husbands and brothers, in contrast to male commoners, were likely to wear a long tunic

maps do not reflect the Earth's curvature, and hence are useless at higher latitudes. Near the equator, however, the charts, which record positions of shift in prevailing winds as a way of determining location, provide valuable and fairly accurate information.

1200s: **The use of moveable type spreads throughout Southeast Asia,** greatly speeding the copying of religious and scholarly texts by Buddhist monks. Their Western counterparts will continue to transcribe books laboriously by hand for another 250 years.

1200s: **Three separate literary traditions prosper in Japan.** In 1203, tanka poetry found in the anthology "Shin kokinshu," with its subtle explorations of symbol and meaning, establishes what some consider the high point of that literary form. Ten years later, Buddhist monk Kamo Chomei writes "Hojo-ki," a collection of meditative ruminations that will inspire a whole genre of imitations. Around 1220, "Heike mongatori," one of the first of a new kind of adventure narrative, also is written. The extremely different natures of these new writings reflect the highly segregated, insular worlds of courtier, monk, and samurai in 13th-century Japan.

the actual motivation is greed. The city is pillaged with a savagery unrivaled in the Mediterranean world. The new emperor grants Venice extensive trading rights, but by mid-century Byzantine resistance has recaptured the city, and the most glorious days of Venetian mercantilism are ending.

1206: **The factional clans of Mongolia are united under Genghis Khan,** giving birth to one of the most powerful empires in history. The Mongols revolutionize warfare with their use of fast-moving cavalry, which they can mass suddenly for devastating attacks. By Genghis' death in 1227, Turkistan, Afghanistan, and most of northern China will be under his control, while the khan's raiders will have swept through locations as distant as Russia, Persia, and India. (6)

1206: **Northern India is conquered by a second wave of Islamic invaders.** Known as the Ghurids, the Turkish migrants crush both Muslim and Hindu resistance and establish the Delhi sultanate. Harsh in conquest (the Ghurids completely exterminate Buddhist monasticism and religion in India), the new rulers show the traditional Muslim capacity for tolerance in governing their subjects. A rich and distinctive society, blending Indian and Turkish cultures,

"My greatest good fortune was to chase and defeat my enemy, conquer his lands and people, and share his riches"

G E N G H I S   K H A N

that looked more like a dress than a shirt.

1200s: **Large-scale brewing begins in Western Europe.** Although never completely forgotten in Germany, the ancient art of using barley to make beer had been lost in most of Europe, preserved only in cloistered monastic communities. With the rediscovery of the 7,000-year-old process by the general populace, the production of beer and distilled liquor begins in earnest throughout the continent. (3)

1200s: **European cities are plagued by rat infestations.** With no means of controlling the rat populations, Europeans sometimes find themselves in a life-and-death struggle with the ubiquitous rodents. Breaking into granaries and storage areas, the rats sometimes eat so much stored food that they cause famines during the winter months.

1200s: **Nautical charts begin to proliferate** in the Mediterranean world. First developed around 1270, the new

1200s: **Stained-glass windows in European churches** often depict images of the individuals or trade guilds who fund their production. The windows, which function as the primary didactic sources on religion for a largely illiterate population, also serve to express the political and economic presence of the guilds. Developing in the new millennium, the guilds are powerful trade organizations who not only regulate the cost and quality of services rendered in a given industry, but also decide who might or might not practice that profession within the city limits. (4)

1200s: **European manuscripts and calendars,** such as this December page, are carefully written and illuminated by hand with painstaking care and miniscule detail. (5)

1204: **Latin crusaders sack the Byzantine capital of Constantinople** and establish a puppet emperor. Thin pretexts are offered for justifying the conquest of the Christian state that requested the First Crusade in the 11th century, but

develops and thrives in the Delhi court for the next 300 years.

1209: **Francis of Assisi receives the approval of Pope Innocent III to establish the Franciscan Order.** Obeying the command of Jesus to wander defenseless into the world, spread the Christian message and trust in God's protection, Francis leads a life of self-imposed homelessness and poverty. Although his order will lose spiritual intensity as it becomes a large, bureaucratic organization, Francis will have more lasting influence as a lover of nature. His writings on this subject will have profound influence on early Renaissance thinkers. (7)

1215: **English barons force King John to sign a primitive draft of the Magna Carta.** The actual articles of the document, which essentially institutes the right to trial by peers and provides relief from excessive taxation, are somewhat unremarkable. What is more important is that the document (8)

Court musician

DAY TO DAY:
TATAR LIFE AND CULTURE

An empire is built from nomadic beginnings

The word "Tatar," originally describing the Tungus tribes of Eastern Mongolia, quickly came to apply to all of the Mongol tribes and nomadic peoples subject to the authority of the great khan. United under a series of great rulers, the Tatars took their culture and lifestyle to the far corners of Asia and Russia.

The Tatars were a nomadic people, living off their herds of horses, mares, camels, oxen and cattle. They moved in a circular migratory pattern based on 12-year cycles. In the summer they migrated away from the heat and winds of the lower plains, heading toward cooler mountain regions where water and vegetation were abundant. With the coming of winter they returned to the warmer lowlands. Their homes, tents of black felt on collapsible wooden frames, easily folded into small carts, and they were adept at maintaining fat, healthy livestock in a variety of landscapes and climates.

With animals marked to clarify ownership, rustling was rare. A strong sense of honor and tribal loyalty, combined with a severe penal code, minimized crime. Depending on the severity of the offense, thieves either were lashed or executed. Capital punishment was administered by cutting the criminal completely in half with a sword.

Tatar religion was bipolar in nature. While the nomads believed in a heavenly god, to whom they made supplications for intellectual and physical health, they also worshipped Natigay, the god of all terrestrial things. Offering this deity burnt incense and ceremonial figurines of a wife and a child, patriarchs hoped to be rewarded with good weather, healthy livestock, and a prosperous family. Tatar peoples also felt personal behavior in this life would determine fate and social station in the next. It was this belief in immortal souls that led Tatar parents to arrange marriages for their dead children. Contracts were written and painted pieces of paper assembled to represent the people, cattle, and artifacts of the wedding. The papers and contract were then burned, consecrating the marriage in the afterlife.

Living men were permitted to take as many wives as they could support, but the first wife always maintained a dominant position in the household. In contrast with European practice, Tatar grooms paid a dowry to the wife's mother. With the exception of their own mother, Tatar men were expected to marry the wives of their dead fathers.

Believing in a physical and spiritual cycle of movement, Tatar culture developed a mobile society capable of adapting to continuously changing circumstances. This inherent flexibility was the spiritual foundation that made the great Mongol conquests of the 13th century possible.

establishes the principle of a system of law and feudal contract that exists above the authority of the king. The idea of a higher law, to which both ruler and ruled are equally subject, becomes one of the founding principles of good Western government.

1217: **In honor of Duke Leopold VI's victories** against the Saracens of Spain, Austrian bakers make the first croissants. The half-moon shape of the pastries are inspired by the Islamic crescent, a religious and military symbol of the defeated Saracens.

1229: **Muslim philosopher Ibn al-Arabi finishes "al-Futuhat al-Makkiyah,"** a comprehensive encyclopedia of the Islamic sciences. The same year he writes "Fusus al-hikam," one of the canonical works of Islamic mysticism. Al-Arabi is the first to develop fully the principles of his religion's mystic branch, Sufism, into a complete system of thought and belief, greatly influencing the spiritual development of the Islamic world.

1235: **The great Arab poet Ibn al-Farid dies.** Al-Farid's poetry takes the form of the traditional "qasidah," a kind of verse used to express a lament over separation from a loved one, but in his poetry the one longed for is his god. The poet's major work, "Nazm as-suluk," will become one of the great artistic expressions of Sufi mysticism.

1237-1241: **Mongol cavalry,** undaunted by bitter weather, conquer central Russia and Hungary. They also launch devastating raids into Poland, where they are introduced to various Western possessions, including reading glasses and distilled alcohol.

1241: **Pope Gregory IX dies.** A sincere, energetic, and dedicated man of the church, Gregory also was uncompromising, overzealous, and quick to lose his temper. Founder of the Inquisition, Gregory established an institution that thought torture an appropriate means of fact-finding. Spurred by personal dislike for Frederick II, the Holy Roman Emperor, Gregory involved the Papal States in costly, losing wars with the German monarch.
⑨

1244: **Egyptian Malmuks recapture Jerusalem.** Fifteen years earlier, the Sixth Crusade had established a Christian kingdom in the city. With the Egyptian victory, the contested fate of the region is decided—it will remain under Islamic control for the rest of the medieval era.

1245: **Thomas Aquinas departs for Paris** to study under the great philosopher Albertus Magnus. In the midst of intellectual conflict between the growing Aristotelianism of philosophers and the church's Platonic doctrines, Aquinas attempts to walk a middle path. In the process, he develops modern Western theology, using Aristotelian rationalism to draw complex conclusions from a relatively basic foundation of fundamental truths revealed by God.
⑩

1247: **Roger Bacon,** one of the first and most vocal proponents of scientific experimentation, returns to Oxford from France. An Aristotelian professor at the University of Paris, Bacon goes on to pursue an interest in methodical experimentation and observation, foreshadowing the development of modern Western science by more than 300 years. His own intellectual development maps in microcosm the

evolution of Aristotelian rationalism into the scientific methods of the 17th century.

1247: **The historical Robin Hood,** if he ever existed at all, apparently dies. Later, legends will make the celebrated bandit a contemporary of Richard I, but this dating seems implausible. Details of the stories also suggest that Robin operated in Yorkshire, making his literary conflict with the Sheriff of Nottingham unlikely. In all probability, the character of Robin Hood, like that of King Arthur, is a composite of many men and events, some real, but most fictitious.
⑪

1248: **The French royal chapel of St. Chapelle,** one of the highest achievements of Gothic architecture, is completed in Paris. Making up less than a quarter of the total wall surface, the opaque structure of the building is brightly painted to match the stained glass. The blending of wall with the large windows gives one the sense of standing in a glass box, surrounded on all sides by the natural light that medieval worshippers associated with God.
⑫

1251: **Mangu, grandson of Genghis, is elected great khan of the Mongol empire.** Mangu, a great warrior like his grandfather, expands the empire into Persia. More importantly, however, he acts as an able administrator and a religiously tolerant ruler. During his reign, a government bureaucracy, composed both of Mongols and subject peoples, will be established, giving the empire the administrative capacity to retain control of the vast territories it has conquered.

1252-1284: **Bagpipes,** and possibly portable organs, are used in the royal court of Spanish king Alfonso X.
⑬

1258-1260: **Mongol conquerors sack the great Islamic cities of Baghdad and Damascus.** The western expansion of the empire is finally checked, however, by the Malmuk rulers of Egypt, who turn back the Mongol cavalry at the Battle of Ayn Jalut.

1274: **Mongol invaders are thwarted in their attempt to conquer Japan** when a typhoon badly damages their supporting ships. Miraculously, a second Mongol invasion fleet also is crushed by a typhoon in 1281, and Japanese society is saved from Mongol domination. The Japanese believe the typhoons to be "kamikaze," or divine wind, sent by the gods to protect them. The double miracle fosters a strong sense of national pride and destiny among the islands' inhabitants.

1279: **After 20 years of warfare, Kublai Khan conquers Southern Sung China** and proclaims the Yuan dynasty. By 1294, the Mongol empire will stretch from Korea to Kiev and from Vietnam to Siberia, essentially constituting the entire continent of Asia and most of Russia. Ruling over Christians, Jews, Buddhists, and Muslims in jungles, mountains, steppes, and deserts, Mongol rulers govern approximately one-fifth of the inhabitable world.

1284: **The legendary Pied Piper,** unpaid after supposedly ridding the German town of Hamelin of yet another rat infestation, extracts revenge. Using the entrancing power of his pipe, he leads all the children of Hamelin out of town, never to be seen again.
⑭

1285: **Florentine painter Cimabue paints "Madonna Enthroned."** Heavily influenced by Byzantine artists, Italian
⑮

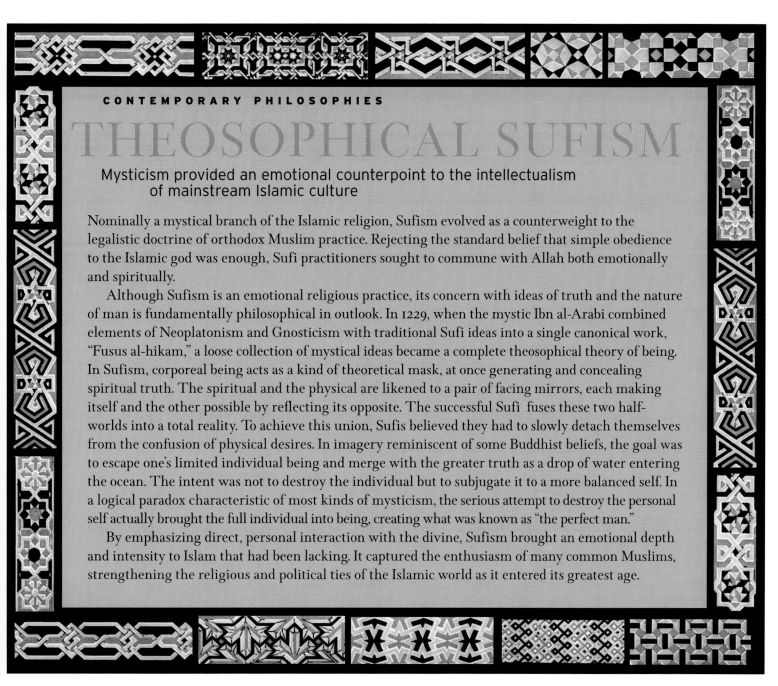

Joel Colton and R.R. Palmer. A History of the Modern World, 5th ed., Alfred A. Knopf, New York, 1978, pp. 22-41.

Horst de la Croix and Richard Tansey. Gardener's Art Through the Ages, 8th ed., Harcourt Brace Jovanovich, New York, 1986, pp. 383-391.

Goetz, Philip W., ed. The Encyclopedia Britannica 15th ed., Encyclopedia Britannica, Inc., Chicago, 1990, vol. 1 pp. 777-778, vol. 2 pp. 700-701, vol. 4 pp. 926-927, vol. 6 pp. 216-217, vol. 7 pp. 496-497, vol. 10 pp. 111-112, vol. 14 pp. 491-492, vol. 18 pp. 451-452, vol. 23, pp. 518-519, vol. 28 pp. 636-639, vol 29 pp. 35-36.

Chandice L.Goucher, Charles A. LeGuin, and Linda Linda A. Walton. In the Balance: Themes in Global History, Vol. 2, McGraw-Hill, Boston, 1998, pp. 438-449, 464-476.

Grun, Bernard. The Timetables of History, Simon and Schuster, New York, 1979, pp. 144-163.

Hanes III, William Travis, editor. World History: Continuity and Change, Holt, Rinehart, and Winston, Austin, TX, 1997, pp. 318, 321-326, 344.

Janson, H.W. History of Western Art, 3rd ed., Prentice Hall Abrams, Englewood Cliffs, NJ, 1986, pp. 306-314.

Muller, Richard A. "Saint Thomas Aquinas" Great Thinkers of the Western World, Ian P. McGreal, ed., HarperCollins Publishers, New York, 1992, pp.107-113.

ON TATAR LIFE
Cottie A. Burland and Werner Forman, The Travels of Marco Polo, McGraw-Hill Company, Boston, 1970.

Komroff, Michael, ed., The Travels of Marco Polo, Random House, New York, 1926.

Oldvhiki, Leonard. Marco Polo's Asia: An Introduction to His "Description of the World," University of California Press, Los Angeles, 1960.

ON SUFI MYSTICISM
Goetz, Philip W., ed.The Encyclopedia Britannica 15th ed., Encyclopedia Britannica, Inc., Chicago, 1990, vol. 22, pp. 22-24.

Nicholson, Reynold Alleyne. Studies in Islamic Mysticism, Cambridge University Press, Cambridge, 1921, pp. 77-148.

Schimmel, Annemarie. Mystical Dimensions of Islam, The University of North Carolina Press, Chapel Hill, 1975, pp. 3-23, 187-192.

BIBLIOGRAPHY AND FURTHER READING:

CONTEMPORARY PHILOSOPHIES

THEOSOPHICAL SUFISM

Mysticism provided an emotional counterpoint to the intellectualism of mainstream Islamic culture

Nominally a mystical branch of the Islamic religion, Sufism evolved as a counterweight to the legalistic doctrine of orthodox Muslim practice. Rejecting the standard belief that simple obedience to the Islamic god was enough, Sufi practitioners sought to commune with Allah both emotionally and spiritually.

Although Sufism is an emotional religious practice, its concern with ideas of truth and the nature of man is fundamentally philosophical in outlook. In 1229, when the mystic Ibn al-Arabi combined elements of Neoplatonism and Gnosticism with traditional Sufi ideas into a single canonical work, "Fusus al-hikam," a loose collection of mystical ideas became a complete theosophical theory of being. In Sufism, corporeal being acts as a kind of theoretical mask, at once generating and concealing spiritual truth. The spiritual and the physical are likened to a pair of facing mirrors, each making itself and the other possible by reflecting its opposite. The successful Sufi fuses these two half-worlds into a total reality. To achieve this union, Sufis believed they had to slowly detach themselves from the confusion of physical desires. In imagery reminiscent of some Buddhist beliefs, the goal was to escape one's limited individual being and merge with the greater truth as a drop of water entering the ocean. The intent was not to destroy the individual but to subjugate it to a more balanced self. In a logical paradox characteristic of most kinds of mysticism, the serious attempt to destroy the personal self actually brought the full individual into being, creating what was known as "the perfect man."

By emphasizing direct, personal interaction with the divine, Sufism brought an emotional depth and intensity to Islam that had been lacking. It captured the enthusiasm of many common Muslims, strengthening the religious and political ties of the Islamic world as it entered its greatest age.

---

artists like Cimabue brought a Greek sensibility to European art, which, when mixed with older Gothic traditions, would eventually lay the aesthetic foundations of the Renaissance.

1288: **Ibn an-Nafis, a great Muslim doctor** and the first to describe accurately pulmonary action in the human body, dies. Correcting the conclusions of the venerated ancient Galen, an-Nafis observes that blood is first passed through the lungs before the heart pumps it through the rest of the body. Although the observation will go unnoticed in Europe for some time, it eventually will revolutionize medical understanding of the cardiovascular system.

1291: **Venetian officials,** anxious to keep the techniques of (16) the city's profitable glass blowing industry a state secret,

order the glass factories moved to the remote island of Murano. The distinctive colors and forms of Venetian glass are to remain the finest in Europe for hundreds of years.

1295: **Niccolò, Maffeo, and Marco Polo return from their 24** (17) **years of travel in the Far East.** Soon after, Marco begins dictating his famous account of their adventures in the Middle East and the Mongolian empire. The resulting book, "Il Milione," is read by European contemporaries as a chivalric romance; its wealth of geographic and anthropological information is largely lost on 13th-century readers.

1298: **The spinning wheel,** an invention from the Indian subcontinent, is introduced to Latin Europe, greatly facilitating the production of cloth and clothing.

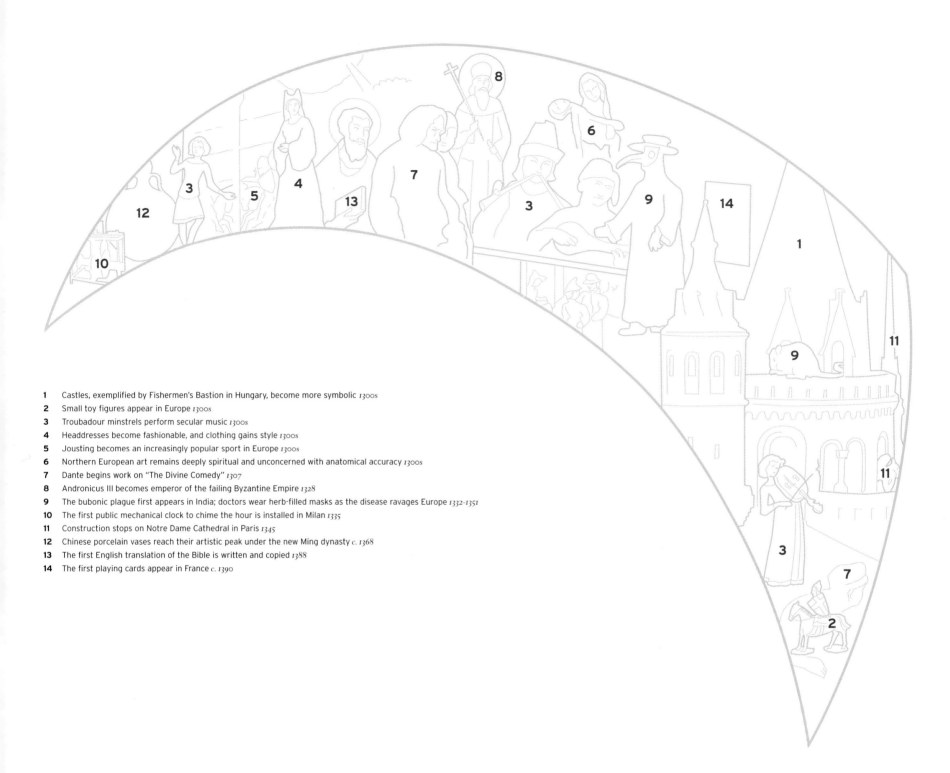

1 Castles, exemplified by Fishermen's Bastion in Hungary, become more symbolic *1300s*
2 Small toy figures appear in Europe *1300s*
3 Troubadour minstrels perform secular music *1300s*
4 Headdresses become fashionable, and clothing gains style *1300s*
5 Jousting becomes an increasingly popular sport in Europe *1300s*
6 Northern European art remains deeply spiritual and unconcerned with anatomical accuracy *1300s*
7 Dante begins work on "The Divine Comedy" *1307*
8 Andronicus III becomes emperor of the failing Byzantine Empire *1328*
9 The bubonic plague first appears in India; doctors wear herb-filled masks as the disease ravages Europe *1332-1351*
10 The first public mechanical clock to chime the hour is installed in Milan *1335*
11 Construction stops on Notre Dame Cathedral in Paris *1345*
12 Chinese porcelain vases reach their artistic peak under the new Ming dynasty *c. 1368*
13 The first English translation of the Bible is written and copied *1388*
14 The first playing cards appear in France *c. 1390*

14

THE FLOWERING
OF THE ISLAMIC WORLD

THE FLOWERING OF THE ISLAMIC WORLD

 ike the rulers of most great empires of conquest, the Mongols ultimately could not maintain the enormous sphere of influence they had forged during the 1200s. In the 14th century, their power and territory gradually diminished in the face of internal dissension and stiffening external resistance. Strong new Islamic states repelled Mongolian encroachment on the Mediterranean, the Duchy of Moscow began to challenge the authority of the Golden Horde, and, in 1368, China regained its independence.

In the wake of this steady collapse, Asia and Europe experienced substantial cultural growth. Chinese opera and the Japanese Noh play developed under new governments in their respective countries. Vernacular European literature, written by masters like Dante and Chaucer, helped lay the intellectual groundwork for the coming Renaissance.

Behind the aesthetic development of these regions, however, real political and social crises were brewing. France and England fell into The Hundred Years War, a continuing dispute over control of Normandy. At the same time, the Western Schism split the Catholic church into political factions, each claiming its own pope. While the hierarchy of the church alienated itself from the laity with its infighting, it was suddenly challenged by a new external threat: the translation of the Bible into vernacular languages. Now able to read the text for themselves, the European laity found themselves less willing to accept the traditional clerical monopoly on interpreting the message of God.

Internal trouble in Japan and China, if less immediately visible, was ultimately no less harmful. In Ming China, inflexible laws and social customs would provide order initially, but over time would produce a government and culture unable to respond creatively to changing foreign and domestic conditions. Japanese government, built on an agricultural feudal system, was destabilized by a developing money economy. Eventually, central authority would collapse, and Japan would dissolve into a host of tiny warring kingdoms.

Unencumbered by internal strife, the real beneficiaries of 14th-century change were the Muslims. Released from a deadly vise by the simultaneous collapse of the Byzantine and Mongol states, the Islamic world exploded. Under strong Malmuk and Ottoman governments, Islamic society experienced an artistic and intellectual renaissance, political stability, and constant military success. For the next few hundred years, Turkish sultans would replace Mongol khans as the leaders of the world's most dominant society.

1300S: **Cairo, the capital of the growing Malmuk state, becomes the greatest city of the Islamic world.** As the Seljuk empire buckled under Mongol attacks in the 13th century, Muslim refugees flocked to Egypt. By the 1300s, Cairo's population, at no less than 500,000 people, is 15 times larger than that of contemporary London. As Malmuk armies drive the threatening Mongols out of Syria, the city becomes the center of a major renaissance in Islamic culture, literature, and art.

1300S: **With the increasing power of national monarchies,** (1) feudal castles, like Fishermen's Bastion in Hungary, become increasingly decorative and symbolic in function.

1300S: **Increasing specialization of labor in Europe** leads (2) to the expanded production of toys, like this lead figurine of a knight. During the subsistence lifestyle of early medieval times, such frivolous expenditure of effort would have been unthinkable. Like all toys, this one educates, encouraging its young aristocratic owner to grow up to be a great warrior.

1300S: **The tradition of secular music** performed by trou- (3) badours continues to thrive in 14th-century Europe. Instruments, no longer strictly relegated to backing up the human voice, increasingly are used in a melodic fashion.

1300S: **European clothing continues to evolve** in the 14th (4) century. Women wear long, loose dresses that are more stylish and are now equipped with buttons. Often smocks or overgarments also are worn. A more elaborate headdress, typically involving columns of hair held on the side of the

1300S: **Jousting becomes an increasingly popular sport** of

(5) European tournaments. Using blunt lances and protected by new advances in armor, jousting knights of the 1300s are in much less physical danger than their 12th-century counter-parts. By the 15th century, jousting will completely replace the more violent mêlée as the competition of choice. By 1600, both sports will be effectively dead.

1300S: **An increase in available hard currency in Japan** indicates the rise of a new mercantile economy. Expensive, urbane tastes move into rural areas, and samurai are forced to spend beyond their means in order to maintain the appearance of their social station. As the economy becomes increasingly financial in character, the fiscal resources of many samurai will dwindle, driving them into poverty.

1300S: **Northern European art remains deeply spiritual in** (6) **the 14th century,** focusing more on religious content than representational accuracy. Even as their southern counter-parts begin to flirt with the artistic sensuousness that will lead to the Italian Renaissance, northern artists remain unconcerned with rendering a world that religion has taught them and experience has shown them to be unpredictable, fleeting, and cruel.

1302: **Osman I, founder of the Ottoman nation, leads his people to their first victory over the Byzantines.** Permanently forced out of Asia Minor by 1337, the Byzantine Empire rapidly begins to decay. In counterpoint, the Ottomans expand rapidly from their homeland in northeast Anatolia, quickly replacing the beleagured Seljuks as the dominant nation of the Turkish world. By the 15th century,

anthropomorphic units establish unchanging values, which, among other things, greatly eases the calculation of property tax.

1306: **Giotto di Bondone finishes "The Lamentation,"** one of his finest paintings. Giotto's work is characterized by a new sense of depth and modelling that separates it from earlier medieval painting. This more lifelike rendering of subjects eventually will evolve into the Renaissance painting of the 14th century.

1307: **Dante Alighieri begins work on "The Divine** (7) **Comedy,"** one of the first great pieces of literature written in a modern vernacular language. Dante's admiration for both the ancient past and the modern present make him a key figure in the development of Renaissance thought and liter-ature, while his metaphoric story of the salvation of a lost human soul establishes him as one of the most poetic writers of Western literature.

1309: **The Order of Hospitalers continues the Holy War** against Islamic nations from their base in Rhodes. After the fall of Acre, the last Christian city in the Holy Land, in 1291, the ultimate failure of the Crusades is undeniable. Nonetheless, the Hospitalers establish island kingdoms, first in Rhodes and later in Malta, from which they vainly continue the fight for 500 more years. Building up a strong navy, the Hospitalers harry Muslim commercial shipping until 1791, when Malta is seized by Napoleon.

1309: **Pope Clement V transfers the papacy to Avignon,**

> "Latin . . . is undoubtedly the nobler language . . .
> The vernacular, on the other hand . . . still shows itself capable
> of much improvement and enrichment"
>
> P E T R A R C H

head with netting, also becomes fashionable. Men, in turn, wear a shorter tunic with a scoop neck, tight hose, and pointed leather shoes. Aristocratic men are seen sporting gloves, and their retainers often wear two-tone tunics and hose in harlequin fashion, reflecting the colors of the house they serve.

their empire will encompass most of the Islamic Mediterranean coast.

1305: **Uniform standard dimensions for the yard and acre are established in England.** Dimensions like the royal foot, based on the distance from the end of the ruling monarch's toes to his heel, were changed every time a new royal took the throne, causing immense confusion. The new, non-

France, beginning a period of church history known as the "Babylon Captivity." Finding Rome politically fractious, Clement hopes to stabilize papal authority from the new cap-ital. Instead, religious policy is dominated by French interests. During the 68 years in which Avignon serves as the papal seat, every pope elected is French. In 1377, Pope Gregory XI finally returns the church government to Rome in an effort to reassert control over the papal states.

1313: **Friar Berthold Schwarz is the first European to make gunpowder.** Although Chinese inventors perfected the explosive several hundred years earlier, it will be Europeans who most effectively harness its power. Western firearms, firing projectiles launched by combusting gunpowder, will help 16th-century Latin armies begin to conquer most of the world.

1325: **Ibn Battutah,** the greatest medieval traveler, leaves home for the first time to travel to Mecca. In his lifetime, Battutah will walk, ride, or sail more than 75,000 miles, dwarfing the distances covered by Marco Polo. By his death in 1368, he will have visited every major Islamic court and much of the Far East.

1325: **The first Noh plays are performed in Japan.** Evolving into a definitive type of theatre during the 14th century, Noh performances develop out of dances and Shinto rituals. Highly stylized and sparing in dialogue, the plays tell short stories primarily through music and subtle body movements performed by the actors.

standing of physical mechanics that might have been deemed sinful at the height of the Christian Middle Ages, the sophisticated device shows a new mastery of the physical sciences, which will become the hallmark of modern Western culture.

1337: **The Hundred Years War begins** when French king Philip VI refuses to acknowledge English claims to Normandy. Rulers of a kingdom established by William the Conqueror, the English monarchs have a legitimate claim to the disputed territory, but differences of language and culture alienate them from the French. The ultimate French victory, earned strictly by perseverance, will not be won until 1453. Until then, half of modern France will be ravaged by continuous warfare.

1338: **The Ashikaga family declares a new shogunate,** regaining control from the brief imperial regime that ousted the Kamakura government. Although the new rulership, known as the Muromachi shogunate, is able to reassert the

meant to cap the towers are never installed. As expressions of faith and civic pride, most cathedrals were such titanic undertakings that they remained incomplete long after the religious fervor responsible for their construction had faded.

1346: **Stefan Dusan declares himself ruler of Serbia and Greece.** The brief flowering of his Latin Christian empire in the Balkans will eat away most of the remaining Byzantine Empire, reducing the last remnant of the Roman world to a territory no larger than Bulgaria.

1353: **Giovanni Boccaccio completes the "Decameron,"** his most famous work. The collected short tales of the book, in which men and women actively influence or take advantage of their fate, sketches an essentially anti-medieval understanding of the human condition, suggesting that, for good or ill, people can at least partially control their destinies. This vision of man as a proactive being is to be one of the fundamental ways that Renaissance thinking will depart from previous Latin ideology.

> "… in men and women alike it first betrayed itself by the emergence of certain tumors in the groin or the armpits, some of which grew as large as the common apple …"
>
> B O C C A C C I O   D E S C R I B I N G   T H E   B L A C K   D E A T H

1327: **The Aztec city of Tenochtitlán is founded** on a swampy island in Lake Texcoco, Mexico. One of many competing city-states located on the central body of water, the Aztec nation will remain fairly undistinguished amongst its neighbors for the next 100 years.

1328: **Andronicus II, the Byzantine emperor, is forced to yield his throne to Andronicus III.** Since the fall of Constantinople to the Fourth Crusade in 1204, the Byzantine empire has been crippled by internal division, including the civil war that forces Andronicus II to capitulate. A period of financial, political, and military decay, the ousted emperor's reign also was a time of renewed vitality in scholasticism, traditional mystic religion, and the arts. His replacement by Andronicus III is seen as a victory for the younger generation, but Byzantine fortunes will continue to crumble for the rest of the century.

1332: **The first recorded outbreak of the bubonic plague strikes in India.** Following the extensive trade routes of the Eastern world, the disease rapidly spreads through Persia, China, and southern Asia. By 1347, the fatal sickness has reached Europe; it will kill 75 million people between 1347 and 1351. In 1349 alone, an entire third of the English population dies from infection.

1335: **The first public mechanical clock,** designed to sound the hour, is installed in Milan. Accurate to within 30 minutes over a 24-hour period, the complex machine is a milestone in the development of Western technology. Requiring an under-

power of the warrior class, it is a weak imitation of the earlier military government. Unintimidated by a central government greatly weakened by changing economic conditions, regional military governors become the real rulers of Japan.

1341: **The city of Rome crowns Francesco Petrarca poet on the Capitoline Hill.** The work of the poet better known as Petrarch will influence greatly Renaissance lyric poetry. His coronation in Rome, capital both of the ancient pagan and modern Latin Christian worlds, mirrors the poet's desire to merge the values of these two periods. This interest in marrying Roman culture with European religion will prove to be one of Petrarch's central contributions to Renaissance thought in the next century.

1343: **William of Ockham finishes his "Dialogues."** The English thinker's famous theory of deductive reasoning, known as Ockham's Razor, will have enormous influence on Western scientific thought. Stating that in the absence of conflicting information, the simplest explanation is the most likely to be true, Ockham's Razor will help move Western thought away from the excessively complex machinations of scholastic Aristotelianism. In time, William's intolerance of artificial structures will become a central pillar of scientific observation.

1345: **Work stops on Notre Dame Cathedral in Paris,** more than 175 years after the foundations were laid. Like most Gothic cathedrals, it will remain incomplete; large spires

1354: **Gallipoli is taken by Ottoman invaders,** making it the site of the first lasting Islamic foothold in Europe. By the 15th century, all of the Balkans will be under Ottoman rule, which will eventually extend to the gates of Vienna.

1356: **Edward, "The Black Prince," wins a decisive battle against the French at Poitiers.** The victory assures English military control of Aquitane, and Edward is made prince of the French region. A classic example of why the English will never win The Hundred Years War, Edward is an excellent soldier but a terrible ruler. Uniting the local French population against him, he loses the entire principality to rebellion by 1372. Throughout the war, English soldiers continuously prove themselves stronger, smarter, and braver than their French counterparts, but demonstrate an utter incapacity to govern competently the territories they conquer.

1360: **The Ca d'Oro is built in Venice.** Although Venice was already past its economic prime by 1360, the Ca d'Oro still represents the fabulous wealth and cosmopolitan sophistication that the city's vast trading empire produced. While the intricate detailing of the façade demonstrates the vast financial resources of its owner, the Islamic motifs of the door and window openings allude to the Eastern world where the owner made his fortune.

1360: **The first francs are minted in France.** The need to produce new specie reflects the growing money economy of Europe, indicating further urbanization and increased break-

CONTEMPORARY PHILOSOPHIES

NEO-CONFUCIANISM

A high sense of individual duty and morality defined Ming culture

During the late 14th century, China began to enjoy the greatest international power and prestige of its long history. The Great Wall and the new capital city of Beijing were constructed, Chinese fleets plied the Indian Ocean, and Chinese borders expanded deep into Mongolia, Manchuria, and Vietnam. Fueling this aggressive growth and accomplishment was an efficient and talented administrative government built on the principles of an ancient Chinese philosophy recently renewed by the leaders of the Ming dynasty: Confucianism.

Through 1,800 years of development, Confucianism had developed as a code of moral social behavior in which individuals played ritualistic roles within the community, emphasizing the good of the populace as a whole over the desires of the individual. The basic building block of culture was understood to be the family, with the leading role of patrician imitated at higher levels of organization. Thus the town leaders were fathers to their communities' residents and the emperor was a father to the nation as a whole. In Confucian thinking, the right and the responsibility to lead were based on a person's virtue and humanity (selflessness), without regard for family or wealth.

The Ming government adopted Confucian principles with a literalness and thoroughness unprecedented in Chinese history. The basic political unit was established as the family, with each group of 100 families organized into a community. The "father leaders" of these communities interacted directly with the lower organs of the national government. Out of this system, a highly rational and efficient government bureaucracy was developed.

The highest achievement in Ming society was to become a civil servant. Those wishing to enter public service were educated in local schools or at the national university; upon completion of their studies, they were required to pass an exam to obtain entry-level positions in the government hierarchy. Educational quotas were installed to insure that wealthy families did not dominate school populations, and positions were assigned according to grades on the exam—those with the highest grades received the first available spots. Positions of high rank were awarded only to those who had been consistently successful in lower offices over a period of time and were frequently filled by men who had risen from inauspicious or humble family backgrounds.

Confucian ideology produced a government with minimal corruption, one in which those of the greatest talent occupied the most important positions. Guided by Confucian ideals of selflessness, self-cultivation, and virtue, Ming administrators led their country to prominence in the world.

> "But the branch
> of philosophy which
> regulates the work …
> is morals or ethics,
> because the whole was
> undertaken not for
> speculation but for
> practical results"

DANTE
"THE DIVINE COMEDY"

down of the feudal barter system. At the same time, the production and distribution of royal currency creates a sense of national identity in France, aiding the French kings in their effort to alienate the English kings from the French populations they claim to rule.

1368: **Chinese troops under Chu Yüan-chang capture the Mongol capital of Ta-tu**, ending Mongol rule in China. Chu, who gained support as a champion of the ousted Sung dynasty, reveals his true intentions by declaring himself the first emperor of the new Ming dynasty. By 1398, all of modern China is under Ming control and an independent Chinese nation firmly reestablished.

Post-1368: **The visual, literary, and performing arts ⑫ flourish in Ming China.** The Ming dynasty's most famous artistic achievement is its distinctive blue and white porcelain, but Chinese opera and drama also come into their own under Ming sponsorship. Scholarship thrives as exhaustively thorough anthologies of history and the sciences are compiled. Extremely strict government regulations, however, quickly stamp out any individual creativity in officially sponsored arts, ultimately creating an environment of stale repetition.

1373: **The Byzantine Empire becomes a tribute state of the Ottoman rulers.** So reduced and weakened that it can no longer defend itself, Byzantium concedes Islamic overlordship. For the remaining 70 years of its existence, the Byzantine state will be little more than a toy of Genoa, Venice, and Turkey in their struggles to control trade in the eastern Mediterranean.

1374: **The highly influential Chinese landscape painter Ni**

DAY TO DAY:
MUSLIM PILGRIMS TRAVEL TO MECCA

Religious caravans to the holiest of cities brought diverse strands of the Islamic world together in a common purpose

The Islamic religion requires all its adherents to make at least one journey to Mecca during their lifetime, unless very specific reasons prevent it. In the 14th century, pilgrims from throughout the Islamic world would gather in Cairo and Damascus, and, from these centers, set out in large caravans on the 40- to 50-day journey into Arabia. Coming from vastly different regions and social classes, the members of these processions made an interesting spectacle. Arab scholars sporting turbans and shawls, wide-sleeved robes, and full beards walked with Persians in short coats and baggy pants gathered at the ankles. Turks in shirts, short-sleeved coats, cloaks, and lambskin fezes traveled with Arab commoners in long shirts and woolen overgarments. Women wore veils of crepe or muslin.

Except for the very poor, who were subsidized by the Malmuk government, pilgrims were expected to furnish their own supplies and transportation. Since civilians were forbidden to use horses, most pilgrims either walked or rode donkeys and mules, carrying with them small tents for shelter from the elements. To pay their way, pilgrims brought wares to trade or provided services to other travelers. Educated men supported themselves as caravan officers, acting as judges or leaders for the temporary community. In this way, the caravans became largely self-sufficient mobile economies.

The Islamic year is 12 lunar months and is not adjusted to the solar year, so, depending on the year, the month of pilgrimages could occur in any season, presenting the travellers with a variety of dangers. On any given pilgrimage, caravans could be destroyed by threats as diverse as exposure, dehydration, sandstorms, and flash floods. Nomadic bandits were a year-round concern.

A few days outside of Mecca, the pilgrims would enter a state of "ihram" in which certain extra obligations were expected of them. While prayer five times a day was still required, the pilgrims also had to abstain from fighting and arguing, wearing jewelry and perfume, engaging in sex, cutting nails and hair, killing plants and animals, and wearing sewn garments. To reflect their changed state, all the men donned an outfit also referred to as an ihram, consisting of two seamless white sheets, and went either barefoot or in open sandals, crying praises to Allah as they travelled the rest of their journey.

Upon entering the city and completing their extensive religious obligations, the pilgrims were rewarded at the markets of the white-robed Meccans. Here, where many worlds came together, figs, walnuts, various exotic fruits and vegetables, cloth, perfume, and medicine all could be gathered for the journey home.

Tsan dies. As Chu Yüan-chang gradually gained control of China, an official Ming style of painting evolved, based on rather unimaginative recreations of Sung- and Tang-dynasty work. Away from his court, however, a group of amateur gentleman painters, including Ni Tsan, develop a new monochromatic style of painting. Characterized by bold brushwork and the high contrast of black ink on a white surface, this new method will influence deeply Chinese and Japanese painting in the coming centuries.

1378: **The Western Schism begins** when disgruntled French cardinals reject the election of the Italian Pope Urban VI and retire to Avignon, where they elect their own French pope. For the next 39 years, two and sometimes three popes will rule simultaneously, dividing the church along political and national lines. Although a single pope finally will be elected in the 15th century, the claim that the papacy is the direct instrument of God, resting high above the worldly squabbles of political Europe, is shattered in the eyes of many Latin Christians. The power and authority of the Vatican will never recover.

1378: **Armies of the Grand Duke of Moscow defeat the Mongol "Golden Horde."** Throughout the 1300s, the Mongol rulers of Russia have relied on Moscow to run local government and exact tribute. The uprising and the initial military success of Moscow against its rulers demonstrate the strength such a position has given it. Although Mongol presence will be felt strongly in Russia for another 100 years, their dominance gradually will pass to the upstart Russians.

c. 1382: **Retired Muslim statesman Ibn Khaldun** completes the first draft of "Muqaddimah," one of the first secular treatises on the science of history. His analytical studies of society are the basis of modern sociology, while his cultural theory of growth, maturity, and decay becomes one of the most prevalent and lasting models of modern history.

1388: **The first English translation of the Bible is written** (13) **and copied.** The availability of the Bible in vernacular languages makes it accessible to a much larger lay audience, restricting the ability of the clergy to control interpretations of the text. Free to draw their own conclusions directly from the source, many Latin Christians will begin to challenge or disagree with Catholic doctrine. The very possibility of the Protestant Reformation is established in part with vernacular translations of the Bible.

c. 1390: **Jacques Gringonneur** develops the four suits of (14) playing cards in the French court of Charles VI. Each suit represents a class of French society: spades for soldiers, hearts for clergy, diamonds for artisans, and clubs for farmers.

1390: **Chaucer begins work on "The Canterbury Tales,"** a collection of stories left largely unfinished at his death in 1400. The completed narratives, told by fictitious pilgrims on their way to Canterbury, capture the essence of English medieval culture in all of its conflicting tensions. Half a religious obligation and half a vacation, participated in by members from all levels of society, the pilgrimage—and the stories it produces—outline the contradictions between spiritual and sensual, rich and poor, noble and base, all of which characterize 14th-century Europe.

1397: **A definitive code of law is established by China's Ming government.** Chinese society is divided into military, artisan, and civilian classes, with the civilian class further subdivided into political units of 10 and 100 families. Large estates are split up and rented to stimulate agrarian redevelopment, slavery is outlawed, and strict government standards of aesthetics are applied to art, literature, and architecture.

BIBLIOGRAPHY AND FURTHER READING

Cahill, James. Chinese Painting, Rizzoli International Publications, Inc., New York, 1977, pp. 107-116.

Joel Colton and R.R. Palmer. A History of the Modern World, 5th ed., Alfred A. Knopf, New York, 1978, pp. 42-49

Horst de la Croix and Richard Tansey. Gardener's Art Through the Ages, 8th ed., Harcourt Brace Jovanovich, New York, 1986, pp. 458-460, 472-475, 528-547.

Goetz, Philip W., ed. The Encyclopedia Britannica 15th ed., Encyclopedia Britannica, Inc., Chicago, 1990, vol. 1 pp. 740-741, vol. 2 pp. 309-310, vol. 6 pp. 149-150, 216-222, vol. 8 p. 736, 867, vol. 9 pp. 339-340, vol. 12 p. 601, vol. 15 pp. 440-443, vol. 16 pp. 112-119, 971-975, vol. 22 pp. 313-343

Grun, Bernard. The Timetables of History, Simon and Schuster, New York, 1979, pp. 182-199.

Hanes III, William Travis, editor. World History: Continuity and Change, Holt, Rinehart, and Winston, Austin, TX, 1997, pp. 237-241, 326, 349-351, 360-366.

Hundersmarck, Lawrence. "William of Ockham," Great Thinkers of the Western World, Ian P. McGreal, ed., HarperCollins Publishers, New York, 1992, pp. 123-128.

Janson, H.W. History of Western Art, 3rd ed., Prentice Hall Abrams, Englewood Cliffs, NJ, 1986, pp. 332-333, 344-349.

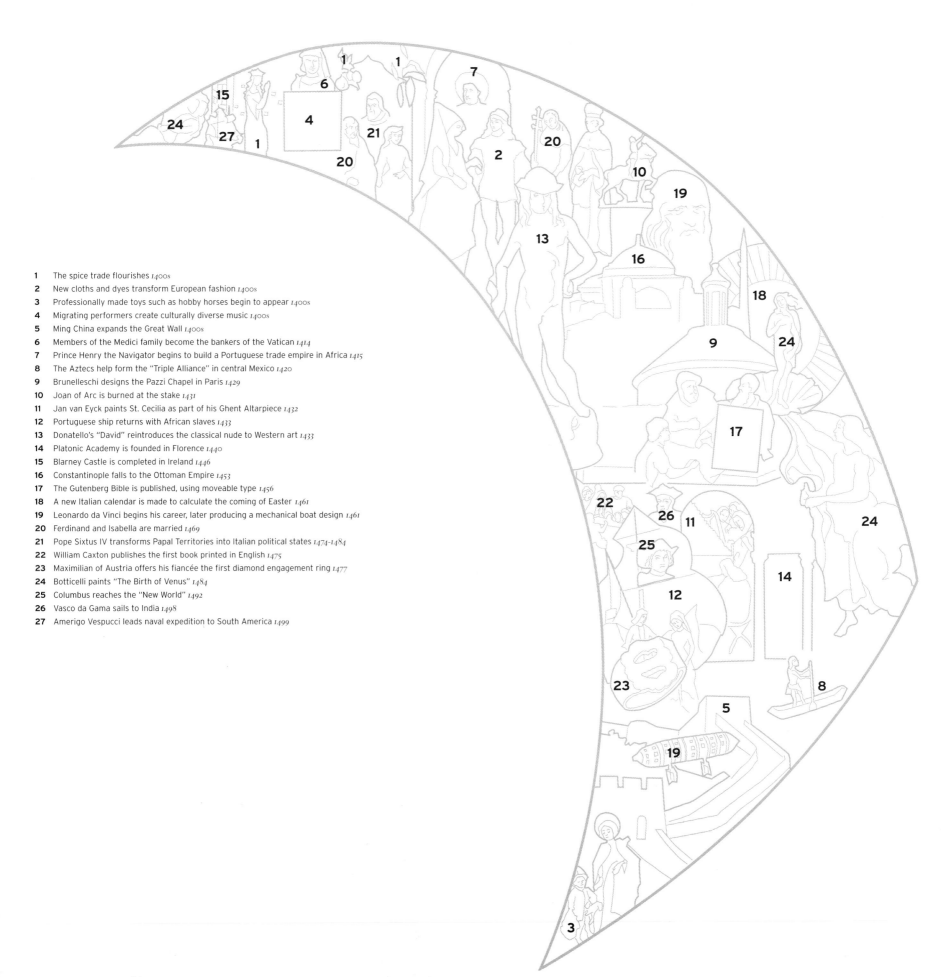

1 The spice trade flourishes *1400s*
2 New cloths and dyes transform European fashion *1400s*
3 Professionally made toys such as hobby horses begin to appear *1400s*
4 Migrating performers create culturally diverse music *1400s*
5 Ming China expands the Great Wall *1400s*
6 Members of the Medici family become the bankers of the Vatican *1414*
7 Prince Henry the Navigator begins to build a Portuguese trade empire in Africa *1415*
8 The Aztecs help form the "Triple Alliance" in central Mexico *1420*
9 Brunelleschi designs the Pazzi Chapel in Paris *1429*
10 Joan of Arc is burned at the stake *1431*
11 Jan van Eyck paints St. Cecilia as part of his Ghent Altarpiece *1432*
12 Portuguese ship returns with African slaves *1433*
13 Donatello's "David" reintroduces the classical nude to Western art *1433*
14 Platonic Academy is founded in Florence *1440*
15 Blarney Castle is completed in Ireland *1446*
16 Constantinople falls to the Ottoman Empire *1453*
17 The Gutenberg Bible is published, using moveable type *1456*
18 A new Italian calendar is made to calculate the coming of Easter *1461*
19 Leonardo da Vinci begins his career, later producing a mechanical boat design *1461*
20 Ferdinand and Isabella are married *1469*
21 Pope Sixtus IV transforms Papal Territories into Italian political states *1474-1484*
22 William Caxton publishes the first book printed in English *1475*
23 Maximilian of Austria offers his fiancée the first diamond engagement ring *1477*
24 Botticelli paints "The Birth of Venus" *1484*
25 Columbus reaches the "New World" *1492*
26 Vasco da Gama sails to India *1498*
27 Amerigo Vespucci leads naval expedition to South America *1499*

AN AGE
OF REBIRTH

15th Century

AN AGE OF REBIRTH

If the 15th century proved to be a period of enormous growth and development in Europe, it also was a political and cultural zenith for other parts of the world. As faith in the divine perfection of the Catholic church crumbled in Europe, new attitudes of investigation and exploration took root. In the northern countries, as technological advances like the Gutenberg Press made books affordable and accessible for the first time, people began to examine the Bible themselves and formed their own opinions outside of church doctrine. Thus the seeds of the Protestant Reformation were sown. To the south, a new secular attitude, committed to the study and enjoyment of the physical world and the celebration of humanity, flourished in the form of the Italian Renaissance. New techniques such as scientific perspective enabled Italian artists to depict the natural world with tremendous accuracy and beauty.

Europe was not the only region experiencing a rebirth, however. In Ming-dynasty China, the expulsion of Mongol conquerors had stimulated a resurgence of traditional Confucian values. As Portuguese explorers tentatively crawled down the west coast of Africa, Chinese fleets confidently traded in East Africa and Persia. While Europe remained divided, disease ridden, and war torn, the Chinese built the Great Wall and an entire new capital: Beijing.

Even more impressive than the Ming dynasty was the Ottoman Empire. Stretching from Morocco to Basra to the very gates of Vienna, the vast Islamic state was a political, social, economic, and military accomplishment utterly beyond the capabilities of the Christian world. Whereas Europe was divided by war, xenophobia, and religious intolerance, Turkish rulers forged a vast multi-cultural empire, united in tolerance and political solidarity.

If the heroic voyages of Columbus and da Gama demonstrated the European character, they were necessary because the Crusades proved that Christian soldiers could not break Islamic control of direct overland trade routes to the Far East. Western exploration was triggered by a need for Eastern goods and an inability to dislodge the Ottomans.

Renaissance painting equalled, but did not exceed, Islamic architecture. Leonardo's musings on mechanics rivalled, but did not overshadow Ottoman astronomy. In the 15th Century, Europe did not eclipse the rest of the world; it simply began to catch up.

1400s: (1) **An active spice trade with the Far East continues to grow in Latin Europe.** Incapable of domestically producing the exotic spices, the Western world establishes an extensive trade network by which to import them. As the industry expands, urbanization, the merchant class, and the money economy all grow to accommodate the transport, distribution, and sale of the highly demanded Eastern products. In the 15th century, this developing economy finally will topple the feudal system in favor of a modern economy.

1400s: **The city of Venice continues to thrive**, even though its mercantile empire has been greatly reduced. Recognizing their slipping influence in Mediterranean trade, the Venetians consolidate their continental holdings, developing a stable agricultural base in northern Italy to support their rich capital. Art, literature, and architecture continue to thrive as Venice evolves into a major cultural center of the developing Renaissance.

1400s: (2) **Increased urbanization and trade** expands access to various new cloths and dyes, changing clothing fashion in Europe. Greater focus on comfort and worldly beauty make Renaissance clothing a far cry from the rough cloth and hair shirts of the Middle Ages. More so than in the recent past, clothing becomes an expression of wealth, taste, and social standing.

1400s: (3) **Specialization of labor**, made possible by improved farming techniques and more plentiful food, leads to an increase in craft goods, including toys such as the hobby horse.

1400s: (4) **Western music flourishes.** Competition between royal courts and church patrons to secure performers leads musicians to travel to more places and play in different environments. As a result, there is a tremendous cross-fertilization of ideas and techniques as migrant performers encounter new musical styles. Flemish musicians, with their distinctive four-part compositions, are in particularly high demand.

1400s: (5) **The Ming dynasty greatly expands the Great Wall of China.** By the end of the century, the massive defense system, designed to keep northern Mongol and Manchurian invaders out, extends more than 2,000 miles in length.

1401: **The port of Malacca is founded in Malaysia**, creating a hub for the interlocking maritime trade worlds of East Africa, the Persian Gulf, the Indian Ocean, and the China Sea. Trade flourishes as Malacca develops into one of the great multicultural centers of the Eastern Hemisphere.

1401: **Legendary Persian conqueror Timur storms Baghdad and Damascus.** The strongest of the many regional khans to emerge after the collapse of the Mongol empire, Timur already has taken control of Central Asia, laid waste to much of India, and subdued the Golden Horde in Russia. In the next few years, he will serve major defeats to the Ottoman Turks, capture Smyrna, and accept the submission and tribute of Egypt and the Byzantine empire. Plans to invade China will be checked only by the khan's natural death in 1405. At the end of Timur's life, Persia seems ready to emerge as one of the principal imperial powers of the globe, but the khan's decision to divide his kingdom among his sons and grandsons will plunge the region into chaos. By the time his empire is largely reestablished by his youngest son, the Ottoman Turks and the Ming Chinese both will be too strong to overcome; the opportunity to recreate the Mongol empire is lost.

1402-1413: **Filippo Brunelleschi studies ancient ruins in Rome.** By the time he returns to his native Florence, the architect has developed scientific perspective, revolutionizing Italian painting, and is preparing to create a new architecture, based on antiquity, which will define Renaissance building. Brunelleschi's new techniques become the benchmark of European architecture for the next 300 years and of Western painting for the next 500.

1405-1433: **Seven Chinese fleets under Zheng He sail the Persian and East African coasts**, reaffirming the Chinese presence in the trade of the Indian Ocean. Harried by northern invaders, economically exhausted, and divided by internal political tensions, the Ming government ends the expeditions after the death of Zheng He in 1433.

1407: **The Genoese bank Casa di San Giorgio introduces credit banking to Europe**, revolutionizing Western finance and eventually leading to such devices as credit cards and checking accounts.

1408: **Completion of the "Yung-lo ta-tien,"** an 11,000 volume encyclopedic compilation of Chinese thought and writing, is completed in Ming China. One of the most impressive collections of human knowledge ever conducted, the 22,000 chapters of the work take five years to assemble and cover every discipline of knowledge known to China. Reproduced in three copies, the compilation is the scholastic counterpart to the political and economic apex enjoyed by Ming China under the emperor Yung Lo.

1409: **The Council of Pisa attempts to end the Great Schism by electing a new pope**, but the Avignon and Roman popes both refuse to step down. For the next six years there are three popes. In 1415, the Council of Constance elects a fourth pope, Martin V, and the other three popes are coerced into abandoning their claims to the papacy. Martin returns the papacy to Rome, but the legitimacy and authority of the office are damaged badly.

1414: (6) **Members of the Medici family become the bankers of the Vatican.** Under the leadership of Cosimo de Medici and his successor Lorenzo, the Florentine family establishes a financial empire that gives them enormous power in Tuscany. Effective leaders of Florence and generous patrons of the arts throughout the 15th century, the family will become the hereditary rulers of the city, produce two popes, and have two of its daughters become queens of France.

1414: **Pope Gregory XII's abdication reunites the divided Catholic church.** The most legitimate of the three claimants

> "O investigator, do not flatter yourself that you know the things nature performs for herself, but rejoice in knowing the purpose of those things designed by your own mind"
>
> LEONARDO DA VINCI

Leonardo's boat design

to the papacy, Gregory's decision to step down clears the way for the election of a single pope and the end of religious chaos in Latin Europe. In many ways, however, the authenticity of the pope as the chief representative of God has been tarnished, and the path has already been cleared for the Protestant Reformation of the 16th century.

1415: **Prince Henry the Navigator's Portuguese forces capture the North African city of Ceuta,** driving out its Islamic occupants and establishing a Portuguese presence at the end of the trans-Saharan trade routes. From this initial foothold, Portuguese trade outposts would slowly creep down the coast of Africa and into the Indian Ocean. In time, the Portuguese will control a vast maritime trade network that stretches from Lisbon to Malacca.

1415: **Badly outnumbered English forces under Henry V decisively defeat the French at Agincourt.** The English, protected behind wooden stakes driven into the ground, decimate the French cavalry with the new Welsh longbow. The weapon, which fires arrows with enough force to penetrate heavy armor, spells the end of the mounted knight's dominance in Western warfare and paves the way for the introduction of the musket into European combat.

1420: **The Aztec nation joins the city-states of Texcoco and Tlacopán** to form the "Triple Alliance" in central Mexico. The new league, in which the Aztec state is the principal partner, quickly conquers the neighboring states around Lake Texcoco, giving birth to the Aztec empire. Aztec society, supported by the booty, slaves, and human sacrifices made available through constant military expansion and conquest, will thrive in Mesoamerica until the arrival of the Spanish in 1519.

1431: **Joan of Arc is burned at the stake for heresy.** Claiming that she had been instructed by God, Joan became a key leader in France's struggle to become a united kingdom and drive the English armies off the continent. In large part, her military and political accomplishments will prove essential in establishing the king of France as something more than just another feudal lord who happens to control Paris. Captured by English allies and turned over to the Catholic church as a heretic, however, Joan is abandoned by her king, who makes no effort to save her from the stake.

1432: **Jan van Eyck completes the Ghent Altarpiece.** In close economic contact with Italy, Flanders is one of the first communities of northern Europe to experience the cultural and artistic impact of the Renaissance. Flemish painters like van Eyck, while strongly influenced by their southern counterparts, develop a distinctive style in the region. Loaded with incredibly dense systems of symbol and allegory, the northern paintings also are typified by extremely precise detail, something made possible by the artists' preference for oil paint over the sloppier Italian tempera.

1433: **For the first time, Portuguese ships return from western Africa with human cargo to be sold as slaves.** Further authorized to enslave Africans by Pope Nicholas V in 1450, the Portuguese will expand the slave trade. Over the next 370 years, more than 20 million Africans will be kidnapped from their homes or taken as prisoners of war and sold to European traders as slaves.

1433: **Florentine sculptor Donatello reintroduces the classical nude** into Western art with his sculpture "David." The new sculpture celebrates the natural human body in a way that earlier artists would have found unthinkable. The

1438: **The Archduke of Austria, from the Hapsburg family, is elected Holy Roman Emperor.** Through cunning, intrigue, and force, the Hapsburgs will be able to keep the position of emperor in the family almost continuously until the time of Napoleon. For the next 350 years, their policies will dominate Central European politics even as they struggle with Rome, France, and the Ottoman Empire for hegemony in Europe at large.

1440: **The Platonic Academy is founded in Florence.** Marsilio Ficino's philosophy of Neoplatonism will have enormous impact on Western thought, which had been more influenced by Aristotle in recent centuries. Neoplatonism, as espoused by the new academy, provides an abstract theoretical framework in which classical and Christian themes and ideologies can be intermingled. The academy's teachings define the intellectual climate of the Italian Renaissance.

1440: **Scholar and priest Nicholas of Cusa finishes writing a piece entitled "Learned Ignorance."** A religious philosopher, Nicholas contends that the educated man is the one who has come to understand his own ignorance, and thus perceives that faith transcends reason or knowing. Himself a mystic, Nicholas will foreshadow the more rational skepticism of 17th-century philosophers such as Descartes.

1446: **Blarney Castle,** replete with magic stone, is completed in Ireland.

1453: **Constantinople falls to the Ottoman Empire**, destroying the last remnant of the 1,500-year-old Roman Empire and securing an Islamic presence in Europe that will eventually extend to the gates of Vienna. The city is declared the new capital of Mehmet II's expansive empire.

> "She comes sent by the King of Heaven, body for body, to take you out of France . . ."
>
> JOAN OF ARC

1421: **The capital of China is renamed Beijing** as the Ming dynasty removes all traces of Mongol occupation and rekindles traditional Confucian values. Construction of the Forbidden City begins.

1425: **Masaccio paints "The Holy Trinity with Virgin and St. John,"** marking the final transition from Gothic to Renaissance art. The artist's mastery of perspective, understanding of anatomy, and willingness to mix pagan and Christian content establish him as one of the first true Renaissance painters.

1429: **Brunelleschi designs the Pazzi Chapel in Paris.** With its carefully defined proportions and its multiple symmetries, the new structure will epitomize the values and methods of early Renaissance architecture. Elegant, serene, and geometrical, the chapel expresses the confidence and rationalism that are at the heart of Renaissance culture.

depiction of a Judeo-Christian subject in a pre-Christian style will become a typical aspect of 15th-century Italian art.

1437: **John Dunstable develops tonal counterpoint in musical composition.** Along with harmonic theory and sequencing, it will become one of the fundamental structures of Western music throughout the millennium.

1438: **The military prowess of Incan Prince Pachacutec transforms the town of Cuzco** into the capital city of a new empire. By 1470, the Incans have replaced the Chimu as the dominant society of western South America. A highly developed system of roads and bridges allows the Incan military to maintain control over a large expanse of mountainous territory inhabited by many different subjugated peoples. During Pachacutec's reign, Cuzco is rebuilt in stone, and its large palaces are equipped with such luxuries as indoor running water and solid silver bathtubs.

1453: **The Hundred Years War ends.** The tide of war was turned by the leadership of Joan of Arc, who helped establish Charles VII as king of France in 1429. Charles repaid Joan by allowing her to be tried as a heretic by English captors and burned at the stake in 1431. By then, however, English dominance in France had been shattered. By 1453, the English have retired from most of the continent, essentially assuring the development of modern France as a state.

1456: **Moveable type, developed by Johannes Gutenberg, is used in Europe for the first time.** Greatly reducing the cost of producing books, the new technique makes texts financially available to larger audiences. An environment of critical thinking and personal interpretation develops as a consequence, laying additional groundwork for the Protestant Reformation of the following century.

c. 1460: **German gunsmiths develop the first matchlock**

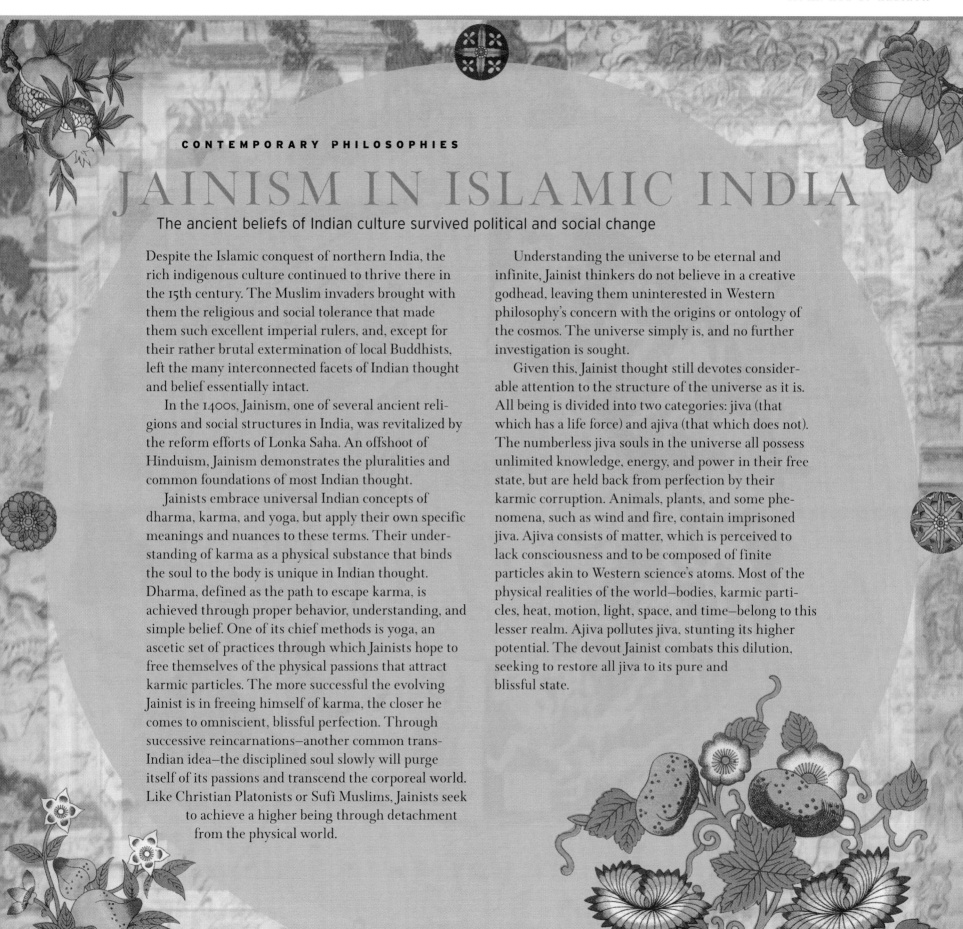

CONTEMPORARY PHILOSOPHIES

JAINISM IN ISLAMIC INDIA

The ancient beliefs of Indian culture survived political and social change

Despite the Islamic conquest of northern India, the rich indigenous culture continued to thrive there in the 15th century. The Muslim invaders brought with them the religious and social tolerance that made them such excellent imperial rulers, and, except for their rather brutal extermination of local Buddhists, left the many interconnected facets of Indian thought and belief essentially intact.

In the 1400s, Jainism, one of several ancient religions and social structures in India, was revitalized by the reform efforts of Lonka Saha. An offshoot of Hinduism, Jainism demonstrates the pluralities and common foundations of most Indian thought.

Jainists embrace universal Indian concepts of dharma, karma, and yoga, but apply their own specific meanings and nuances to these terms. Their understanding of karma as a physical substance that binds the soul to the body is unique in Indian thought. Dharma, defined as the path to escape karma, is achieved through proper behavior, understanding, and simple belief. One of its chief methods is yoga, an ascetic set of practices through which Jainists hope to free themselves of the physical passions that attract karmic particles. The more successful the evolving Jainist is in freeing himself of karma, the closer he comes to omniscient, blissful perfection. Through successive reincarnations—another common trans-Indian idea—the disciplined soul slowly will purge itself of its passions and transcend the corporeal world. Like Christian Platonists or Sufi Muslims, Jainists seek to achieve a higher being through detachment from the physical world.

Understanding the universe to be eternal and infinite, Jainist thinkers do not believe in a creative godhead, leaving them uninterested in Western philosophy's concern with the origins or ontology of the cosmos. The universe simply is, and no further investigation is sought.

Given this, Jainist thought still devotes considerable attention to the structure of the universe as it is. All being is divided into two categories: jiva (that which has a life force) and ajiva (that which does not). The numberless jiva souls in the universe all possess unlimited knowledge, energy, and power in their free state, but are held back from perfection by their karmic corruption. Animals, plants, and some phenomena, such as wind and fire, contain imprisoned jiva. Ajiva consists of matter, which is perceived to lack consciousness and to be composed of finite particles akin to Western science's atoms. Most of the physical realities of the world—bodies, karmic particles, heat, motion, light, space, and time—belong to this lesser realm. Ajiva pollutes jiva, stunting its higher potential. The devout Jainist combats this dilution, seeking to restore all jiva to its pure and blissful state.

muskets. Throughout the 15th century, the logical application of gunpowder technology revolutionizes warfare. By the 1420s, heavy artillery has made castles obsolete, easily knocking thick walls down with heavy shot. The musket, operable by a single man and able to penetrate heavy armor at considerable distances, gradually antiquates both the longbow and the mounted knight. The heroic individual of medieval warfare, charging on horseback, is slowly supplanted by anonymous masses of musket-bearing infantry.

1461: **An Italian calendar,** illustrated with images of Christ
(18) and the four authors of the Gospels, is published to help the faithful calculate the coming of Easter.

1461: **Leonardo da Vinci enters the workshop of the master**
(19) **artist Verrocchio.** In 1495, he paints a mural of "The Last Supper." Painter and theoretical inventor, da Vinci will make numerous contributions to mechanics, including sketch proposals for helicopters, shaft propellers, and parachutes, and careful observations of anatomy and various physical phenomena such as capillary action.

1464: **Royal mail service is introduced in France.** The distribution of mail is one of the chief ways that the central government establishes a national bureaucracy, placing local offices throughout the country. Through these regional institutions, monarchs are able to assert their presence and keep tabs on developments in distant localities, facilitating the development of a large modern state with strong central leadership.

1469: **King Ferdinand and Queen Isabella are married,**
(20) uniting the two kingdoms of Castile and Aragon under a dual monarchy that will evolve into modern Spain.

1472: **Ivan III of Moscow marries the niece of the last Byzantine emperor.** By doing so, Ivan effectively becomes the leader of the Orthodox church and shifts the locus of power in Eastern Europe from the lost Constantinople to Russia. In 1480, Ivan declares himself czar of the Russias and begins to unite local fiefdoms into the modern Russian state.

1474-1484: **Pope Sixtus IV effectively transforms the**
(21) **Papal Territories into one of many Italian political states.** With the failure of the Crusades, the defiant independence of the Russian Orthodox church, and the de facto submission of the French church to its country's king, the international influence of the Vatican has greatly weakened. Consequently, Sixtus turns his attention to local concerns, becoming in effect a regional prince. Like other domestic rulers of Italy, he engages in petty wars, is a patron of the arts, and fills important offices with incompetent friends and cronies. The days of widespread papal authority have passed.

1475: **William Caxton engages a Belgian publishing house**
(22) to produce the first book printed in English. Caxton follows up his first book, "The Recuyell of the Historyes of Troye," with a second book, "The Game and Playe of Chesse," in 1479.

1477: **Maximilian of Austria seals his contract to wed**
(23) **Mary of Burgundy** with a diamond ring, beginning the Western tradition of diamond engagement rings.

1478: **The Spanish Inquisition begins.** Receiving permission from Rome to expose and try heretics, Ferdinand and

DAY TO DAY:
THE URBAN LIFE

As trade flourished and feudalism collapsed, the cities of Western Europe offered new opportunities for all classes

Over the course of the 15th century, Europe's population, which in the previous century had approached 45 million people, grew nearly 65 percent. With improved farming techniques actually reducing the need for people in rural areas, the vast majority of this new population gathered in rapidly developing urban environments. As trade flourished and the feudal system began to collapse, the city became the focus of life for all classes of European society.

Increasingly diverse social stratification heavily impacted most European families. In London, numerous distinct social districts developed—small groups of wealthy fishmongers and cloth traders congregated near the river, for example, while middle-class goldsmiths, skinners, and drapers gathered in the city center.

These middle-class homes often were of reasonable comfort and size. Typical furniture included folding chairs, tables assembled from boards and sawhorses, and chests, which served simultaneously as cupboards, closets, and seats. One tailor's will outlined an estate including a house with a hall, a parlor, and three chambers (including one for the maid), two butteries, a kitchen, a counting house, and a garden. Properties included a few tables, one chair, and some stools. In his cupboards were some pewter ornaments and typical clothing, including cloaks lined with wool fleece and dyed violet, green, red, and blue.

The city offered new opportunities for rural immigrants, especially adolescent boys who could apprentice with town craftsmen. Apprenticeship began at age 18 and included 10 years directly under the master and two more as a "bachelor" in his service.

Fewer opportunities existed for women, who were typically kept at home. In 1400s European society, they were valued primarily as child-bearing machines. Usually moving directly from their father's house to that of their husband, women often were impregnated yearly in an effort to counteract high infant mortality.

City dwellers enjoyed a healthier, more diversified diet than did their rural counterparts of the previous century. Government regulation of the sale of products such as meat, poultry, fish, eggs, and cheese in neighborhood markets allowed common people to meet their basic nutritional needs. In addition to this basic fare, the extremely wealthy were likely to sup on swans, herons, and peacocks. Poorer, rural populations, who were less fortunate, probably could expect a diet of cereal, vegetables, turnips, and pork.

Isabella begin a vigorous persecution of religious dissenters as they attempt to forge a national identity on the basis of common Catholic belief. Converts of Jewish or Moorish background are particularly scrutinized by an investigative system that accepts undefined suspicion as a justification for prosecution and prolonged torture as a legitimate means of extracting truthful confession.

1484: **Sandro Botticelli paints "The Birth of Venus" for members of the Medici family.** The confident and frank depiction of pagan subject matter demonstrates how successfully philosophies of the time, especially Neoplatonism, have smoothly integrated pagan thought and ideology into a nominally Christian society.

1484: **Portuguese explorer Diego Cam discovers the mouth of the Congo River in West Africa.** Previously restricted to the coastal regions of the continent, European explorers, colonists, and slave traders now will be able to penetrate deep inland along the river, which provides access to inner Africa's rich natural resources. With Cam's discovery, 400 years of European exploitation in central Africa will begin in earnest.

1485: **Henry Tudor becomes Henry VII of England, bringing an end to 30 years of civil war in that country.** Henry, from the House of Lancaster, marries a daughter from the rival House of York to produce an heir with bloodlines from both factions, effectively ending the dispute. Advances in military technology, laws forbidding the maintenance of private armies, and a strong central government under Henry broke the power of local nobles, ending feudalism and thus creating a modern state in England.

1492: **Ferdinand and Isabella drive the Moors out of southern Spain,** freeing Iberia of Islamic presence for the first time in hundreds of years. Immediately, Spain's entire Jewish population, who had peacefully coexisted with the Moors for centuries, is expelled from the two Spanish kingdoms. The Jews take with them almost all of Spain's middle class, including the knowledge of banking, accounting, and investing that might have saved Spain from its endless economic insolvency over the next few hundred years.

1492: **Christopher Columbus reaches the "New World" while searching for a western route to the Far East.** Spain rapidly conquers, colonizes, and plunders large sections of the continents, supplying the European nations with a gigantic supply of precious metals with which to support their unsteady economies. In the meantime, Europeans are introduced to a new American vice: tobacco.

1492: **Martin Behem builds the first globe in Nurenberg.** Beham's presentation of the world as a sphere is one of the first indications that scientific observation is beginning to overtake quasi-religious medieval rhetoric in the description of the Earth. The courage of men like Behem and Columbus, who dare to declare the world a round solid and not a flat plane, sets the stage—at least culturally—for the work of men like Galileo, Copernicus, and Kepler.

1494: **Florentine monk Savonarola leads a popular religious coup in Florence.** Not everyone accepts the classical ideology of Neoplatonism, and Savonarola is able to expel the Medici briefly from Florence, throwing the city into an orgy of book, painting, and heretic burning as the monk tries to purge Tuscany of pagan impurity. Eventually Rome intervenes, however, restoring the Medici to power and burning Savonarola at the stake in 1498.

1494: **Luca di Pacioli finishes his paper "Algebra."** A sophisticated work, which includes an exploration of cubic equations, Pacioli's treatise is one of many indicators that the mantle of advanced mathematics is passing from Islamic to Western thinkers. Advancing in complexity with increasing speed, the European understanding of abstract math will help propel the explosion in Western technology that will bring the Latin world to the forefront of global power, wealth and prestige.

1495: **The first recorded outbreak of syphilis** infects the French army as they invade Italy in an attempt to subdue the Vatican's political power. The Italians cannot stop the French, but the disease does. As the army retires to northern Europe, it takes the disease with it, distributing it throughout Europe.

1498: **Vasco da Gama sails to India via the southern tip of Africa.** Da Gama's voyage finally establishes a direct European presence in the rich trade world of the Indian Ocean and the China Sea. Bringing in precious metals from outposts in West Africa and spices straight from the Far East, Portugal now is able to circumnavigate the trans-Saharan caravan routes and avoid expensive, indirect trade with the East through Venetian and Islamic merchants in the Mediterranean. As a result, the overland African trade routes dry up, and the Venetian merchant empire collapses.

1499: **The Venetian fleet is defeated by the Ottoman navy at the Battle of Sapienza.** The Mediterranean Sea, long the lake of the Venetians, comes under the dominion of the Ottoman Empire, which controls its coast continuously from the Straits of Gibraltar to the Dardanelles and into the Balkans. With the exception of Italy, France, and Spain, the Mediterranean world is a decisively Islamic one for the next 200 years.

1499: **Amerigo Vespucci leads his first naval expedition to the Caribbean and South America.** Working for Spain, the Florentine navigator makes detailed explorations of the American coast, discovering, among other things, the mouth of the Amazon river. His precise observations and records make it clear that the territory in question is not, as Columbus hoped, Asia, but is in fact a continent previously unknown to the modern West. The "new" continents are called the Americas, after Amerigo, in honor of the explorer's realization.

BIBLIOGRAPHY AND FURTHER READING:

Joel Colton and R.R. Palmer, A History of the Modern World, 5th ed., Alfred A. Knopf, New York, 1978, pp. 49-69.

Horst de la Croix and Richard Tansey, Gardener's Art Through the Ages, 8th ed., Harcourt Brace Jovanovich, New York, 1986, pp. 458-461, 548-577.

Friedman, Robert, editor. The LIFE Millenium, Life Books, New York, 1998, pp. 32, 62-63

Chandice L.Goucher, Charles A. LeGuin, and Linda Linda A. Walton. In the Balance: Themes in Global History, Vol. 2, McGraw-Hill, Boston, 1998, pp. 468-480, 528-536, 555-557, 562-570.

Goetz, Philip W., ed.The Encyclopedia Britannica 15th ed., Encyclopedia Britannica, Inc., Chicago, 1990, vol. 24, pp. 552-555.

Grun, Bernard. The Timetables of History, Simon and Schuster, New York, 1979, pp. 198-220.

Hanes III, William Travis, editor. World History: Continuity and Change, Holt, Rinehart, and Winston, Austin, TX, 1997, pp. 201-203, 330-339, 349-350, 360-379, 418-441.

Janson, H.W. History of Western Art, 3rd ed., Prentice Hall Abrams, Englewood Cliffs, NJ, 1986, pp. 391-463.

ON NEO-CONFUCIANISM
Goetz, Philip W., ed. The Encyclopedia Britannica 15th ed., Encyclopedia Britannica, inc., Chicago, 1990, vol. 16, pp. 653-662.

ON LIFE IN LONDON
Hanawalt, Barbara. Growing up in Medieval London: The Experience of Childhood in History. Oxford 1993.

Fritz, Jean, et al. The World in 1492. New York: Holt and Co., 1992.

Cardini, Franco. Europe 1492: Portrait of a Continent Five Hundred Years Ago. Milan: Anaya Editorial, 1989.

1   A student of Botticelli paints a scene inspired by Boccaccio's "Decameron" *1500s*
2   European depictions of African tribal scenes are dominated by superstition *1500s*
3   Some wives and daughters of European men must wear chastity belts *1500s*
4   European explorers often fight with indigenous inhabitants as portrayed in "Death of Magellan" by Russeu *1500s*
5   Western world adopts the manner of modern fashion, which changes quickly and varies between social classes *1500s*
6   Armor is relegated to a symbolic function *1500s*
7   Elaborate gunpowder flasks are made of bone and ivory *1500*
8   The Americas are named after Amerigo Vespucci *1501*
9   Michelangelo sculpts "David" *1504*
10 Leonardo da Vinci paints "Mona Lisa" *1505*
11 Bosch completes his triptych "The Garden of Earthly Delights" *c. 1510*
12 Ponce de Leon searches for the fountain of youth *1511*
13 Balboa, shown on Spanish coin, crosses the Isthmus of Panama *1513*
14 Martin Luther posts his "95 Theses" *1517*
15 Hernán Cortés conquers Aztec Mexico *1519*
16 Magellan's crew circumnavigates the world *1520*
17 Pizarro subjugates the Incan empire *1531*
18 Henry VIII is named leader of the Anglican church *1534*
19 Copernicus publishes "On the Rotation of the Heavenly Spheres" *1543*
20 Cast-iron artillery becomes common in warfare *1543*
21 Nostradamus writes his prophetic "Centuries" *1555*
22 Elizabeth Tudor becomes Queen of England *1559*
23 St. Basil's Cathedral is completed in Moscow *1561*
24 Globes influence depictions of longitude and latitude on flat maps *1569*
25 The Villa Rotunda by Palladio is completed in Vicenza, Italy *1569*
26 Sir Francis Drake raids Spanish America *1577*
27 Sir Walter Raleigh colonizes North Carolina *1584*

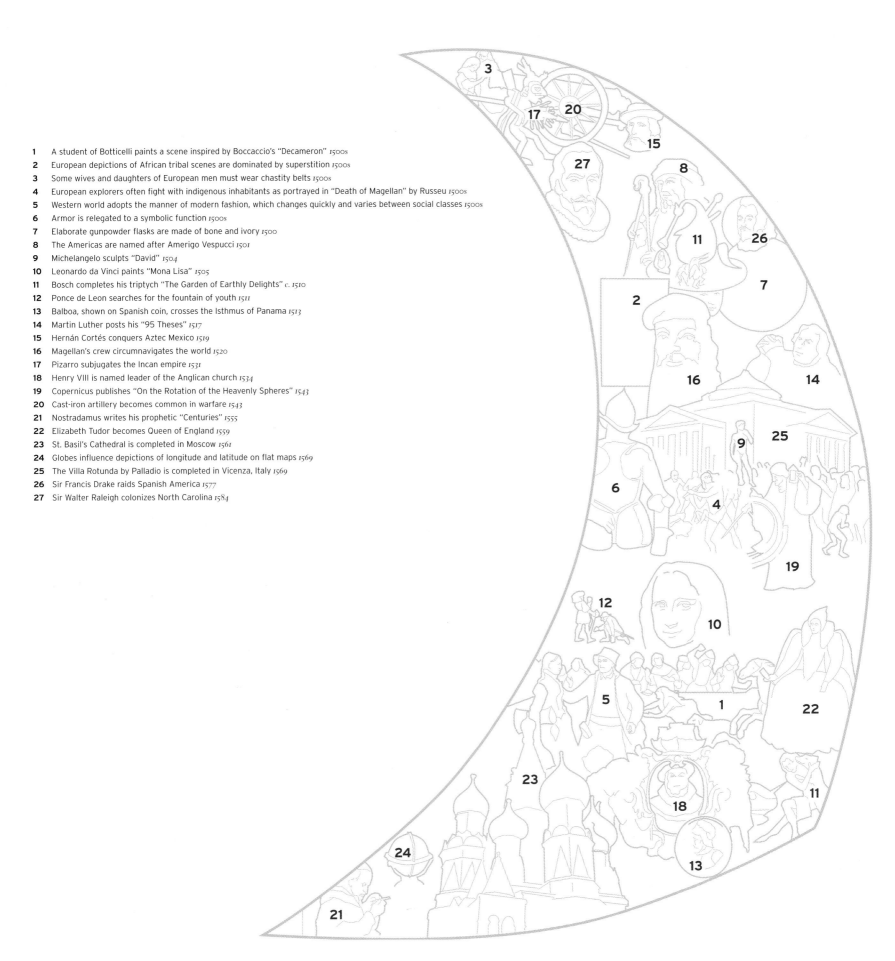

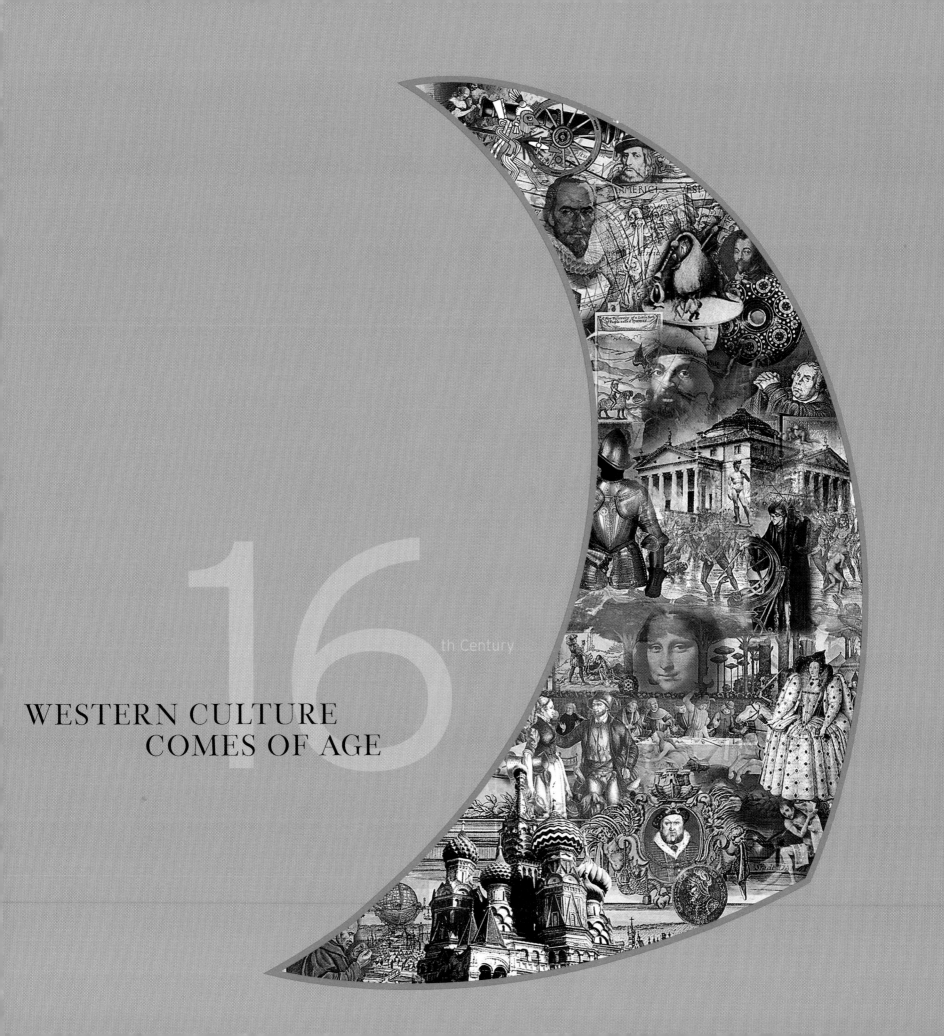

16
th Century

WESTERN CULTURE
COMES OF AGE

WESTERN CULTURE COMES OF AGE

Throughout the 1500s, the Islamic and Latin Christian worlds vied for undisputed global dominance. The Ming dynasty of China, the other potential player in the equation, slowly slipped into an isolationist shadow world of political, economic, and cultural stagnation. The divided tribes of Mongolia, although destined to partial reemergence in the 17th century, were long past the peak of their influence. Japan would spend most of the century embroiled in civil conflict, and the libertarian political structure of sub-Saharan Africa would prevent it from emerging as a global force. Weakened by internal strife and their own brutal governing policies, the Aztec and Inca civilizations left themselves open to outside intervention.

This left the Europeans and the Muslims, two cultural groups with their own set of problems. Both societies were to be wracked by religious conflict in the 16th century. Shiite and Sunni Muslims fought on the frontiers of Persia even as the Protestant Reformation tore the Latin world apart. As these religious disputes intensified, they became vehicles to resolve political disagreements as well, adding to the turmoil and confusion.

Despite this challenging environment, or perhaps because of it, both Europe and the Islamic world politically, economically, and culturally thrived. Four great Islamic empires—the Songhay, Ottoman, Safavid, and Mughal—blossomed in the 1500s, producing great cultural centers in Timbuktu, Cairo, Isfahan, and Constantinople. Between civil wars (in France, the Netherlands, and Germany) and the terrors of the Inquisition (in Spain and Italy), Europe enjoyed the highest artistic and intellectual achievements of the Renaissance, and Western explorers established great trading empires in the Americas and the Far East.

In the end, it was the Portuguese navy's ability to wrest control of the Indian Ocean away from the Muslim nations that decided who would ascend to world domination. The Islamic states, dependent on military conquest for economic stability, found themselves hemmed in on all sides. The Holy Roman Empire checked the Ottomans' westward expansion toward Vienna, the growing strength of Russia formed a boundary to the north, and the Himalayas blocked movement to the east. With the Portuguese victories to the south, the fence was closed on the Islamic world. With their only real competitor contained, European soldiers, merchants, missionaries, and diplomats began to bring the entire globe under their dominion.

1500s: **Nostagio Degli Onesti,** a student of Botticelli, paints ① in the Florentine Renaissance style a rowdy scene inspired by Boccaccio's "Decameron."

1500s: **Ever more introspective, the Ming dynasty of China restricts trade** with the outside world, limiting the size and number of ships leaving Chinese ports. Economically burdened by the new policy, many coastal Chinese take up piracy as a means of employment. Less and less interested in the outside world, China finds its borders increasingly threatened by its more active Manchu and Japanese neighbors.

1500s: **Pirates and privateers flourish** around the globe. English and Dutch raiders harry Spanish shipping in the Atlantic, while the Barbary Corsairs terrorize Christian merchants in the Mediterranean. In the Far East, Chinese and Japanese pirates plunder coastal China. In most parts of the world, pirate culture is tolerant and fluid. Foreigners, women, convicts, and escaped slaves enjoy equal status and are not unlikely to become leaders within their communities.

1500s: **European concepts and depictions of African tribal** ② **life** remain crude and dominated by superstition.

1500s: **Europe's population expands** from 70 million to 90 million between 1500 and 1600. By century's end, both Paris and London will boast communities of more than 200,000. The populations of Lisbon, Antwerp, and Seville, stimulated by increased maritime trade, all will exceed 100,000 by 1600.

1500s: **Modern economic policies begin to emerge** in European nations. New concepts of self-sufficiency, production for export, trade deficit, and unemployment rates—later loosely combined into the theory of mercantilism—become issues of utmost importance to many Latin governments.

1500s: **Hand watches appear in Europe.** Typically four or five inches in diameter and three inches thick, the new portable timekeepers can run for up to 40 hours. Made possible by the use of springs, which replace bulky weights in driving the gears, the new chronometers usually employ four hands to mark the passage of time.

1500s: **Some European men begin to force their wives** ③ **and daughters to wear chastity belts.** Designed to control the promiscuous and protect the vulnerable, the new devices are only marginally effective.

1500s: **Perfumes become extremely popular in Europe.** In the 1500s, hygiene reaches an all-time low in Latin culture, chiefly because of the common belief that bathing is unhealthy. Predictably, the corresponding increase in body odor makes perfume a particularly attractive commodity for those who can afford it.

1500s: **Constant warfare and civil strife,** motivated by the religious conflicts of the Protestant Reformation, reduce the Germanies from an intellectual center to a cultural backwater of Western Europe. Protestant rebels shut down many monasteries, the traditional centers of learning in the region. More concerned with survival than erudition, many Germans lose interest in intellectual pursuits.

1500s: **European explorers** often fight with indigenous ④ inhabitants, as portrayed in "Death of Magellan" by Russeu.

1500s: **Clothing in the Western world adopts the manner** ⑤ **of modern fashion,** changing quickly and varying amongst different social classes. Wealthy men continue to wear longish doublets and stockings, while trousers are common in the lower classes. Women still wear kirtles and gowns, the latter becoming progressively wider or bell shaped toward the end of the century. In some countries, men and women of fashion adopt the highly recognizable neck ruff after 1550. A constantly changing parade of cloaks, capes, hats, shoes, headdresses, and jewelry adorn these outfits.

1500s: **Armor,** made obsolete by the longbow and the mus- ⑥ ket, remains an important symbol of rank, wealth, and taste among Western military officers.

1500: **Isma'il, leader of the Shiite Muslim Safavid family, comes out of hiding in Persia.** Persecuted by other Persians, the kizilbash, a group of Shiites devoted to the Safavid clan, had gone into hiding. Upon the emergence of their leader, the kizilbash quickly rally an army around his banner. Within a year, they have established a militant religious state in Persia that will push against neighboring Islamic states. Throughout the century, Safavid cavalries will wage holy war on the Sunni Ottomans to the west, but ultimately they will find the gunpowder weapons of the Turks too much to overcome. Its aggression contained, the radical religious government of the Safavids still will influence the modern political culture of Iran.

1500: **Highly decorative gunpowder flasks,** like this one with ⑦ ivory inlay, are common among European musket owners.

1500: **Lead pencils are used** for the first time in England. They are followed in 1503 by the first vegetable gum erasers.

1500: **Jakob Nufer performs the first successful Caesarean section on a living woman.** Jakob is deemed qualified for the emergency procedure based on his professional experience gelding pigs.

1501: **The Americas** are named after Amerigo Vespucci. ⑧

1502: **Vasco da Gama** leads his second expedition into the Indian Ocean and the Persian Gulf. It is strictly a voyage of conquest. Twenty-one Portuguese warships crush Islamic competition for trade in the region, burning docks, pillaging cities, and butchering fallen enemies. By 1509, Portuguese forts control trade all the way from Lisbon to Malacca, and spices from the Far East are selling in the Portuguese capital for 20 percent of the going Venetian rate. Having secured a southern route, Portuguese traders finally circumnavigate the Turkish juggernaut between them and Asia. Behind the advance of soldiers and merchants, Jesuit missionaries like Francis Xavier slowly filter into the Eastern world.

1503: **Pocket handkerchiefs** become fashionable in Europe.

1504: **Michelangelo finishes his sculpture "David,"** ⑨ announcing the arrival of the High Renaissance in Italy. In contrast to Donatello's youthful depiction of the same subject in the previous century, Michelangelo's work is a powerful man. The figure, poised and arrogantly calm, undisturbed but ready for sudden action in the face of the approaching Goliath, is a metaphor for the sculptor's home city of Florence, standing nonplussed before the territorial aggressions of neighboring Milan. Along with Bramante's design for St. Peter's Cathedral and Raphael's painting "The School of Athens," Michelangelo's sculpture will stand as one of the highest artistic expressions of Renaissance culture.

1505: **Leonardo da Vinci completes the "Mona Lisa,"** one ⑩ of the few paintings the obsessive perfectionist actually will finish in his lifetime. Easily distracted and prone to bold (and often disastrous) experiments with pigment, Leonardo will leave many of his works incomplete. Incredibly fond of the "Mona Lisa," which contains a gentle mystery in its soft light and deep shadows, the artist will refuse to surrender the painting to the client for years.

1505: **Bramante submits his design for the new St. Peter's Cathedral in Rome.** Boasting that the design places the Pantheon on top of the Basilica of Constantine, the architect develops an image and design fitting for the megalomaniacal ambitions of his client, Pope Julius II. Metaphorically, the huge dome becomes the center of the world, from which the authority of the Catholic church radiates. Calm, powerful, and poised, the building, as it is initially designed, is the architectural equivalent of Michelangelo's "David."

1506: **Albrecht Dürer returns to the Low Countries from a trip to Italy,** where he drank in the artistic revolution of the Italian Renaissance. Sometimes referred to as the "Leonardo of the North," Dürer becomes the champion of Italian style and technique in his home country. Author of treatises on perspective and proportions, Dürer also is one of the century's finest engravers. His incredibly refined touch, developed

during his training as a goldsmith, produces prints of a quality that will essentially remain unchallenged through the 20th century.

1509: **Erasmus of Rotterdam writes "Praise of Folly,"** a satire of contemporary society focusing on the failings and abuses of the Catholic church. Although highly critical of the clergy, Erasmus is a humanist, and hence by nature a moderate. His respect for tolerance, peace, and critical distance encourages him to seek reform of the church, rather than its complete dismantling. In the emotional turmoil of the Protestant Reformation, his voice of reason will be overshadowed by calls for violence and destruction.

c. 1510: **Hieronymus Bosch completes his triptych "The Garden of Earthly Delights,"** one of the most unique, disturbing, and at times opaque works of European art. Mixing objects and scale in a manner that prefigures Surrealist art, Bosch's panels are symbolic landscapes filled with hidden symbols of alchemy, magic, sexuality, and witchcraft. In somewhat of a throwback to medieval thought, Bosch warns through his paintings that humans are destroyed by physical gratification and that earthly joy is fragile and fleeting. Music seems to be a particularly dangerous evil in Bosch's work—many of the victims in the "Hell" panel are crucified, impaled, or otherwise tortured on giant musical instruments.

1511: **Raphael paints "The School of Athens,"** one of the finest expressions of Italian Renaissance culture. In the painting, great philosophers of the ancient world, such as Plato, Aristotle, Euclid, Pythagoras, and Diogenes, are imagined to gather together in a building that looks remarkably like St. Peter's Cathedral as designed by Bramante. The balanced symmetry of the composition marks a high point in Renaissance aesthetics, but it is the painting's content, which depicts Rome as the great inheritor of ancient intellectual traditions, that is most interesting. This almost arrogant Roman confidence will not survive the next 20 years.

1511: **Ponce de León sets out in search of the Fountain of Youth.** Interested as much in the precious metals that supposedly surround the fountain as he is in the prospect of eternal life, the former governor of Puerto Rico embarks from that island at the head of a sizeable expedition. Although he never will find the fountain, his search will lead him to discover Florida.

1512: **Michelangelo completes the painting of the Sistine Chapel.** The scene depicting the creation of Adam demonstrates the evolution of Renaissance society beyond the medieval awe of God. Adam seems to have reached for God before the divine spark is delivered; his gaze may already have passed to Eve, who hovers just behind the creator. Magnificent and beautiful, the High Renaissance vision of Adam seems to have a power independent of the Christian godhead.

1512: **The British Royal Navy begins building double-deck warships.** Each of the new vessels can carry 70 guns. A country of limited natural resources and population, England will blunt the aggression of its larger European neighbors with the world's most celebrated navy. In time, English sea power will make Britain the mother country of the most powerful empire on Earth.

1513: **Spanish explorers** under Vasco Núñez de Balboa cross the Isthmus of Panama, becoming the first Europeans to see the Pacific Ocean.

1513: **Niccoló Machiavelli writes "The Prince,"** one of the first explorations of politics as a practical science. Believing humans to be selfish and cruel by nature, the Florentine author rejects moral systems of government in favor of expediency. Cruelty, dishonesty, and manipulation all are legitimate tools of government as long as they preserve the combined interests of the ruler and the state.

1514: **Portuguese ships enter Chinese waters for the first time.** By 1520, a temporary Portuguese settlement exists on the Chinese mainland. Over the next 400 years, the European presence in China will steadily grow, gradually taking advantage of weak Chinese governments to exploit the nation's rich, natural resources. Western domination of the country will not be broken until the early 20th century.

1516: **Pope Julius II formalizes the king of France's role as head of the Gallican church.** Throughout the 16th century, many European monarchs will become Protestant to gain control of church property and influence within their territories. By granting religious authority to the French kings, Julius ultimately helps preserve France as an officially Catholic state.

1516: **Titian is named Painter to the Republic of Venice.** Famous for the rich color and texture of his paintings, the Venetian painter will, during his long career, gradually move away from the Arcadian subjects and Renaissance compositions of his early works. In later pieces like "Madonna of the Pegaro Family," his compositions will take on the strong diagonals, extreme foreshortening, and sweeping movement characteristic of Mannerist and Baroque painting.

1516: **Englishman Thomas More writes "Utopia,"** a hypothetical exploration of the ideal Christian society. Arguing that the best civilization is the one that is concerned for all its members, More concludes that private property, by benefiting some at the expense of others, is a great evil. In later times, this position will be read as a prototypical call for socialist or communist forms of government.

1517: **Coffee is introduced to Latin Europe.** Developed in the Middle East, the habit of drinking coffee slowly spreads along major trade routes, finally reaching Western Europe in the early 16th century.

1517: **Martin Luther posts his "95 Theses," setting off the Protestant Reformation.** Among other things, Luther denies the redemptive value of good works and the indulgences, insists that all believers are priests through their duty to interpret the Bible for themselves, and rejects monasticism. Impossible to reconcile with traditional Latin doctrine, Luther's beliefs establish a new branch of Christianity in opposition to Catholicism. As many Christians embrace the new beliefs, Europe is divided along militant religious lines and plunged into widespread civil war.

1517: **Ottoman armies led by Selim the Great capture Cairo,** bringing an end to the Malmuk empire. With the victory, the northern Turks greatly expand their dominion, which now includes all of Egypt, Arabia, Syria, Anatolia, and the Balkans.

DAY TO DAY:
CITY OF TIMBUKTU

*An Islamic oasis
of culture and trade*

Eight miles north of the Niger river, Timbuktu is situated in an isolated oasis, wedged between the southern edge of the Sahara desert and the northern limits of the West African jungle. During the late 16th century, the city flourished as the capital of the powerful Songhay empire. Home to 60,000 Arab and West African residents, Timbuktu served as the Islamic world's westernmost hub of trade, manufacture, and scholastic learning.

African pilgrims gathered here for their religious journey to Mecca. In the markets, merchants from Wadan, Tuwat, Ghudamis, Augila, and Morocco met to trade West African gold, cloth, and slaves for Saharan salt or North African horses. Artisans and weavers were open for business. Men and women worked side by side, and female retailers often removed their veils to conduct business. When barter was insufficient for a transaction, gold nuggets and Persian cowrice shells were used for currency.

Around this active trade economy, a peaceful, luxuriant lifestyle emerged. Within their wattle-and-daub, thatch-roofed homes, most families had sizeable households of male and female slaves. City squares bustled at night as young people gathered to sing, dance, and play music. Inhabitants enjoyed an abundance of grains, milk, butter, and meat in their diets. Despite the neighboring desert, sweet water was plentiful, filling the city's wells.

Intellectual pursuits were cherished, and advanced education was available to foreigners and the poor. Students who could not afford the five to 10 cowrice shells of weekly tuition worked as apprentices in the city's tailoring industry. More than 25 tailor houses supported approximately 50 students each in this way, giving many of the less wealthy access to the city's 150 schools of Islamic science, religion, and law. To commence their studies, students often entered into a relationship with a scholar, or master, who would serve as a tutor. Upon completion of their studies, many of the educated would be appointed to government positions as elementary school teachers, mosque functionaries, scribes or secretaries.

The Songhay kings deeply valued education within the society, recognizing that, along with a vibrant trade economy, education was one of the prime pillars of the empire's prosperity.

1519: **A small expedition of Spanish soldiers,** led by Hernán Cortés, invade Aztec Mexico. Many of the Mesoamerican empire's non-Aztec subjects, rebelling against harsh imperial rule, join the Spanish in overthrowing the Aztec emperor Montezuma. Unfortunately, they will not be any happier with their new rulers. Within 50 years, smallpox and influenza brought by the Spanish will kill more than 90 percent of the indigenous adult population. Those who survive will find their domination by the Spanish only slightly less oppressive than that suffered under the Aztecs.

1520: **Explorer Ferdinand Magellan leads a Spanish ship** around the southern tip of the Americas and into the Pacific. Having found a route past South America, his expedition will

1524: **Giovanni da Verrazzano leads the first extensive European exploration** of the North American Atlantic coast. An Italian in the service of France, Verrazzano searches for a western sea passage to Asia. Unsuccessful in this aim, the expedition still is the first from Europe to enter what will later become known as New York harbor.

1526: **Mbemba Nzinga, Christian monarch of the Congo region of Africa,** issues a formal protest to the king of Portugal over the growing slave trade. Nzinga, whose population is being whittled away as entire villages agree to be kidnapped and sold into slavery by Portuguese raiders, demands that the practice come to an end. Powerless to stop the Europeans, however, Nzinga finds his objections ignored. By

1531: **Francisco Pizarro, with less than 200 Spanish soldiers, subjugates the Incan empire.** Taking advantage of superior military technology and an internally divided Incan state, Pizarro quickly gains control of the capital of Cuzco, where he appoints a puppet government to rule until a more permanent Spanish authority can be installed.

1534: **Pope Paul III ascends to the head of the Catholic Church.** Accepting his position's loss of direct political power, Paul is the first modern pope to understand his office as one of moral influence rather than political leadership. Abandoning the secular practices of his Renaissance predecessors, Paul attempts to reform the church into a legitimate religious authority.

> "...our works cannot reconcile God or merit forgiveness of sins...
> ...we obtain this only by faith"
>
> MARTIN LUTHER

be the first to circumnavigate the globe. Magellan himself will not finish the voyage–dying in the Philippines–and only about 20 members of his crew will survive the journey to see Spain again.

1520: **Süleyman the Lawgiver becomes padishah of the Ottoman empire.** During his 46-year reign, the new emperor will guide the Ottoman state to the apex of its glory. Under Süleyman, government and taxation are efficiently overhauled, urban growth is stimulated by vast building campaigns, borders are expanded by military conquest, and the arts flourish. New political representation for the empire's religious minorities establishes a general sense of domestic stability and social harmony.

1520: **The Spanish discover chocolate.** Imported from Mexico, the sweet becomes a favorite delicacy amongst the Spanish aristocracy.

1520S: **Peasant revolts against church governments** in northern Germany reveal the social and political aspects of the Protestant Reformation. Although Luther was motivated by belief, most of the German religious wars of the 16th century are not. Peasants revolt in church territories to protest oppressive taxes and working conditions, not Catholic doctrine. In a similar manner, free towns of middle-class burghers use the Reformation as a tool to break their feudal obligations to church rulers. Princes and kings see Lutheranism as an opportunity to reinforce the independence of their territories from papal or imperial influence. For many German Protestants, religious freedom serves as a vehicle to more pragmatic ends.

1523: **François Rabelais, physician and humanist, writes "Pantagruel,"** the first of his great contributions to French satiric comedy. A mockery of the chivalric romance, the book serves as a general satire of medieval thought and values. Aesthetically, the text is a collection of brilliant writing, a celebration of the linguistic wit of a great wordsmith.

1600, more than 100,000 African slaves will be working in Spain's American colonies alone.

1527: **Imperial troops sack Rome.** Hatred of the Roman clergy, which has festered in Germany for years, drives the barbarous pillaging of the city. Shocked by the brutality of the event, northern Italian society loses the confidence that has propelled the Renaissance. In the aftermath, artistic and intellectual movements expressing uncertainty, such as Mannerism, emerge in the region.

1527: **The first Protestant university** is established in the city of Marburg. With the development of its own formal institutions of education, the Protestant movement insures its own lasting presence in Europe. In new universities like Marburg, the future leaders and intellectuals of Protestant Christianity will be formed.

1529: **Ottoman armies are repelled** in their attempt to capture Vienna. The Austrian victory secures the safety of Eastern Europe, halting Ottoman expansion. Denied the continuing conquest and expansion upon which it economically and politically depends, the Turkish state slowly begins to destabilize after Süleyman's death in 1566.

1530: **The Portuguese establish a colony in Brazil,** where a rich sugar cane industry is developing. The only Portuguese colony in the Americas, the new settlement is intended to offset Spanish colonization of the Philippines. In a moment of supreme arrogance, the two Iberian nations agree to divide the world between them, Spain taking the Americas and Portugal taking Africa and Asia. Brazil and the Philippines constitute the singular exceptions to this agreement. Unfortunately for the two nations, other states, European and otherwise, will have more to say on the issue than allowed for by their agreement.

1530: **The potato, discovered by Spanish colonists** in the Andes of South America, is introduced to Europe.

1534: **English Parliament passes the Act of Supremacy,** establishing Henry VIII as the leader of the new Anglican church. Henry's desire for a son, a wish unfulfilled by five of his six wives, left him in constant need of annulments of his unfruitful marriages. When he asks that his marriage to a close relative of the Holy Roman Emperor be invalidated, the Pope, caught in a political vise, balks. Undaunted, Henry declares England a Protestant nation, and as the head of the new Anglican church, annuls his own marriage. Henry's act is the supreme example of the secular ends to which the religious crisis in Europe is used during the 16th century.

1535: **Jacques Cartier leads a French expedition** up the St. Lawrence River in North America, establishing outposts at Quebec and Montreal. For the next 200 years, these locations will serve as the major centers of the French colonies in Canada.

1536: **John Calvin releases the first edition of "Institutes of the Christian Religion,"** a synthetic Protestant reading of the Bible. Calvin's interpretation, most distinctive for its militant development of predestination, gives rise to more radical Protestant sects. Unlike the followers of Luther, who seek authority and administrative structure through local secular rulers, Calvinists recognize no final worldly authority.

1540: **Ignatius Loyola receives papal permission to found the Society of Jesus.** The front line of the Catholic church's attempt to reclaim Protestants and spread Catholicism throughout the world, the organization will establish missionary schools around the globe. Following a strict military discipline within their order, the Jesuits are progressive and open-minded instructors, educating their charges in a humanistic, Renaissance manner. As the tutors of the upper classes, Jesuit monks will rise to positions of great political influence, serving as the councilors and advisors of many state leaders.

Copernicus

1542: **The Roman Inquisition, a tribunal dedicated to exposing heresy,** is established in Italy. Although less notorious than the Spanish Inquisition, which earns a well-deserved reputation for outright barbarism during a crackdown on Calvinists in the Spanish Netherlands, the Roman tribunal is not above torturing its victims before burning them at the stake. Revealing the diminished reach of papal authority, the Roman Inquisition's influence will never really extend beyond northern Italy.

1543: **Portuguese traders introduce firearms to Japan.** Rapidly mastering the new technology, Japanese gunsmiths revolutionize warfare in the archipelago.

1543: **Blasco da Garaq submits a design for a steamboat** to Austrian Emperor Charles V. Garaq's proposal, a little ahead of its time, is left unexplored by the emperor's scientists. Almost 300 years will pass before nautical engineers seriously consider steam propulsion again.

1543: **Polish astronomer Nicolaus Copernicus publishes "On the Rotation of the Heavenly Spheres,"** the first modern text to contend that the sun is the center of the solar system. Theorizing that the apparent movement of the stars across the night sky is caused by the axial rotation of the Earth, Copernicus goes on to conclude that many astronom-

Miraculously, the Spanish government simply will spend its enormous wealth without any thought to investment or improvement of the country's shaky domestic economy. When the colonies are lost, Spain will experience a devastating financial collapse.

1545-1547: **The first meeting of the Council of Trent** attempts to outline a Catholic response to the new Protestant threat. Minor reforms are implemented and Catholic doctrine reasserted. Traditional beliefs of salvation through good works, celibacy of the clergy, monasticism, services in Latin, and the seven sacraments are reiterated. Most importantly, the central authority of the Pope is emphasized, allowing the Catholic church to remain unified while Protestant believers fragment into a multitude of sects.

1546-1555: **Open warfare between imperial troops and the Protestant League** of Schmalkand devastates German regions. Holy Roman Emperor Charles V feels the need to uphold Catholicism, but his attempts to suppress Luther are seen by many German princes as a threat to local freedom, and war breaks out. In a typical demonstration of the Reformation's political character, Catholic France supports the Protestant princes throughout the war. In 1555, the Peace of Augsburg establishes religious independence by principality

the Spanish will successfully establish a widespread Iberian culture in their American colonies.

c. 1553: **Andrea Amati makes the first modern violin.** Developed in Cremona, Italy, the violin quickly replaces the cruder viol as the primary string instrument of Western music. An answer to the demand for a more expressive instrument, the violin reflects a growing Latin interest in non-vocal music.

1553: **The Russia Company, one of the first modern corporations, is established in London.** Partly funded by the government, the company is created to develop trade with Russia across the recently discovered White Sea. Beyond the financial capacity of individual merchants, trade along the new route is made possible by the pooled fiscal resources of a larger organization. An influential model for European trade and colonization, the Russia Company will serve as a corporate template for English colonies and trading concerns throughout the world.

1555: **Tobacco is shipped from the Americas to Spain,** where cigarette smoking becomes a popular habit. Portuguese merchants also will introduce Europeans to snuff in 1558.

"The greatest thing in the world is to know how to be one's own"

M O N T A I G N E

ical observations are most easily explained if the sun, and not the Earth, is the focal point of the solar system. His elegant model of the sun and its satellites replaces the excessively complex geocentric theories supported by ancient philosophy and Catholic ideology.

1543: **Flemish physician Andreas Vesalius completes "Fabrica,"** the first comprehensive Western study of modern anatomy. Influenced by Arab medicine, Vesalius breaks with Latin tradition and secretly dissects human cadavers. Ancient medicine, which extrapolated its theories of internal human anatomy from animal dissections, is revealed to be wrong in many of its conclusions. Vesalius's seven-volume record of direct anatomical observation becomes the European basis of all further study on the subject.

1543: **Improvements in metalworking techniques** allow English armories to begin producing cast-iron artillery. The new cannons are heavier than their bronze counterparts, rust quickly, and tend to explode into fragments when they fail, but are remarkably inexpensive to make, cutting production costs by as much as two-thirds. Cheaper to build and mounted on wheeled chassis for greater mobility, heavy artillery plays an increasingly important role in Western warfare.

1545: **Rich silver deposits are discovered in Peru.** Technical improvements in the extraction process greatly accelerate the mining process, and production soars. For the rest of the century, Spain's American colonies will produce 500,000 pounds of silver and 10,000 pounds of gold annually.

throughout the empire, finally bringing peace to a weak and exhausted Germany.

1546: **Michelangelo takes over the construction of St. Peter's Cathedral.** With Pope Julius dead and the swelling confidence of 1506 long gone, the famous sculptor scales back Bramante's ambitious project. In his hands, the reduced design takes on some of the movement and energy more typical of Mannerist architecture.

1548: **Francis Xavier establishes the first Jesuit mission in Japan.** Several warlords are converted to the new religion, but they and their followers remain a distinct minority among the general population.

1550: **The game of billiards** is played for the first time in Italy.

1550: **Ukiyo-e** ("painting of the floating world"), a kind of popular genre painting, begins to emerge in Japan. Depicting the scenes and events of everyday life, the new art portrays groups of individuals interacting on a neutral background. With their concern for details of typical dress and social relationships, the paintings enjoy a popular appeal. Like kabuki theatre, which is developing at the same time, ukiyo-e is an art form intended for common audiences.

1551: **The University of Lima** becomes the first European-style institution of higher learning in the Americas. The University of Mexico follows quickly in 1554. While the Portuguese will remain a hostile ruling minority in the Far East, controlling trade routes from isolated fortress outposts,

1555: **Nostradamus, a prominent French physician, writes "Centuries,"** a collection of prophetic poems. With astrology at the peak of its popularity in France, the author's cryptic verses become wildly popular as predictions of the future. Invited to court by the queen of France, Nostradamus will serve as astrologer and physician to two French kings.

1558: **Gioseffo Zarlino** publishes "Institutioni harmoniche," in which he defines the 12 major and minor scales of modern Western music.

1558: **France annexes Calais, the last English possession in continental Europe.** The dispute that caused the Hundred Years War is finally put to rest. Accepting reality, the English monarchs relinquish their claim to any hereditary rights in northern France.

1559: **Elizabeth Tudor is crowned queen of England.** Taking control after the turbulent reign of her Catholic half-sister Mary, Elizabeth reestablishes the Anglican church, which Mary had dissolved. Under Elizabeth, the religious instability that emerged in England after Henry VIII's death ends, and the nation becomes decidedly Protestant. The Catholic minority eventually shrinks to three percent of the total English population.

c. 1560: **The modern religious boundaries of Europe are essentially established.** France, Spain, Italy, southern Germany, and Ireland remain predominantly Catholic, while England, Scotland, Scandinavia, northern Germany, and

CONTEMPORARY PHILOSOPHIES

HUMANISM

For Renaissance thinkers, pragmatism outweighed idealism

Humanism, an intellectual movement that began in the 14th century with thinkers such as Petrarch and Boccaccio, reached the peak of its influence in early 16th-century Europe.

Encompassing the work of men with backgrounds as diverse as those of Erasmus and Rabelais, incorporating views as apparently contradictory as those of Sir Thomas More and Niccoló Machiavelli, humanistic thought dominated Renaissance culture. First and foremost a renewed interest in humanity and the human world, humanism constituted an outright rejection of the anti-corporeal philosophies of medieval thinkers.

For an alternative to medieval texts, the humanists looked to ancient Roman writers for their inspiration. Absorbing and critically considering the wisdom of authors like Cicero, Pliny, and Ovid, Renaissance men would attempt to apply it to their social and political lives.

Virtue, the central theme of humanism, really constituted appropriate and well-executed action. Humanistic study, comprised of history, rhetoric, philosophy, and grammar, was not considered valuable unless it was actively applied to daily affairs. As philosophical and spiritual beings, humanists had no interest in transcending the human world and the human condition, but rather sought to fulfill their considerable potential within themselves. Power, material success, and positive social influence all were highly valued goals of the movement's adherents.

In keeping with their practical mindset, humanist thinkers tended to reject abstract, unsubstantiated theory in favor of thoughtful analysis and detailed observation. Consequently, a book like Machiavelli's "The Prince" is not an outline of perfect governments based on ideal human behavior and morals but a rough and ready theory of effective rule within an imperfect political system. The moral undertones of previous treatises on government, like Plato's "Republic," are rejected for their lack of correspondence to reality. Even Thomas More's "Utopia," which is an exploration of an ideal society, reflects humanist pragmatism. More's hypothetical community is not based on "perfect" human behavior, but is instead a proposal for how man's most destructive impulses might be contained or deflected. By abolishing personal property, More is not attempting to deny man's selfish nature; he is merely trying to minimize its damage to society as a whole.

With its passion for observation and practical application, humanism is the final stone in the intellectual foundation of Western science. Driving men to excel, to fulfill their human potential in a pragmatic way, humanism became the impetus for the explosion of European science and technology which, after 1600, shaped the modern world.

parts of the Low Countries adopt various forms of the Protestant religion.

c. 1560: **The Catholic church establishes the Index of Prohibited Books**, a list of titles the faithful are forbidden from reading. Throughout the 16th century, Catholic and Protestant bishops alike will attempt to limit reading within their dioceses.

1560: **Hsü Wei writes Ching P'ing Mei, the first genuine Chinese novel.** A rude, murderous drunkard (he beat his second wife to death), Hsü Wei is also a man of multiple artistic talents. In addition to writing the first Chinese novel, he paints and is renowned for his fiery, impressionistic brushwork.

1561: **St. Basil's Cathedral is completed in Moscow**, physically establishing the city as the new religious capital of the Orthodox church. The building is a beautiful example of a distinctive Russian visual culture that flowered briefly after the withdrawal of the Mongols. Infatuated with French culture, later Russian rulers and nobles would suppress this indigenous expression in favor of Western styles and methods.

(23)

1562: **French Catholics and Protestant Huguenots divide their nation in religious civil war.** Many minor Protestant nobles, wishing to control religion within their principalities, rebel against Catholic rule. An untraditional war, the conflict is characterized by bands of marauders roaming the countryside. Left vulnerable by a central government too weak to control either side, the real victims of the war are the French peasants caught in its midst.

1562: **John Heywood's "Woorkes,"** a collection of the comedic playwright's interludes and ballads, is published in England. A major figure in the evolution of early Elizabethan comedy, Heywood is best known for catchy sayings like "Love me, love my dog," "Out of the frying pan, into the fire," and "Beggars shouldn't be choosers."

1566: The first newspaper, "Notizie Scritte," is printed in Venice.

1567: Japanese warlord Oda Nobunaga deposes the ineffective shogunate government, making himself the dictator of central Japan. Gradually expanding his borders, Nobunaga continues to subjugate the daimyo rulers of neighboring fiefdoms, slowly reuniting Japan into a single state under a strong central authority.

1569: Flemish cartographer Gerardus Mercator develops a flat map of the Earth, showing lines of longitude and latitude. Making the lines of reference a perfect grid, Mercator distorts dimensions in the northern and southern edges of the map to match the distances of the spherical globe to his rectangular chart. His method will become the standard convention of European mapmakers, lasting through the 20th century.

1569: The Villa Rotonda, architect Andrea Palladio's most famous work, is completed in Vicenza, Italy. Located in one of the outlying districts of the Venetian Empire, the new building is behind the times, serving as one of the finest examples of Renaissance architecture even though the Renaissance has long since ended in major cultural centers such as Rome. Set on top of a local hill, the villa's four porches provide a panoramic view of the surrounding landscape, effectively claiming the world in all directions as the domain of the villa's owner. Standing beneath the central dome, with

dies. One of the most influential of the Jewish mystics, Luria's ideas of reassembling a fractured universe through the recreation of Adam, the "primordial man," are not unlike Islamic Sufi beliefs. His doctrines, known as Lurianic Kabbala, will become one of the principal sources of future Jewish mysticism.

1573: Wan-Li becomes the emperor of Ming China. Introspective and unconcerned with affairs of state, the new ruler will oversee the gradual deterioration of central authority in the empire. As the government grows progressively weaker, regional officials will abuse their domestic authority, while foreign threats increasingly will destabilize national security.

1577: An English naval expedition under Sir Francis Drake sets out to raid the Spanish Americas. Successfully navigating the Straits of Magellan, Drake's one remaining ship inflicts terror on Spanish shipping; its holds are soon stuffed with captured gold, silver, and precious stones. Unable to find a northern passage back to the Atlantic, Drake turns his ship westward. In 1580, he becomes the first English captain to circumnavigate the globe, arriving at Plymouth in September of that year.

1579: Under the Cossack leader Yermak, a Russian military expedition subdues the Mongol populations of Siberia. Drawn eastward by timber, wax, fur, salt, and fish-

by elaborate but obviously fake sets, modern theatre will remain detached from daily life in a way that medieval drama never was.

1582: Pope Gregory XIII establishes the Gregorian Calendar. Inaccurate by approximately an hour every year, the old Julian calendar had slipped 14 days since Roman times. Adjusting the date to account for the accumulated inaccuracy, the Pope also institutes a more precise system. The new calendar, accurate to within one day every 20,000 years, becomes the modern standard for the European world.

1582: With the death of Oda Nobunaga, his lieutenant Toyotomi Hideyoshi becomes the dictator of Japan. In 1590, the new ruler accomplishes his predecessor's goal, uniting all of Japan under his singular authority.

1582: The first English colony in North America is established in Newfoundland. On the same island that their Nordic ancestors tried to settle 582 years ago, the English establish the first community of what will soon be a large colonial empire.

1583: The first known life insurance policy is written in England.

1584: Sir Walter Raleigh finances the establishment of an English colony on the coast of North Carolina. The com-

> ## "...none have had a greater effect on the human spirit than Copernicus. The world had scarcely become known...when it was asked to waive the tremendous privilege of being the center of the universe"
>
> GOETHE

views radiating out in all four directions, the building's occupants rest at the metaphorical center of the universe.

c. 1570: The Iroquois League, a confederation of five major Native American nations, is formed. United under the leader Dekanawidah, the Mohawk, Cayuga, Onondaga, Seneca, and Oneida tribes form a pact of mutual protection against the encroaching Mohican and Huron nations. As the European presence in North America expands during the 17th century, the Iroquois will become one of the chief blocks of resistance against the Eastern invaders.

1571: Akbar, one of the great rulers of the Mughal dynasty in India, builds the city of Fatehpur Sikri. Famous for its distinctive mosque and city gate, the city shows a blending of Islamic, Hindu, and Persian architectural styles that reflects the various cultural strands of the Mughal state. In contrast to their zealous Safavid neighbors, the Mughal rulers are distinctive for their religious tolerance and acceptance of indigenous Indian custom and thought.

1572: The great Syrian Kabbalist Isaac ben Solomon Luria

ing, the Russians slowly stretch across northern Asia throughout the 16th century. On the Siberian frontier, indigenous Mongols will mix with migrant Cossacks, peasants escaping feudal obligations in the west, and prisoner communities known as gulags. Around them, Russian territory will stretch west to Poland and south to the Amur River and China.

1579: A great astronomical observatory is constructed in Constantinople. In addition to astronomy and astrology, Islamic scholars excel in mathematics, the physical sciences, history, geography, and theology. Their astronomical charts, maps, and geographical texts, particularly "The Book of the Sea" by Piri Reis, are among the finest of the century.

1580: The last miracle play is performed in Coventry, England, marking the end of the powerful medieval form. While the plays of the 16th century will be more sophisticated in their plots and dialogues, the authenticity felt by medieval audiences will be lost forever, a fact bemoaned by playwrights like William Shakespeare. Raised up on stages, placed behind prosceniums and curtains, and surrounded

plete disappearance of the colonists is one of the great mysteries of early American history, but is somewhat typical of Raleigh's numerous abortive undertakings. A one-time favorite of Queen Elizabeth, he loses influence when he marries another woman. After exploring parts of South America, he bungles an attempt to establish an English mining colony there. An angry King James reactivates a 15-year-old stayed order of execution against Raleigh (who once had been accused of treason), and the hapless nobleman's life comes to an uneremonious, headless conclusion.

1585: Saint John of the Cross writes "Living Flame of Love," one of many mystic Catholic texts to be written in late 16th-century Spain. With other mystical thinkers like Saint Teresa of Avila, John contributes to the recreation of a personal, emotional, and anti-scientific approach to Christianity. The resurgence of Catholic mystic belief offers the faithful an alternative to the deductive reasoning and detached intellectualism of Protestant thinkers.

1586: The first performances of kabuki theatre are staged in Japan. A far cry from the restrained elegance of Noh performance, kabuki is an exuberant and playful art form, focusing more on the showcasing of artists' talents than the relation of plots or deep social messages. The first popular theatre in Japan, kabuki is performed in day-long festivals where audience members come and go as they please, eat at meal times, actively interact with the cast, and are utterly nonplussed by the frequent invasion of the audience space by the performers.

1586: **El Greco paints "The Burial of Count Orgaz" in Spain.** A student in Venice, the Greek painter had worked with Titian before moving to Spain. In the younger painter's hands, the diagonal movement of the Venetian artist becomes a swirling field of energy. The figures of the painting are elongated and distorted, almost as if the spiritual power of the scene is literally stretching space. The height of Mannerist painting, El Greco's pulsing compositions, in which physical reality takes a back seat to a higher power, meshes perfectly with the mystic spiritualism of 16th-century Spain.

1587: **Italian composer Claudio Monteverdi** releases his first book of madrigals. Toward the end of the 16th and the beginning of the 17th centuries, the composer's music gradually will turn more experimental as he becomes one of the major figures in the development of Italian opera.

1587: **Under 'Abbas the Great, Safavid culture achieves its greatest success.** 'Abbas arms his elite troops with gunpowder weapons, greatly strengthening the military. In the meantime, the Shah's government helps turn Iranian carpet production into a national, factory-driven export industry, greatly strengthening the economy through trade. Chinese potters are brought in to train Persian craftsman in the tile work for which they will become famous.

1588: **Michel de Montaigne's "Essays" are published** in France. A harbinger of Enlightenment thought, Montaigne establishes the need for self-knowledge, acceptance of human limitations, and a love of moderation over excess as the fundamental prerequisites of living well.

c. 1588: **English playwright Christopher Marlowe** writes "The Tragical History of Doctor Faustus," perhaps his finest play. Written in the blank verse that Marlowe has introduced to English theatre, the work is a transition between medieval morality plays and Renaissance theatre. Faustus, the tragic hero, is both magnificent and foolish, the powerful man of the Renaissance and the flawed and sinful wretch of the Middle Ages.

1588: **The Spanish armada,** a vast invasion fleet intent on landing a Spanish army in Protestant England, is badly defeated in the English Channel by a British navy under Sir Francis Drake. Spanish king Philip II, self-proclaimed Catholic crusader against the heretic Protestants, launched the fleet to conquer England after Elizabeth I openly helps rebelling Protestants in the Spanish Netherlands. Instead, the Spanish navy is shattered, setting the stage for England to become the great naval power of the modern world.

1589: **Henry of Navarre, leader of the Huguenots, becomes the first Bourbon king of France.** As Henry IV, the new king will convert to Catholicism in the name of peace. His announcement of the Edict of Nantes in 1598, however, provides for the safety and security of French Protestants. By skillfully walking a middle path, Henry finally brings an end to 40 years of religious civil war in France.

1590: **Edmund Spenser** finishes his epic poem "The Faerie Queen."

1591: **The great Songhay empire, located in modern Nigeria, is conquered** by Moroccan armies. Under the rule of Askia the Great, the Songhay city of Timbuktu was the westernmost cultural and commercial hub of the Islamic world. Its fabulous university attracted scholars from the far reaches of Muslim territory, while its markets traded European, Indian, and Far Eastern wares. Less admirable in the eyes of the modern reader, Songhay ports also were the main distribution centers for a continental slave industry that delivered human cargo throughout the Mediterranean region.

1591: **The practice of "enclosing" the bulls in the streets of Pamplona is begun.** Part of a traditional festival celebrating the city's first bishop, the dangerous sport of herding the bulls is an integral part of the annual eight-day bullfighting marathon.

1595: **European shoes,** much broader than their 14th-century ancestors, begin to feature hard heels.

1597: **Shakespeare writes "Henry IV,"** one of his finest history plays. Writing primarily histories and comedies during the late 16th century, the great playwright will not begin producing his tragic masterpieces until the 1600s.

1598: **Philip II, King of Spain, dies.** He leaves behind an economy living hand to mouth on American gold, a society contemptuous of labor and intrigued by mysticism, and a shrinking population burdened by heavy taxes. Spain, the strongest nation of the 16th century, will fade rapidly into the background of the 1600s.

1598: **Toyotomi Hideyoshi dies,** having completed his social, political, and economic restructuring of the Japanese state. During his reign, the Japanese ruler instituted a rigorous feudalism, severely segregating the warrior, farmer, tradesman, and artisan classes. Thorough "sword hunts" disarmed the peasants, preventing revolt, while many castles and fortifications of the daimyo lords were destroyed to weaken their military independence. Artisans and merchants were strictly prohibited from living in agricultural communities. By keeping the different social classes divided and limited in their military autonomy, Hideyoshi secured the power of his central government, protecting against the return of political chaos.

1599: **Isfahan becomes the capital of Safavid Persia.** The urban planning of the city, featuring a grand boulevard that connects the imperial palace to the monumental gate before the Shah's mosque, is celebrated throughout the world. The mosque, famous for its beautiful polychromatic tiles, is balanced in splendor only by the expansive city park in front of the palace. Surrounded by the covered arcades of the Isfahan market, where products from throughout the Eastern world are sold, the park is the cultural and economic heart of the thriving community.

BIBLIOGRAPHY AND FURTHER READING:

Adams, Laurie Schneider. Art Across Time: Vol. 2, McGraw-Hill College, Chicago, 1999, pp. 547-624.

Allen, W. Loyd. "John Calvin," Great Thinkers of the Western World, Ian P. McGreal, ed., HarperCollins Publishers, New York, 1992, pp. 155-158.

Cahill, James. Chinese Painting, Rizzoli International Publications, Inc., New York, 1977, pp. 125-149, 158-159.

Joel Colton and R.R. Palmer. A History of the Modern World, 5th ed., Alfred A. Knopf, New York, 1978, pp. 49-134.

Erasmus of Rotterdam. Praise of Folly, Betty Radice, trans., Viking Penguin Inc., New York, 1971.

Horst de la Croix and Richard Tansey. Gardener's Art Through the Ages, 8th ed., Harcourt Brace Jovanovich, New York, 1986, pp. 598-653.

Frye, Robert. "Michel de Montaigne," Great Thinkers of the Western World, Ian P. McGreal, ed., HarperCollins Publishers, New York, 1992, pp. 164-166.

Giles, Mary. "Desiderius Erasmus," Great Thinkers of the Western World, Ian P. McGreal, ed., HarperCollins Publishers, New York, 1992, pp. 129-132.

Giles, Mary. "St. John of the Cross," Great Thinkers of the Western World, Ian P. McGreal, ed., HarperCollins Publishers, New York, 1992, pp. 167-171.

Chandice L. Goucher, Charles A. LeGuin, and Linda Linda A. Walton. In the Balance: Themes in Global History, Vol. 2, McGraw-Hill, Boston, 1998, pp. 590-591, 595-607.

Goetz, Philip W., ed. The Encyclopedia Britannica 15th ed., Encyclopedia Britannica, Inc., Chicago, 1990, vol. 4 pp. 211-212, vol. 5 p. 476, vol. 6 pp. 390-391, 671-672, vol. 7 pp. 568, 863-864, vol. 8 pp. 285-287, vol. 9 pp. 101, 872-873, 913-914, vol. 11 pp. 321, 881, vol. 12 pp. 328, 333-334, 483, 513-514, vol. 17 pp. 452-453, vol. 22 pp. 314-317, vol. 24 p. 495, vol. 29 pp. 543-545.

Grun, Bernard. The Timetables of History, Simon and Schuster, New York, 1979, pp. 220-267.

Hanes III, William Travis, editor. World History: Continuity and Change, Holt, Rinehart, and Winston, Austin, TX, 1997, pp. 332-346, 356

Helm, Thomas E. "Thomas More", Great Thinkers of the Western World, Ian P. McGreal, ed., HarperCollins Publishers, New York, 1992, pp. 145-149.

Hundersmarck, Lawrence F. "Martin Luther" Great Thinkers of the Western World, Ian P. McGreal, ed., HarperCollins Publishers, New York, 1992, pp. 150-154.

Hundersmarck, Lawrence F. "Niccolo Machiavelli," Great Thinkers of the Western World, Ian P. McGreal, ed., HarperCollins Publishers, New York, 1992, pp. 133-139.

Janson, H.W. History of Western Art, 3rd ed., Prentice Hall Abrams, Englewood Cliffs, NJ, 1986, pp. 436-498.

Lever, Burton M. "Nicholas Copernicus" Great Thinkers of the Western World, Ian P. McGreal, ed., HarperCollins Publishers, New York, 1992, pp. 140-144.

Machiavelli, Niccolo. The Prince, George Bull, trans. Viking Penguin Inc., New York, 1986.

Terakazu, Akiyama. Japanese Painting, Rizzoli International Publications, New York, 1990, pp. 123-140, 159-165.

ON THE CITY OF TIMBUKTU
Gardner, Brian: The Quest for Timbuctoo. London: Cassell and Company, 1968.

Maalouf, Amin: Leo Africanus. Trans. Peter Sluget. New York: W.W. Norton, 1986.

Reading About the World, Volume 2, edited by Paul Brians, Mary Gallwey, Douglas Hughes, Michael Myers, Michael Neville, Roger Schlesinger, Alice Spitzer, and Susan Swan. American Heritage Custom.

Saad, Elias N. Social History of Timbuktu: The Role of Muslim Scholars and Notables, 1400-1900. Cambridge: Cambridge University Press, 1983.

Shah, Tahir. "The Islamic Legacy of Timbuktu." Aramco World, 1995.

ON HUMANISM
Erasmus of Rotterdam. Praise of Folly, Betty Radice, trans., Viking Penguin Inc., New York, 1971.

"Humanism," The Encyclopedia Britannica, Philip W. Goetz, editor, 15th ed., Encyclopedia Britannica, Inc., Chicago, 1990, vol. 20 pp. 665-676

Helm, Thomas E. "Thomas More," Great Thinkers of the Western World, Ian P. McGreal, ed., HarperCollins Publishers, New York, 1992, pp. 145-149.

Machiavelli, Niccolo. The Prince, George Bull, trans. Viking Penguin Inc., New York, 1986.

1 32-point compasses are used to navigate *1600s*
2 The backstaff becomes a standard tool of nautical navigation *1600s*
3 Molds are used to make buttons *1600s*
4 The harpsichord changes Western music *1600s*
5 Increased volume of sea travel results in more shipwrecks *1600s*
6 American turkeys are imported by Europe *1600s*
7 Italian inventor Galileo Galilei develops the first thermometer *c. 1600*
8 William Shakespeare finishes "Hamlet" *1601*
9 King James I introduces Scottish golf to England *1608*
10 Galileo publishes "The Sidereal Messenger" and further develops the microscope *c. 1610*
11 Bernini carves a Baroque "David" and the Piazza Navona fountain in Rome *c. 1623*
12 "Blessing of the Bay" is the first ship built in America *1631*
13 Monteverdi completes the first truly modern opera *1640*
14 Rembrandt van Rijn paints "The Night Watch" *1642*
15 Construction of the Taj Mahal is completed *1648*
16 Blaise Pascal advances probability theory based on a study of triangles *1650s*
17 John Milton finishes "Paradise Lost" *1667*
18 Diverse fashions of dress develop in Europe *c. 1670*
19 The French royal palace of Versailles is completed outside Paris *1670*
20 Flintlock muskets revolutionize firearms *c. 1675*
21 Christiaan Huygens develops the first modern watch *1675*
22 Isaac Newton publishes "Philosophie naturalis principia mathematica" *1687*
23 The Salem witch trials result in 19 executions *1692*
24 William and Mary College is founded in Virginia by the Rev. J. Blair *1693*

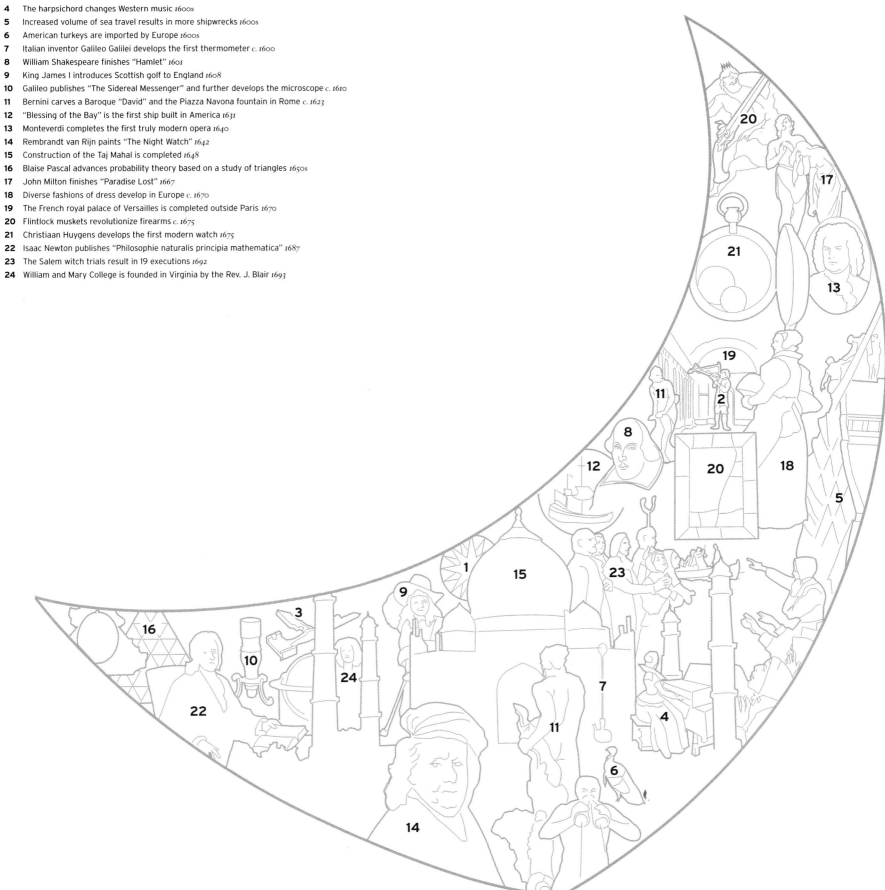

17
th Century

THE EMERGENCE
OF THE MODERN WORLD

THE EMERGENCE OF THE MODERN WORLD

During the 1600s, the world began to develop much of the political and national character that it would carry through the 19th century. In Europe, England and Scotland were united under a single crown, paving the way for the creation of Great Britain. Under the leadership of Richelieu, Mazarin, and Louis XIV, France emerged as the great Western power, a status it would enjoy off and on until a disastrous war in 1870. In the central continent, Prussia and Austria began to define themselves as the major players in German politics, while to the east a growing Russian state began to overshadow its Swedish and Polish neighbors.

In the non-European world, important political shifts also were occurring. In Japan, the Tokugawa family established a stable culture under a new shogunate that would last until 1860. Immediately to the west, the Manchurian Qing would gain control of China, forming the dynasty that would rule that nation through the early 20th century. In the Americas, European colonial societies established political frameworks that would eventually evolve into the United States, Canada, and the modern states of Latin America.

The 17th century is not, however, simply a story of stable growth. Many powers that had been centers of the 16th-century world, particularly Portugal, Spain, Poland, and the Ottoman Empire, suffered serious setbacks in the 1600s that marked the beginnings of decay and collapse. The Iberian nations saw their vast trade empires slowly devoured by the more aggressive English, Dutch, and French interests. Robbed of their wealth, Spain and Portugal faded into the shadows of insignificance. In the meantime, a disastrous siege of Vienna in 1683 broke Ottoman military power in Europe, and the loss of strength and prestige that accompanied the defeat weakened Turkish influence in the Arab world. Poland, incapable of uniting its factious nobles under a strong king, became an easy target for the more integrated Austrian, Russian, and Prussian nations that quickly began to annex territory along their Polish frontiers.

As these nations began to deteriorate politically, they created power vacuums that would have to be filled in later centuries. As Europe and the Far East settled into their modern forms and structures, the African, Asian, and American empires of Portugal, Spain, and the Ottoman Empire collapsed, later to become the setting for the most dynamic changes of the 18th, 19th, and 20th centuries.

1600s: (1) **Typical European compasses** of the age have 32 points and indicate the direction north with a decorative fleur-de-lis. A stylization of the letter T, the fleur-de-lis stands for Tramotana, a nautical name for the north wind.

1600s: (2) **The backstaff becomes the principal instrument** by which Western sailors determine their latitude at sea. A substantial improvement over the cross staff, which required its user to look directly into the sun, the new instrument spares many sailors permanent eye damage.

1600s: **Metal alloys like brass** become increasingly important in the production of precision instruments such as astrolabes. The alloys, distinctive for their light weight and considerable strength, will be particularly useful in the production of small, accurate watches and clocks.

1600s: **Japan prospers.** After the chaos of the 16th century, the archipelago thrives under new, stable forms of national government. Internal commerce and infrastructure redevelop, cities grow, cultural life evolves, and the overall standard of living improves. By 1700, the city of Edo, with a population of one million will be the largest metropolis in the world. Under the new Tokugawa shogunate, Chinese

1521 by Gerolamo Bolognese, the instrument will become a favorite of Baroque composers, reigning supreme until it is eclipsed by the superior expressive qualities of the piano in the 18th century.

1600s: (5) **Increasing sea traffic leads to increasing numbers of shipwrecks.** As more and more sailors set out for distant locations, they find themselves more susceptible to disaster on the open sea or along unfamiliar coastlines.

1600s: (6) **Spanish and English explorers return to Europe with American turkeys.** Along with chocolate, tobacco, and corn, turkeys will be one of several American resources to transform the European diet.

1600s: **Cultural diversity and segregation leave Poland weak and fragmented.** So many different vernacular languages are spoken in the kingdom that Latin is used as the official language. German and Jewish urban populations remain largely isolated from rural ethnic Poles, a division further exacerbated by laws that require Jews to live in segregated ghetto communities. Without a strong middleclass to link together urban and rural production or a central government powerful enough to direct economic policies,

London. The Dutch East India Company will follow in 1602. Together with stiffening Islamic resistance, the new companies slowly drive the Portuguese out of their trading fortresses in Africa and Asia. By 1652, large Dutch colonies will be established in Java and South Africa, while major English outposts in Bombay, Ceylon, and Madras will dominate Indian exports.

1601: (8) **William Shakespeare finishes "Hamlet," the most famous of his tragedies.** While maintaining the fine writing and comedic wit of his 16th-century work, Shakespeare's later tragedies sound the human condition with remarkable force and power. Tackling tough spiritual, philosophical, and ontological problems, Shakespeare explores his themes thoroughly without drawing definitive conclusions, leaving his work as a platform for endless discussion and interpretation.

1603: **Tokugawa Ieyasu declares himself shogun,** reestablishing national military government in Japan. Asserting himself as the dominant leader after Toyotomi Hideyoshi's death, Ieyasu is the first of the recent Japanese strongmen to establish a political system that lasts beyond his death. By 1615, all potential rivals to Ieyasu's successors will be elimi-

"It is not certain that everything is uncertain"

Confucianism is promoted in place of traditional Shinto and Buddhist social values, providing cultural legitimization to the nation's rigid feudal structure. While traditional institutions, such as the tea ceremony and Noh theatre, continue to thrive on the islands, new, more modern forms of cultural expression also develop.

1600s: **Russian culture maintains its distinctive Eastern qualities through much of the century.** Upper-class women continue to wear veils, while their male counterparts sport long beards and largely Asian dress. Arabic numerals are unknown in the region, and the Eastern abacus is used to calculate financial transactions. As the century progresses, however, Russia will become increasingly Western both in its political and cultural orientation.

1600s: (3) **The first cast buttons,** usually made from pewter or brass, are poured in molds.

1600s: (4) **The harpsichord emerges as an increasingly important instrument in Western music.** First developed in

a healthy national economy fails to develop.

1600s: (7) **Early thermometers** begin to come into common use. First developed by Italian inventor Galileo Galilei in 1596, the new instruments make it possible to measure thermal changes during experiments, greatly expanding the amount of data available to researchers and accelerating the development of Western science.

1600s: **Dutch merchant ships,** numbering more than 10,000 individual vessels, dominate the shipping of northern Europe. Dutch culture, with a wider national identity forged by its 16th-century wars with Spain, flourishes under the commercial prosperity of maritime trade. A classic period of literature emerges, painters like Vermeer and Rembrandt expand the arts, Huygens and Leeuwenhoek push the limits of scientific knowledge and technological innovation, and Dutch explorers and settlers establish colonies in the Americas and the Far East.

1600: **The English East India Company is organized in**

nated. For the first time in more than a century, Japan enjoys lasting political and social stability.

1605: **"El ingenioso hidalgo Don Quixote de la Mancha,"** a new novel by Miguel de Cervantes Saavedra, is printed in Spain. As the high point of a particularly fertile period in Spanish literature, "Don Quixote" proves itself to be one of the greatest Western novels ever written. A brilliant mix of comic farce and tragic realism, Cervantes' novel will remain fresh and relevant throughout the centuries, providing new meanings and interpretations for each new generation of scholars and readers.

1607: **The colonial village of Jamestown is established in Virginia.** Part of a corporate venture seeking gold, the settlers find themselves in crisis when the yellow metal proves elusive. Attempting to recoup company losses, they resort to growing tobacco. Financially, the desperate measure proves to be a stunning success—by 1638 more than three million pounds of the weed are being imported to England annually. Unable to keep up with growing demand, Virginian leaders

William Shakespeare

augment their population, first with indentured servants, then with African slaves.

1608: **Powhatan princess Matoaka Pocahontas** intercedes to save English settler John Smith from execution in Virginia. As a reward, the British colonists of Jamestown kidnap the young girl and hold her as insurance against future Powhatan attacks. In time, Pocahontas will marry one of the Englishmen, ending the violence between the two peoples during her lifetime.

1608: **King James I of England,** a man of Scottish birth, (9) introduces his native sport of golf to southern England.

1608: **Samuel de Champlain establishes Quebec** as the headquarters of the French fur trade in North America. Trading European wares and weapons for pelts brought in by American trappers, French outposts rapidly spread along the St. Lawrence River and throughout the Great Lakes region. Competing for French business and pelt-rich lands, the Iroquois and Huron nations will drive each other to open warfare in 1640.

1609: **Henry Hudson establishes a Dutch trading post on Manhattan island.** In 1624, the Dutch West India Company will establish a 30-family settlement, called New Netherland, in the region. After formally buying the island from its Canargee owners in 1626, the Dutch will establish the city of New Amsterdam, later known as New York. By 1650, the colony's population will swell to 5,000. Concerned about the growth, the company will restrict further immigration to ease tensions with its increasingly restless American trading partners.

1609: **With the creation of the Bank of Amsterdam,** the Dutch Republic becomes the financial center of Europe. Establishing stable exchange rates for Europe's wildly diverse currency, minting gold florins of consistent value, and guaranteeing deposits through the Dutch government, the new bank offers an attractive atmosphere of fairness and consistency that draws investors from throughout the continent.

1610: **Britches and knee stockings replace trunk hose** as the standard attire of European men. Low, wide-brimmed hats and tall boots folded over at the knee also become fashionable. Wide laced collars, lying flat across the chest and shoulders, replace the 16th-century neck ruff both in men's and women's clothing.

1610: **Galileo Galilei publishes "The Sidereal Messenger,"** in (10) which many of his groundbreaking astronomical observations are recorded. By refining and improving telescope design, Galileo is the first to see the rings of Saturn, lunar mountains, and sunspots. Observing the phases of Venus, he accepts the heliocentric model of the solar system. This blasphemous conclusion leads to his persecution by the Catholic church. More than an astronomer, Galileo makes important contributions to the physics of friction, periodic vibration, material strengths, parabolic trajectories, and concepts of force, as well as the development of the microscope.

1610: **Flemish painter Peter Paul Rubens creates "The Raising of the Cross,"** a highly representational masterpiece of Baroque painting. Influenced by painters like

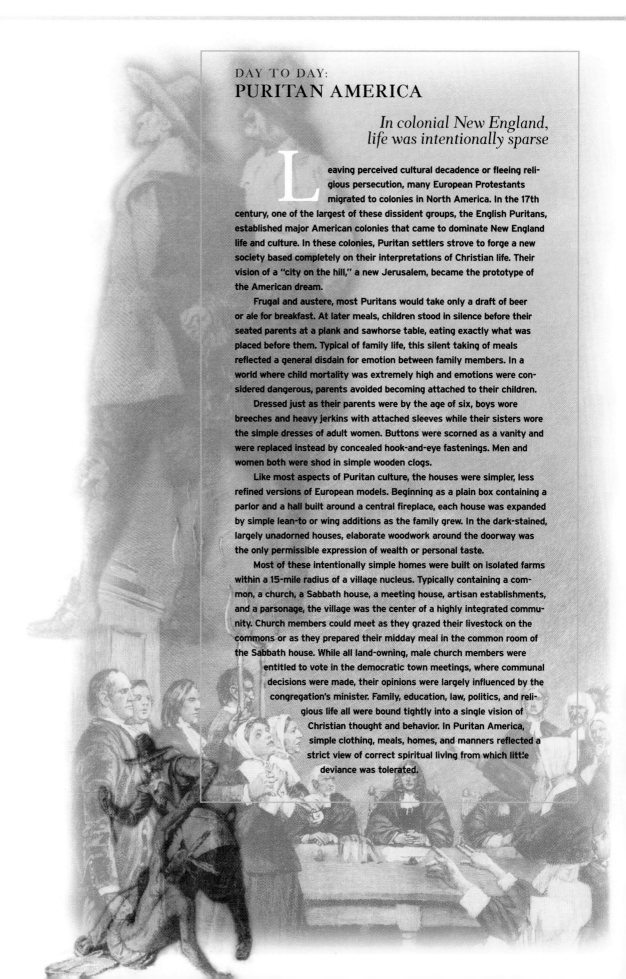

DAY TO DAY:
PURITAN AMERICA

In colonial New England, life was intentionally sparse

Leaving perceived cultural decadence or fleeing religious persecution, many European Protestants migrated to colonies in North America. In the 17th century, one of the largest of these dissident groups, the English Puritans, established major American colonies that came to dominate New England life and culture. In these colonies, Puritan settlers strove to forge a new society based completely on their interpretations of Christian life. Their vision of a "city on the hill," a new Jerusalem, became the prototype of the American dream.

Frugal and austere, most Puritans would take only a draft of beer or ale for breakfast. At later meals, children stood in silence before their seated parents at a plank and sawhorse table, eating exactly what was placed before them. Typical of family life, this silent taking of meals reflected a general disdain for emotion between family members. In a world where child mortality was extremely high and emotions were considered dangerous, parents avoided becoming attached to their children.

Dressed just as their parents were by the age of six, boys wore breeches and heavy jerkins with attached sleeves while their sisters wore the simple dresses of adult women. Buttons were scorned as a vanity and were replaced instead by concealed hook-and-eye fastenings. Men and women both were shod in simple wooden clogs.

Like most aspects of Puritan culture, the houses were simpler, less refined versions of European models. Beginning as a plain box containing a parlor and a hall built around a central fireplace, each house was expanded by simple lean-to or wing additions as the family grew. In the dark-stained, largely unadorned houses, elaborate woodwork around the doorway was the only permissible expression of wealth or personal taste.

Most of these intentionally simple homes were built on isolated farms within a 15-mile radius of a village nucleus. Typically containing a common, a church, a Sabbath house, a meeting house, artisan establishments, and a parsonage, the village was the center of a highly integrated community. Church members could meet as they grazed their livestock on the commons or as they prepared their midday meal in the common room of the Sabbath house. While all land-owning, male church members were entitled to vote in the democratic town meetings, where communal decisions were made, their opinions were largely influenced by the congregation's minister. Family, education, law, politics, and religious life all were bound tightly into a single vision of Christian thought and behavior. In Puritan America, simple clothing, meals, homes, and manners reflected a strict view of correct spiritual living from which little deviance was tolerated.

Caravaggio, Rubens uses sharp contrasts of dark and light, strong compositional diagonals, and muscularly powerful figures to produce a distinctively Baroque style of painting.

1611: **The first edition of the King James Bible is released in England.** Forty-seven scholars, personally approved by the English monarch, have taken seven years to compile the "Authorized Version" from older texts. The new volume will serve as the standard Bible of the English language for the next 300 years.

1612: **The last recorded burning of heretics in England takes place.** Although religion will continue to be a source of violence in Europe throughout the century, it will tend to be more of an excuse for political or social action than an expression of spiritual zeal, a tendency illustrated by the decline of religious executions in the 1600s.

1613: **Michael Romanov, son of the Patriarch of Moscow, is elected czar of Russia.** Still a boy, Michael has no affiliations with any of the bickering factions that have left Russia in domestic turmoil. The hope that his election will bring stability to the region is not disappointed: Russia is reunited under the new monarch. Quickly establishing absolute monarchy, the Romanovs will claim a hereditary right to the throne, ruling Russia without interruption until 1917.

1614: **Scottish mathematician John Napier publishes "Mirifici Logarithmorum Canonis Descriptio,"** in which he explains the use of logarithms. In addition to logarithms,

1618: **The Elector of Brandenburg inherits the Duchy of Prussia on the Polish Baltic coast.** Although only a series of isolated pockets throughout the 17th century, the growing possessions of the Elector slowly will evolve into Prussia, the prototypical form of modern Germany.

1618-1648: **The Thirty Years War begins in Germany.** Like the religious wars of the previous century, the conflict is a variety of disputes combined into one large chaotic violence. Protestants fight Catholics while rebellious princes fight against the authority of the Holy Roman Emperor. French, Spanish, and Swedish troops only add to the confusion as they try to promote their own interests through the conflict. In 1648, the Peace of Westphalia ends the fighting, effectively dividing the Holy Roman Empire into 300 autonomous states. Although emperors will continue to be crowned, their political significance and authority is largely curtailed.

1619: **A Dutch privateer sells 20 African slaves to settlers in Virginia,** the first such transaction in the American colony. By 1741, 60,000 West African slaves will be brought to the Americas every year. Put to work as miners and agricultural hands, they will be the key labor force behind American exports of precious metals, tobacco, cotton, and sugar cane. Prisoners of war or victims of kidnapping, the slaves are sold by other Africans to European traders for Western iron, alcohol, and firearms.

1620: **The Puritan colony of Plymouth is established on**

will represent a high point of productive interaction between the Chinese imperial government and Jesuit missionaries. Later in his life, however, he will be accused, tried, and convicted of corrupting his astronomy students, of whom some are subsequently executed. Although Schall von Bell will be cleared eventually of wrongdoing, the trial announces a deterioration of Sino-Western relations, which will accelerate in the 18th and 19th centuries.

1623: **Giovanni Lorenzo Bernini completes his sculpture "David."** A reinterpretation of the Biblical theme, Bernini's dynamic figure provides a striking contrast to Michelangelo's calm and resolute version of the same subject. Typical of the new Baroque art, Bernini's "David" is depicted in action, shown just as he completes his throwing motion. In contrast to Renaissance sculpture and architecture, which tends to be self-centered, Baroque work has tremendous directional energy, an aspect well-illustrated in the intent gaze and implied projectile emanating from the Bernini sculpture.

1624: **Cardinal Richelieu is appointed by Louis XIII as the chief minister of France.** A key player in preventing France from devolving into further religious civil war after the assassination of Henry IV in 1610, Richelieu rises to courtly prominence as the personal chaplain of the queen. As the effective head of state, he will be instrumental in establishing absolute monarchy in France.

1625: **Charles I becomes king of England.** An absolutist like

---

"For the laws of nature … without the terror of some power, to cause them to be observed, are contrary to our natural passions"

THOMAS HOBBES

---

which he develops to simplify astronomical calculations, the Scottish intellectual invents a prototypical slide rule, establishes the convention of the decimal point, and makes important contributions to spherical trigonometry.

1614: **The first puppet play, or "jojuri," is performed in Japan.** Chikamatsu Monzaemon, the first great "jojuri" playwright, will compose more than 100 performances in the 1600s, most of which will focus on crises of individual conscience, honor, and duty.

1615: **A Portuguese fleet is defeated by English ships off the coast of Bombay.** The victory insures British control of European trade with India, marking another key moment in the accelerating collapse of Portugal's colonial empire.

1615: **John Donne is made an ordained minister of the Anglican church.** Famous in his own day for his brilliant sermons, Donne will be remembered best for his metaphysical poetry. His opening lines "Death be not proud" and "No man is an island" will become some of the most famous phrases in the English language.

the New England coast of North America. Partly designed as an escape mechanism for religious malcontents, the English colonies in the Americas will become the new homes of more than 60,000 Puritans during the 17th century. In 1630, a much larger Puritan community will be established by the Massachusetts Bay Colony. Later that decade, English Catholics will found Maryland, and dissenters within the Massachusetts colony will break off to form communities in Rhode Island and Connecticut.

1620: **English intellectual Francis Bacon writes his natural philosophy, "Novum Organum."** Rejecting the human tendency to structure nature artificially through patterns of thought and language, Bacon is one of the strongest proponents of obtaining scientific knowledge through observation. His call for extensive experimentation, while not the first in Western culture, will be one of the most influential on modern European science. Statesman, scientist, author, and courtier, Bacon is one of the great influential personalities and celebrities of 17th-century England.

1622: **Jesuit astronomer Father Schall von Bell arrives in China.** As the director of imperial astronomy, Schall von Bell

his father, Charles lacks his predecessor's political tact, which puts him at odds with Parliament. Dissolving the legislative body, Charles attempts to collect taxes without its consent. When he is finally forced to call Parliament back to session in 1642, radical members of the body attempt to restructure the government completely, and civil war erupts.

1625: **Russian common law establishes that the penalty for killing a peasant** is to furnish his master with another one. Growing trade, which effectively destroyed feudalism in Europe, actually strengthens it in Russia, where profitable agricultural exports solidify the power of the landed ruling class. Throughout the century, Russian peasants gradually are reduced to de facto slavery. In 1646, they are officially bound to the land they work. In 1675, landowners also are granted ownership of the people who work their farms, receiving the right to sell their serfs as property.

1626-1640: **Economic depression,** an ineffective government, and a harvest shortfall combine to ravage domestic China. As Ming authority continues to deteriorate and conditions become desperate, rogue armies and bandits emerge throughout the nation, terrorizing the general public.

1631: **"Blessing of the Bay," the first ship built in the English colonies,** is launched in Boston Harbor. Shipbuilding, stimulated by the cheap lumber of America's vast forests, becomes a major colonial industry. With the cost of ship construction reduced by the ready availability of wood, fares for passage across the Atlantic also diminish, accelerating emigration from Europe.

1632: **Swedish king Gustavus Adolphus is killed in battle in southern Germany.** One of the most energetic monarchs of the 17th century, Gustavus had transformed Sweden into a modern political state and revolutionized

> ## "A man of war is the best ambassador"
> ### OLIVER CROMWELL

warfare with the unique organization of his army. His timely entry into the Thirty Years War saved the Protestant principalities just as complete Catholic victory seemed inevitable, guaranteeing that the fighting would continue without resolve long after his death.

1632: **The first public coffeehouse is opened in England.** The new establishments instantly become major centers of social interaction and commercial transaction; one of the new houses will in time evolve into Lloyd's of London.

1635: **Japanese citizens are forbidden to make overseas journeys.** Abandoning the active trade policies of Ieyasu, future shoguns will become increasingly suspicious of foreign influence. For the next 200 years, Japan will exist in a political vacuum with surprisingly little harm to its robust culture.

1636: **The Qing dynasty is pronounced at the Manchu capital of Mukden.** Mixing with Chinese populations on their frontier, the Manchu form a powerful state on the northern borders of Ming China. Adapting Chinese civil organization and technology to its Mongolian society and military, the Qing state becomes the obvious favorite for Asian dominance as the Ming dynasty continues to implode.

1637: **René Descartes publishes "Discourse on Method,"** the first cohesive theory of modern scientific method. Descartes exhorts one to believe only what is absolutely known, to avoid speculation, to start with the simple and gradually move to the complex, and, in short, always to move in a clear and rigorous manner from the known to the unknown. Illustrating his method in an example of philosophical inquiry, Descartes begins with the only absolutely certain assertion he can make: "I think, therefore I am." The mathematical sections of the book also introduce the use of letters to represent unknown algebraic quantities.

1637: **A long, bloody rebellion of Christian samurai** against the shogunate is put down in Japan. Christianity is outlawed in the archipelago, and isolationist tendencies are reinforced. Foreign books are banned, and international commerce is restricted to a single Dutch trading post near Nagasaki.

1640: **Claudio Monteverdi completes "The Return of Ulysses to His Country,"** the first truly modern opera. Over the course of his career, the avant-garde Italian will develop the form of the aria, create a musical and narrative structure within which to place his arias, and establish himself as the first composer to use dissonant chords effectively in his music. The tension and release created by subsequent dissonant and consonant chords will become an essential aspect of Western composition.

1640: **Frederick William, "The Great Elector," is crowned King of Prussia.** Under Frederick William's rule, Prussia is transformed into a powerful military state. More than 50 percent of state income is dedicated to maintaining a remarkably large standing army. Most aristocratic males become officers, and basic government functions, including tax collecting, are carried out by military personnel. Seeking a more robust economy to support his troops, Frederick William invites foreign professionals to immigrate to the capital of Berlin, transforming the city into a major cosmopolitan center.

1642: **Roger Williams writes "Queries of Highest Consideration,"** in which he makes the first Euro-American argument for separation of church and state. Banished from Massachusetts for his religious ideas, Williams established the first colony in Rhode Island in 1636. From his new home, he becomes one of the first and strongest voices of religious tolerance in the North American colonies.

1642: **Rembrandt van Rijn paints "The Night Watch."** The Protestant answer to the Catholic Rubens, Rembrandt is one of the first modern commercial artists. While most of his work is portraiture, he tries to sell it on the basis of its fetish value as a "Rembrandt" rather than on its specific quality or depiction of the subject. In many ways a typical Baroque painter, Rembrandt shares Rubens' interest in high contrasts of dark and light and strong compositional diagonals.

1642: **The English Civil War begins.** Fought between Anglican King Charles I and a Puritan minority of Parliament, the war is both political and religious. Puritan elements, physically dominating Parliament with an army under Oliver Cromwell, force 450 of Parliament's 500 members out of office during the war. The remaining 50, having secured military victory over the Royalists, order Charles decapitated in 1649.

1644: **After the suicide of the last Ming emperor,** Chinese generals ask for Qing assistance in expelling bandits from Beijing. Once the Mongolian armies cross the border, they never leave. With the brigands defeated, the Qing emperor occupies Beijing and declares a new dynasty in China.

1648: **The Taj Mahal is completed in Agra, India.** Built as a mausoleum for the dead wife of Shah Jahan, the monument continues a long tradition of indigenous Indian funerary architecture. Its distinctive Islamic style, however, also identifies the building with the Shah's Persian ancestry. Like so much in India, the Taj Mahal embodies a rich blending of different cultures. Elegantly proportioned and lavishly finished with precious stones, the Taj Mahal remains one of the most beautiful buildings ever constructed.

c. 1650: **The new Qing Dynasty of China begins constructing the Forbidden City in Beijing.** Building their new complex over the old Ming city (just as the Ming had built over the old Mongol capital), the Qing establish a compound of monumental scale and grandeur. The vast open spaces and underlying geometric order of the capital express reassuring power and stability in the wake of the chaotic Ming collapse.

1650: **Modern four-part harmony** and modulation begin to develop in European music.

1650: **A new university, later known as Harvard, is established across the Charles River from Boston.** The new community is named Cambridge, after the famous college town in England. When clergyman John Harvard donates his library to the school a few years later, the university takes his name. The first English university in the Americas, Harvard will become one of the most prestigious institutions of higher learning in the world.

1651: **Thomas Hobbes publishes "Leviathan,"** one of the most famous political arguments for absolute monarchy or dictatorship. Asserting every man's right to self-preservation, Hobbes argues that individual security is purchased through the surrendering of one's freedoms to a supreme leader. If all of society submits to the paternal overlord and obeys his laws, then a chaotic state in which the strong abuse the weak is avoided. In an odd way, Hobbes' theories foreshadow Rousseau's social contract of the 18th century.

1653: **Oliver Cromwell dissolves Parliament and declares himself Lord Protector of England.** Ironically, having won a war that was fought to protect England from absolute monarchy, Cromwell becomes the military dictator of England. Finding Parliament as difficult to deal with as did the now headless King Charles I, the Puritan general eliminates the legislative body. During his rule, Puritan interpretations of moral behavior become law, and theatre is banned throughout England.

1657: **Tea is sold in London for the first time.** Imported by the East India Company, the 3,400-year-old Chinese beverage already has become popular in the Dutch Republic. A national institution in Japan, the social drinking of tea also will become a major feature of English cultural life.

1658: **English natural philosopher Robert Hooke develops the balance spring**, an invention later applied to the modern watch by Dutch scientist Christiaan Huygens. Most famous for Hooke's Law, which describes the elastic properties of materials under stress, Hooke also will coin the biological term "cell" during his microscopic observations, make detailed sketches of Jupiter and Mars through a telescope, and develop the first principles of evolution through his study of fossils.

1658: **Aurangzeb assumes the throne of Mughal India.** Although the Mughal empire will continue to dominate most

CONTEMPORARY PHILOSOPHIES

CARTESIANISM

Radical skepticism laid at the heart of 17th-century Europe's most influential philosophical system

In 1637, French-born writer and thinker René Descartes published an original text entitled "Discourse on the Method for Rightly Conducting One's Reason and Seeking Truth in the Sciences." Best remembered for its famous conclusion "Cogito ergo sum" (I think, therefore I am), the book represents a fundamental shift in European thought that would permanently alter the focus and interests of Western philosophy.

In "Discourse on Method," as the book is more popularly known, Descartes outlines an approach to the problem of knowledge that is built on unyielding skepticism. According to the author, any argument about reality must be constructed strictly from immediately self-evident truths. Conjectures, assumptions, and guesses are to be militantly purged from the deductive process. Later in the book, as a demonstration of his method, Descartes examines what he can actually conclude about his own existence. Through this example, the philosopher reveals the radical extremity of his thought.

Descartes begins his inquiry by questioning whether or not he even exists. In the course of examining this issue, he establishes that knowledge of the external world is essentially impossible. There is no reason to assume that the information we receive through our physical senses is objectively true. Our senses may be defective or deceptive in their presentation, a greater being or force may be manipulating our perceptions, or the world may simply be a product of our own imagination. Each individual is not only incapable of establishing the nature of an external object, place, or thing, but also incapable of determining that the outside world even really exists.

Denied the use of his senses, Descartes finds himself limited to the use of pure reason in establishing his own existence. How does he know, for instance, that he is not the product of someone else's imagination? It is in this context that the famous "I think, therefore I am" emerges. Since he has consciousness, Descartes accepts as self-evident that in some fashion he exists. The exact nature of that existence may prove elusive, but the fundamental truth of Descartes' reality is undeniable to himself. It is from this first principle, accepted beyond doubt, that Descartes constructs his beliefs.

Through the rigor of his methods and his identification of pure reason as the only reliable source of establishing certain truths, Descartes transformed Western thought. Imbued with a radical skepticism, European philosophers after Descartes began relentlessly challenging unsubstantiated assumptions about the fundamental nature of individual and cosmic existence. The rift between the mind and the body, long an issue of Latin thought, became through Descartes a division between what was known truth and what was simply unknowable.

---

of India and Bengal during his reign, Aurangzeb lacks the religious tolerance of his predecessors. A devout Sunni Muslim, he will persecute Hindus, Sikhs, and Sufi mystics. Combined with the traditionally harsh taxes of the Mughal rulers, this discrimination will lead to many revolts, greatly weakening the power and cultural unity of the state.

1658: **Blaise Pascal finishes "On the Geometrical Mind and on the Art of Persuasion,"** outlining the limits of human knowledge. Inventor of an adding machine that prefigures the modern computer and a major contributor to probability theory and the study of vacuums and gaseous behavior, Pascal also firmly acknowledges the shortcomings of scientific inquiry. Observing that repeated experiment can only disprove, and never prove, scientific theories, Pascal concludes that absolute certainty and truth lie beyond the grasp of science.

1660: **Charles Stuart is asked to return from exile** in France to become King Charles II of England. After Cromwell's death, the Puritan dictatorship rapidly collapses under his son, and the English Parliament gratefully restores monarchy to the nation. Although the future reign of his brother James will be turbulent, Charles' tenure as king is a happy time in England. The theatres are reopened, strict Puritan laws are repealed, and most people avoid political extremity as they try to forget the hardships of the English Civil War and its aftermath.

1661: **With the death of Cardinal Mazarin, Louis XIV takes active control of French policy and government.** During his reign, France will be the greatest power in Europe, and almost all of Europe will have to unite to contain Louis' expansionist aspirations. While French court life will become the model of high society throughout Western Europe and in Russia during the 17th century, this will be the ultimate extent of French influence. Too obvious in his aggression and might, Louis will unite his enemies against him even as the cost of his interminable wars, huge standing army, and gigantic building projects bring long-term instability to the French economy.

1662: **"L'École des femmes," the first major play of French writer and actor Jean Baptiste Poquelin Molière**, is performed for the first time. Exposing the follies of society through satire, Molière's sharp wit and powerful command of language will make his plays the cornerstone of all subsequent French comedy.

1663: **Otto von Guericke builds the first electric generator**, producing static electricity by applying friction to a rotating ball of sulfur. Also interested in vacuums, von Guericke will

build the first air pump and demonstrate the force of atmospheric pressure through his famous Magdeburg hemispheres.

1664: **Chinese painter Kun-ts'an paints the Pao-en Temple.** With the fall of the Ming dynasty, many Chinese gentleman painters like Kun-ts'an withdraw from society to protest the Qing. Their work tends to be based more on personal interpretation and observation than tradition, and their work is very creative in terms of brushwork technique, style, and content. In contrast, those painters who accept the new dynasty continue the Chinese artistic tradition of creatively reinterpreting past styles and work. Seeking essential qualities, their work is highly restrained, often to the point of sterility, but their best paintings show a refined sensitivity to abstract form and composition.

1664: **Dutch painter Jan Vermeer completes "Woman Holding a Balance,"** one of his most famous works. Vermeer's rigorous, formal compositions, sedate depictions of daily life, and precise brushwork make his work a

1667: **Russian serf Stepan Razin leads a revolt against oppressive landowners in eastern Russia.** The revolt quickly turns into a popular rebellion—armies sent to crush Razin's followers join him—and cities open their gates to the rebels. Until their leader's capture and execution in 1671, the rebels will terrorize landowners along the coast of the Caspian Sea and the banks of the Volga river. Once the rebellion is subdued, however, serf life will further deteriorate as harsh countermeasures are put in place by the ruling class.

1669: **Crete**, the last colonial possession of Venice, is conquered by the Ottoman Turks.

c. 1670: **Two completely different fashions of dress have developed in Europe.** English Anglicans and French male courtiers wear long coats with turned-back sleeves, waistcoats, and wigs. Their Dutch and English radical Protestant counterparts wear more somber colors in their costumes and forego wigs. Women wear dresses with wide puffy sleeves, often with multiple slits, and skirts bunched at the

lense grinder, the Dutch scientist builds short, single-lense microscopes of extraordinary power (300x) and quality. Over the next decade, van Leeuwenhoek will become the first biologist to describe accurately red blood cells and spermatozoa, while his careful observation of small insects will disprove popular theories of spontaneous generation.

c. 1675: **Flintlock firing mechanisms**, which make it possible to fire muskets without a continuously burning match or rope, make firearms a legitimate hunting tool. Having eliminated armor from the battlefield, muskets also become available in smaller, lighter versions. Able to move and aim the barrel quickly and fire at a moment's notice, the hunter's chances of hitting an opportunistic target are enhanced greatly.

1675: **Christiaan Huygens uses the recently invented balance spring to develop the first modern watches.** In 1656, the Dutch scientist had developed the first pendulum clocks. Over his long career, Huygens also will improve telescope design, observe the rings of Saturn, and propose the wave theory of light.

> ## "To every action there is always opposed an equal reaction; or the mutual actions of two bodies upon each other are always equal, and directed to contrary parts"
> ### NEWTON'S THIRD LAW

far cry from the thunderous quality of most Baroque painting. In his motionless scenes, light is depicted with such scientific precision that it creates a palpable atmosphere, a sense of physical and spiritual stillness appropriate for his often reflective subjects.

1666: **The Great Fire of London destroys the central districts of Europe's second largest city.** In the ensuing building campaign after the fire, London takes its modern form, and Sir Christopher Wren emerges as the most prominent of English architects. His design for a new St. Paul's Cathedral will evolve into one of London's most distinctive landmarks.

1667: **Russia seizes the Polish cities of Smolensk and Kiev.** Protective of their liberties, the Polish nobility refuse to elect a strong king, often nominating a foreigner to be their next monarch. While this approach maintains a constitutional monarchy with certain guaranteed rights and freedoms, it leaves the kingdom with a weak central government largely incapable of preserving its borders. Russia, Sweden, Prussia, and Austria all will be tempted to eat away at Polish territory throughout the 17th century.

1667: **John Milton finishes "Paradise Lost," the great epic poem of the English language.** Blind by 1652, Milton compares himself to the blind bards of antiquity, placing his work in the tradition both of the Greek poet Homer and the Roman author Virgil. Beautiful for its blank verse, "Paradise Lost" also is famous for its compelling depiction of Satan, one of the first great antiheroes of Western literature.

bottom to reveal a petticoat. Court women wear wigs while the simpler Puritan headdress consists of a plain white cloth placed over fairly short hair.

1670: **The new French royal palace of Versailles is completed outside Paris.** Of unprecedented scale and cost, the new complex is an architectural expression of raw power. From the palace, diagonal boulevards extend out in all directions, suggesting the expansive power and influence that radiate from the French throne. Here, the long axis of Baroque architecture, manifested both in the boulevards and the long halls of the palace, exerts a kind of visual and psychological power, forcing visitors of the king to cross great distances while exposed to the scrutiny of his observation.

1672: **French armies invade the Spanish Netherlands and the Dutch Republic.** The invasion unites the somewhat libertarian Dutch states under William of Orange, who is made hereditary stadholder in 1673. It also aligns longtime enemies Spain, Austria, and the Dutch Republic in a common front against France. The notion of the balance of power, in which weaker states, regardless of their history or different domestic cultures, form alliances to contain the aggression of stronger nations, will become the fundamental basis of European diplomacy for the next three centuries. Worn down by a long war, France will surrender its claims to the Low Countries in the 1678 Treaty of Nimwegen.

1674: **Antoni van Leeuwenhoek is the first man to observe bacteria and protozoa through a microscope.** Trained as a

1679: **Italian composer Alessandro Scarlatti writes his first opera, "Gli equivoci nel sembiante."** Inventor of the overture form and a key developer of chromatic harmony, Scarlatti will foreshadow 18th-century symphonies in his writing. His work will have considerable influence on later composers such as Mozart and Schubert.

1679: **P'u Sung-ling writes "Liao-chai chih-i,"** one of the great short story collections in the Chinese romantic prose tradition.

1682: **Peter Romanov, later known as Peter the Great, becomes czar of Russia.** A nation always in the past more concerned with Persia and the Far East, Russia enters the European sphere under Peter. In 1698, almost 1,000 Western European technicians are invited east to "modernize" the state. French culture is adopted at court, and French Baroque architecture is built in the growing city of St. Petersburg. Throughout his reign, Peter's efforts to secure Russia's borders and acquire a year-round port of trade will leave Russia in an almost perpetual state of war.

1682: **Japanese author Ihara Saikaku composes his first novel, "Kóshoku ichidai otoko."** A great writer of prototypical haiku poetry (in 1685 he will compose 23,500 of the 17-syllable poems in a 24-hour period), Saikaku eventually will abandon the form entirely in favor of prose. In contrast to earlier Japanese literature, which tended to grapple with cosmic themes, his novels explore human desire on a simple, material level.

1683: **Encouraged and funded by France, the Ottoman Turks invade Hungary and lay siege to Vienna.** German and Polish troops under Polish king Jan Sobieski arrive quickly, however, relieving the city within two months. Crushing the Ottoman armies in 1697, Austrian forces will drive the Turks completely out of the Balkans, a condition formalized by the Treaty of Karlowitz in 1699. While Germany is distracted, however, French troops occupy Alsace and Lorraine. The disputed territories will remain a continuing source of Franco-German conflict well into the 20th century.

1683: **English composer Henry Purcell releases a new series of compositions** that utilize the recently developed violin. In time, Purcell will abandon chamber music for more popular songs. His writing for the human voice, incredibly beautiful and expressive despite insipid lyrics, will prove central to the development of 18th-century English opera.

1683: **English doctor Thomas Sydneham** introduces opium, a pain-killer, to Western medicine.

1683: **French explorer René Robert de La Salle** becomes the first European to reach the Gulf of Mexico by navigating the Mississippi river.

1683: **The last Ming stronghold of Taiwan is captured by Qing forces,** establishing the undisputed authority of the new Chinese dynasty. Much as the rulers of the earlier Mongol dynasty had done, the Qing emperors leave much of China's traditional structure unchanged; Chinese language and principles of Confucian civil service are retained by the new government. A reorganization of the higher administrative organs, however, insures stronger centralized authority than had been present under the late Ming.

1684: **Powered by agricultural reform and the reopening of ports to foreign trade, the Chinese economy thrives.** Tax breaks on new farms encourage resettlement in northern China, while the introduction of European corn and potatoes, tobacco, sugar, and peanuts diversifies Chinese agriculture and reduces the threat of famine. Once the country is stabilized, the Qing emperors avoid major economic interference, allowing a thriving free-market economy to develop. Contractual labor slowly replaces servitude, and state monopolies are turned over to private enterprise.

1685: **Louis XIV revokes the Edict of Nantes,** and French Calvinists are driven from France. Already beleaguered by expensive wars, the French economy will be damaged badly by the loss of the largely middle-class commercial Protestants, much as the expulsion of the Jews and Moors hurt Spain in 1492. Ultimately, economic hardship fostered in the late 1600s will lay the groundwork for the French Revolution in the 18th century.

1687: **English scientist and academic Isaac Newton** publishes the first edition of his famous "Philosophie naturalis principia mathematica." One of the most important thinkers in the history of Western science, Newton will establish the basic laws and related mathematical equations of physical mechanics, accurately grasp the concept and behavior of gravitational force, and demonstrate white light as the composite of all the colored lights. His invention of the reflecting telescope also will prove to be an important contribution to optical technology, greatly expanding the ability of astronomers to study the night sky.

1688: **William of Orange, statholder of the Dutch Republic,** is invited by the English Parliament to become king of England. Mortified by the Catholicism of King James II, Parliament asks fellow Protestant William to usurp the throne. When a sizeable Dutch army lands in England, James flees to France. William is crowned in 1689 after accepting that he and all future monarchs of England will be bound by the laws of Parliament.

1690: **John Locke anonymously publishes "Two Treatises of Government."** In part a rejection of the political absolutism propounded by Thomas Hobbes' "Leviathan," Locke's concern with individual rights, freedoms, and property will become the cornerstone of 18th-century democratic thought. Among others, the English author will heavily influence Thomas Jefferson, whose 1776 Declaration of Independence largely reflects principles first espoused by Locke.

1690: **English chemist Robert Boyle publishes "The Christian Virtuoso,"** an argument for scientific exploration as a fundamental Christian duty. Boyle's theory of a clock-work universe, set in motion by God but now run by secondary laws, will become a key bridge between religion and science during the 18th-century Enlightenment.

1692: **The Salem witch trials result in the hanging of 19 "witches" in Salem, Massachusetts.** Stirred by the voodoo stories of a Caribbean slave girl named Tituba, several girls claim they have been possessed by Satan, beginning a wave of hysteria and accusation. Public outrage halts the trials after 19 executions, and in 1697 the town observes a day of atonement and fasting as an expression of shame and remorse.

1693: **William and Mary College is founded in Virginia by Reverend James Blair.** Chartered by the English monarchy to educate the clergy and civil administrators in the growing colony, the new school is the second oldest (after Harvard) in North America. The original chapter of Phi Beta Kappa will be established there in 1776, and alumni will include Thomas Jefferson, John Marshall, and James Monroe.

1694: **Matsuo Basho, perhaps the greatest haiku poet of 17th-century Japan,** writes "Oku no-hosmichi," a lasting favorite of Tokugawa literature. A narrative travel account ("The Narrow Road through the Deep North"), the prose passage is written as a signpost within a larger collection of poetry. Basho's account is one of the defining moments in an already rich tradition of Japanese literature.

1694: **The Bank of England is created in London.** For the right to be responsible for handling government accounts and minting specie, a consortium of London businessmen grant Parliament a £10 million loan, establishing the first modern national debt.

BIBLIOGRAPHY AND FURTHER READING:

Adams, Laurie Schneider. Art Across Time: Vol. 2, McGraw-Hill College, Chicago, 1999, pp. 627-674.

Clark, Bowman L. "Rene Descartes," Great Thinkers of the Western World, HarperCollins Publishers, Inc., New York, 1992, pp. 195-199.

Joel Colton and R.R. Palmer. A History of the Modern World, 5th ed., Alfred A. Knopf, New York, 1978, pp. 134-188, 269-289.

Horst de la Croix and Richard Tansey. Gardener's Art Through the Ages, 8th ed., Harcourt Brace Jovanovich, New York, 1986, pp. 475-479, 708-767.

Goetz, Philip W., ed. The Encyclopedia Britannica, Inc., Chicago, 1990. vol. 5 p. 348, vol. 9 pp. 537-538, vol. 16 pp. 119-123, vol. 22 pp. 316-320, 344-345.

Chandice L.Goucher, Charles A. LeGuin, and Linda A. Walton. In the Balance: Themes in Global History, Vol. 2, McGraw-Hill, Boston, 1998, pp. 489-509, 668-671.

Grun, Bernard. The Timetables of History, Simon and Schuster, New York, 1979, pp. 266-321.

Hall, Donald E. "Galileo Galilei," Great Thinkers of the Western World, HarperCollins Publishers, Inc., New York, 1992, pp. 178-181.

Hall, Donald E. "Isaac Newton," Great Thinkers of the Western World, HarperCollins Publishers, Inc., New York, 1992, pp. 232-236.

Hanes III, William Travis, editor. World History: Continuity and Change, Holt, Rinehart, and Winston, Austin, TX, 1997, pp. 390-409.

Hobbes, Thomas. Leviathan, Viking Penguin Inc., New York, 1985.

Janson, H.W. History of Western Art, 3rd ed., Prentice Hall Abrams, Englewood Cliffs, NJ, 1986, pp. 499-563.

Laslett, Peter, ed. Locke: Two Treatises on Government, Cambridge University Press, New York, 1988, pp. 45-122.

Leiser, Burton M. "Thomas Hobbes," Great Thinkers of the Western World, HarperCollins Publishers, Inc., New York, 1992, pp. 187-190.

Leiser, Burton M. "John Locke," Great Thinkers of the Western World, HarperCollins Publishers, Inc., New York, 1992, pp. 223-227.

Muller, Richard A. "Gottfried Wilhelm Leibniz," Great Thinkers of the Western World, HarperCollins Publishers, Inc., New York, 1992, pp. 237-242.

Popkin, Richard H. "Blaise Pascal," Great Thinkers of the Western World, HarperCollins Publishers, Inc., New York, 1992, pp. 209-212.

Riley, Mark T. "Johannes Kepler," Great Thinkers of the Western World, HarperCollins Publishers, Inc., New York, 1992, pp. 182-186.

Scott-Kakures, Dion. "Francis Bacon," Great Thinkers of the Western World, HarperCollins Publishers, Inc., New York, 1992, pp. 172-177.

Wootton, David. Ed. Divine Right and Democracy: An Anthology of Political Writing in Stuart England, Viking Penguin, Inc., New York, 1986, pp. 21-86, 238-246, 390-395, 450-492.

ON CARTESIANISM
Clark, Bowman L. "Rene Descartes," Great Thinkers of the Western World, HarperCollins Publishers, Inc., New York, 1992, pp. 195-199.

Goetz, Philip W., ed. The Encyclopedia Britannica 15th ed., Encyclopedia Britannica, Inc., Chicago, 1990. vol. 5

Wilson, Margaret D., ed. The Essential Descartes, Penguin Books USA Inc., New York, 1983, pp. vii-xxxii, 106-153.

ON PURITAN COLONIAL AMERICA
Glubok, Shirley, ed. Home and Child Life in Colonial Days, Macmillan Publishing Co., Inc., New York, 1969.

Stannard, David E. The Puritan Way of Death, Oxford University Press, New York, 1977, pp. 31-71.

Tunis, Edwin. Colonial Living, Thomas Y. Crowell Co., New York, 1957, pp. 22-23, 24-25, 29-63.

1   Feminine fashions are layered and ruffled *1700s*
2   Men wear breeches and waistcoats *1700s*
3   Single-lens microscopes become widely available *1700s*
4   Spanish coins are the standard of trade *1700s*
5   Child's hoop and stick toy of the day *1700s*
6   Pocket watches come into fashion *1700s*
7   Traverse boards aid sailors *1700s*
8   Astronomers map the solar system *1700s*
9   Period map of the zodiac *1700s*
10 Vivaldi begins teaching music to orphaned girls *1703*
11 St. Paul's Cathedral is completed in London *1710*
12 Parlor musicians begin to appear in the salons of Paris *1715*
13 Ch'ien-lung emperor ascends the throne of China *1735*
14 G.F. Handel composes "The Messiah" *1741*
15 The original Liberty Bell arrives in Philadelphia and
    soon after begins to crack *1752*

16 George III is crowned King of England *1760*
17 The Boston Tea Party drives England to close down Boston Harbor *1773*
18 King Louis XVI of France rides in this carriage *1774*
19 The American Revolution begins *1775*
20 The Declaration of Independence is drafted and signed *1776*
21 Benjamin Franklin signs the Treaty of Paris, ending Anglo-American hostilities *1783*
22 The French Revolution begins at the Bastille *1789*
23 George Washington is elected president of the United States *1789*
24 Kitagawa Utamaro paints in the okubi-e style *c. 1790*
25 Mozart composes "The Magic Flute," and dies in the same year *1791*
26 Hadyn composes Austria's national anthem *1797*
27 The Rosetta Stone is discovered in Egypt *1799*

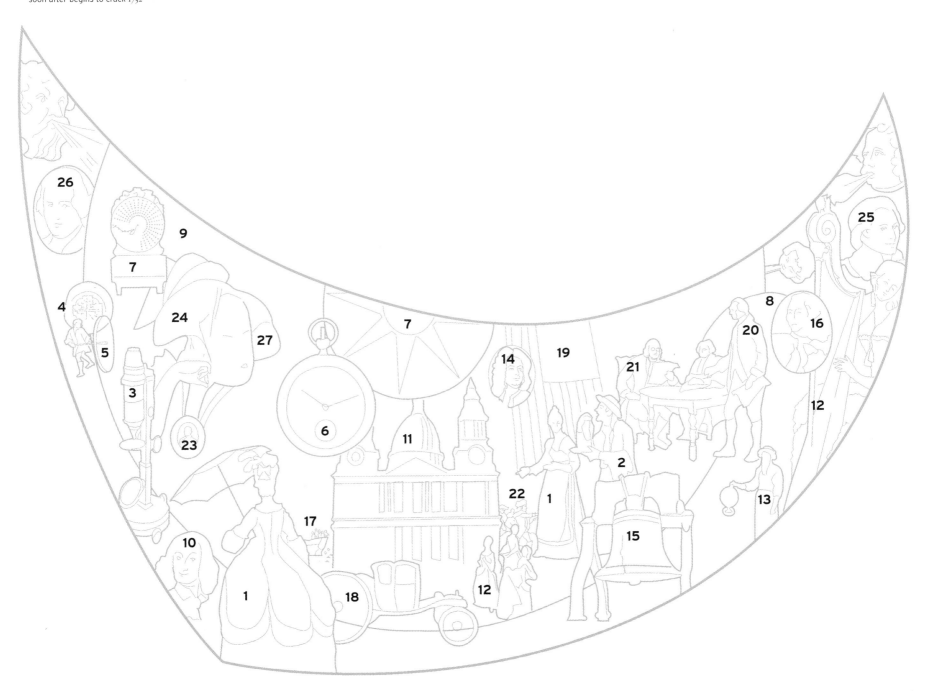

INTRANSIGENCE & REVOLUTION

INTRANSIGENCE & REVOLUTION

The theme of the 18th century was revolution. Across the globe, older systems of thought, economics, and politics increasingly reflected an incapacity to adapt to a world in transition, often forcing sudden, sometimes violent transformations.

Although this tendency for explosive change was not limited to Western Europe, it certainly was best illustrated there. The profligate spending of the emperor Ch'ien-lung would give rise to the same conditions that Louis XIV and Louis XV helped create in Revolutionary France, but China's economic subservience to the West and its suffering at the hands of a growing opium trade lack the symbolic immediacy of the guillotine. While England and Japan experienced similar pressures to move away from outmoded agricultural social structures, the social unrest and Band-Aid measures of the Japanese government are ultimately more forgettable than the factories and steam engines of the Industrial Revolution. It is not that changes in other parts of the world were really so different or less significant; it is just that Western writings, economic transformations, and political reorientations expressed a larger global transformation in unequivocal and memorable fashion.

In many ways a single revolution with different faces, the rapid shift in European culture began in the middle of the century and quickly proceeded to influence all aspects of Western life. If the American Revolution was largely economic in motivation, it was heavily influenced, or at least justified, by the intellectual writings of men like Montesquieu. Similarly, if the Industrial Revolution was propelled by numerous technological inventions, it was made possible by a capitalist spirit supported both by the intellectual world of men like Adam Smith and the political world of the English Parliament. The violence of the French Revolution was triggered by economic distress, but the cultural life of the Paris salons and the writings of the "philosophes" gave direction to the social unrest, providing it with a tangible goal to be attained by overthrowing the king. The simultaneous convergence of capitalism, representational government and political rights, industrial invention, and the radical secularism of ideologies like Deism is not coincidental. Rather, these different fragments show aspects of a total picture in which the autocrat, whether landowner, king, or God, lost much of his control over the world's population and was replaced by a new order.

1700s: (1) **European and colonial American women wear full dresses** with angled bodices, scooped necks, and close-fitting sleeves often ruffled at the elbow. When hoop skirts are worn, the upper parts of the dresses are typically very tight, necessitating a corset underneath. Parasols serve as sunshades for fashionable opera-goers.

1700s: (2) **European and colonial American men wear mid-thigh-length coats** over slightly shorter waistcoats, tight breeches, and stockings to the knee. In the early 1700s, wigs are popular among the wealthy, but by 1800 natural hair, either powdered or unaltered, will become the fashionable norm. Tricorner hats will be replaced in the final years of the 1700s by the short-brimmed prototype of the top hat.

1700s: (3) **Single-lens microscopes become widely available.** Focused with a simple screw-barrel and steadied on a firm brass stand, the new microscopes are a substantial improvement over their predecessors. Limited by weak resolution and color distortions, however, simple microscopes will begin to be replaced by ones equipped with multiple achromatic lenses in the early 19th century.

1700s: (4) **Spanish coins are the principal medium of exchange** between Western merchants and Chinese trade monopolies. While Europeans crave Chinese tea, silk, and porcelain, the West possesses little that interests the Qing other than precious metals. More than 10 million Spanish silver dollars will be imported to Qing territory annually for much of the 18th century.

1700s: (5) **Late in the century, bowling hoops with sticks** begin to develop into the popular recreation of the 19th century. Hoops, used in a variety of games and contests, are one of the most universal and ubiquitous toys in the world, entertaining a wide diversity of cultures, races, and nations.

1700s: **Pocket watches** are coveted by Europe's wealthy. (6)

1700s: (7) **Traverse boards** help sailors record their changing locations.

1700s: (8) **Astronomical discoveries** result in new maps and charts of the solar system.

1700s: (9) **Increasingly accurate astronomical data leads to the refinement of astrology.** The use of scientific advances to improve upon techniques of divination reveal that, beneath an ever more dominant and visible scientific culture, the Western mind continues to be fascinated with the zodiac.

1701: **Jethro Tull invents the seed drill, revolutionizing farming in the British Isles.** Allowing the deep, uniform placement of seeds in the soil, the new device greatly reduces labor. Combined with new crop rotation techniques from Holland, the seed drill will help lay the groundwork for the Industrial Revolution by concentrating land ownership and freeing labor for non-agricultural purposes.

1702: **The War of Spanish Succession begins in Europe.** A continuation of the 17th-century conflict for political supremacy on the continent, the war demonstrates yet again that Louis XIV's France cannot overpower the combined resistance of England, Austria, and the Dutch Republic. Louis' ambition to combine the thrones of France and Spain is deflected by the Peace of Utrecht, and, beyond producing a great military hero in the future English Duke of Marlborough, the war accomplishes little except loss of life and economic exhaustion.

1703: (10) **Antonio Vivaldi, future composer of "The Four Seasons," is ordained as a minister in Italy.** Working in a conservatory for orphaned girls, Vivaldi will establish an international reputation with the compositions he writes for the children's weekly recitals. A talented violinist, the Italian composer will be best remembered for his concerti, distinctive in their dramatic contrast of ensemble and solo sections.

1709: **Englishman Abraham Darby develops a new process for smelting iron** that uses coke instead of charcoal. Freed from dependence on charcoal extracted from England's limited forest resources, iron production skyrockets on the island. Suddenly plentiful, iron will be used to build the machines, bridges, and locomotives of a new Europe.

1710: (11) **Construction is completed on St. Paul's Cathedral in London.** Designed by architect Christopher Wren, it is considered a high point of English Baroque design.

1712: **English writer Alexander Pope publishes his famous mock-epic "The Rape of the Lock."** A man of great sensitivity, Pope is driven to satire by the jealous, relentless mockery of less talented writers. In between lampooning his enemies, Pope will bemoan an artistic and moral decay in Britain that he associates with the Hanoverian monarchs and a growing sense of English commercialism.

1714: **Daniel Gabriel Fahrenheit constructs the first mercury thermometer.** Able to achieve greater accuracy than alcohol thermometers, Fahrenheit establishes the approximate temperature of the human body at 96 degrees.

1714: **Englishman John Harris invents the chronometer,** making the accurate prediction of longitude at sea possible for the first time. In effect, the chronometer is a glorified clock of extreme precision, designed to keep accurate time in the turbulent environment of a moving sea vessel. Comparing the solar time of their current position with the time of their home port as shown by the chronometer, English sailors are able to determine their time zone difference from home, making it possible to establish their distance from home and hence their longitudinal position.

1715: (12) **Parlor musicians begin to appear in the salons** of the French middle class and aristocracy. With the death of Louis XIV in 1715, French social life begins to shift away from Versailles and into the houses of the urban elite. The new social gatherings, usually run by middle-aged wives, focus on the arts and intellectual conversation, providing original forums for French women to express their opinions.

1716: **Tokugawa Yoshimune becomes the eighth shogun of Japan's Tokugawa shogunate.** The last of the truly great shoguns, Yoshimune will combat financial and social crises in his nation. After his retirement in 1745, however, the Edo government will be plagued by corruption and inefficiency. As the nation's economy and social practices change, a rigid feudal structure will become increasingly incapable of meeting the financial needs of the farming and warrior classes.

1718: **The first inoculation against smallpox is developed in Europe.** While effective at controlling the disease in Europe, it will do nothing to protect the Americans, Africans, and Asians whom European explorers expose to their latent infections. Particularly in America, Western explorers marvel at how entire communities of indigenous people mysteriously die in a matter of weeks or months, never realizing that they themselves are the cause of the devastation.

1721: **Johann Sebastian Bach finishes his "Brandenburg Concertos."** The definitive composer of Baroque music, Bach succeeds in forging diverse national and historical traditions into a new music. A busy court composer, he works as a craftsman, using formulaic responses to keep pace with demands for new music.

1721: **The construction of the Lombe silk factory is completed in Derby, England.** A herald of the Industrial Revolution, the water-powered facility processes some 318 million yards of cloth every 24 hours.

1726: **English satirist Jonathan Swift finishes "Gulliver's Travels."** A voice of skepticism in an age of European confidence, Swift is not enthralled with humanity's greatness in the way many of his fellow intellectuals are. An idealist at heart, Swift remains disappointed with mankind's failure to live up to its full potential. In simple, biting prose, he reminds his readers of their legion shortcomings and absurdities.

1726: **The Mogul Empire of India collapses,** leaving the politically and religiously fractured subcontinent vulnerable to exploitation by British and French trading companies. The

British East India Company thrives in the new chaotic environment. Building forts, maintaining their own army, and playing local rulers off one and other, company officers establish a broad base of power in India through which they garner extremely profitable trade arrangements.

1729: **Weekly Bible reading meetings held by John Wesley and other English religious intellectuals** result in the development of Methodism. Wesley's radical interpretations of doctrine and the Bible prove too extreme for the Church of England, and after his death Methodism will become its own separate form of Christianity. Beyond its religious particularities, Methodism will deeply impact English culture with its strong opposition to slavery and its call to expand the social role of women.

1735: **The emperor Ch'ien-lung ascends the throne of China.** (13) Inheriting a sound bureaucracy and financial system reorganized by his father, the new ruler leads China through its most glorious period. Until his death in 1796, the emperor will guide his nation to the apex of political and military prominence. Much like Louis XIV in France, however, he will exhaust the treasury with his endless military and artistic expenditures, leaving his successor bankrupt and burdened by a growing opium trade.

1739: **Scottish thinker David Hume, the great philosophical skeptic of the English language,** releases "A Treatise of Human Nature." In the tradition of Descartes, Hume argues the impossibility of knowing any form of objective reality through intellectual reason or sensual observation. By establishing belief and judgment as legitimate human practices independent of reason, however, Hume avoids having his skepticism devolve into nihilism or overly simplistic hedonism.

21-year reign, bequeathing a powerful state to her de facto successor Catherine the Great.

1744: **The publication of Tom Thumb's "Pretty Songbook"** brings such famous nursery rhymes as "Hickory Dickory Dock" and "London Bridge" into English literary traditions.

1745: **Denis Diderot becomes the chief editor of the "Encyclopedie,"** an ambitious survey of Western knowledge being assembled in France. Including 17 volumes of text and more than 3,000 engravings, the first modern encyclopedia in Europe is also a political tool for the radicals who sponsor it. Many of the articles express the growing revolutionary attitudes of the French populace that will lead to the uprisings of 1789. As an individual writer and thinker, Diderot will become the first modern art critic, promote social tolerance and sexual freedom, and foreshadow Social Darwinism in his materialist thinking.

1745: **Madame de Pompadour becomes the mistress of Louis XV.** As Louis' private secretary, the Frenchwoman holds enormous power at Versailles. Until her death in 1764, she will be largely responsible for cultivating French art and architecture, including the building of the future Place de la Concorde and a renowned porcelain factory at Sévres. Although she proves unable to dislodge Louis' fundamental distrust of intellectuals, she is at least able to protect Voltaire and the other "philosophes" from governmental repression.

1748: **Montesquieu's "Spirit of Laws" explicitly introduces the political concepts of separation of powers and checks and balances into Western thought.** One of the most conservative of the French "philosophes," Montesquieu advocates a return to medieval feudal structures in which the

need of money, he still finds the time to write essays, poems, and drama. Typical of Enlightenment thinkers, Johnson endorses detached observation, favors direct experiment and experience over abstract theory, warns against the danger of unrealistic goals or fantasies, and tends to see humanity as an even mix of virtues and shortcomings.

1758: **French social critic and wit Voltaire writes "Candide,"** the most famous of his sardonic comedies. Rejecting complex 17th-century philosophies, Voltaire's work is a call for tolerance, simple pleasure, self-knowledge, and social equality.

1760: **George III ascends the throne of Great Britain.** Unlike (16) his grandfather George II, the new king is determined to live up to his responsibility and take an active role in British government. A basic lack of ability, combined with bouts of madness in his later years, will hinder his noble aspirations, however, and his influence on England will be largely negative. During his reign, Britain will wrest control of North America from the French, only to lose it to rebellious Americans enraged by the incompetent policies of George's ministers.

c. 1760: **Private canal systems improve transportation** in Great Britain, accelerating the Industrial Revolution. With the cost of transporting food, iron, charcoal, and other commodities greatly reduced, prices drop while urbanization and overall population increase rapidly.

1762: **French social critic Jean-Jacques Rousseau writes "The Social Contract."** Having established in earlier works that modern society is a corruptive and damaging influence on the ideal "natural" man, Rousseau attempts to define a perfect society in which this corruption does not occur.

"A little rebellion now and then is a good thing, and as necessary in the political world as storms in the physical"

THOMAS JEFFERSON

1740: **Frederick the Great becomes King of Prussia.** Under his rule, the Germanic state prospers. Prussian territory is greatly expanded as Frederick agrees to partition Poland with Austria and Russia. Ruling completely on his own and training no successor, however, Frederick leaves Prussia weak and disorganized after his death in 1786, paving the way for France's domination of central Europe in the early 19th century.

1741: **George Frideric Handel's oratorio "Messiah" is performed for the first time in England.** (14) The German-born composer, who wrote the famous "Water Music" and more than 40 operas early in his career, switches to the more popular choral form of the "Messiah" in mid-career.

1741: **Peter the Great's daughter Elizabeth becomes Czarina of Russia.** Ending a 15-year period of domestic chaos after Peter's death, Elizabeth reestablishes Russia as a strong European and Middle Eastern presence during her

absolute power of the central monarchy is limited by local government. Ironically, his reactionary ideas will serve as a model for the progressive democratic systems of countries like the United States.

1752: **The original Liberty Bell, manufactured in England, is installed in the Pennsylvania State House in Philadelphia.** (15) It is cracked almost immediately by an incompetent bell ringer, and despite numerous attempts at repair, has an unpleasant tone throughout its working life. Its ringing, however, will protest the Stamp Act, announce the Declaration of Independence, celebrate the victory at Yorktown, and mourn the deaths of George Washington, the Marquis de Lafayette, and Chief Justice John Marshall. As such, it becomes an icon of early American history.

1755: **English author Samuel Johnson completes his ambitious "Dictionary."** Aided by only a handful of menial assistants, Johnson compiles his dictionary largely by himself. In

Although his terms are vague and his propositions difficult to apply in practice, his discussion of a society that transforms natural virtue into moral virtue will have enormous influence on 18th and 19th century European dialogue.

1762: **Catherine the Great becomes Czarina of Russia.** A woman of minor German nobility, Catherine seizes the throne by participating in the palace coup that murders her mildly retarded husband Peter III. Initially an enlightened monarch and a patron of Diderot, Catherine is driven by peasant rebellions to become a harsh, autocratic ruler, abandoning Russia's vast population of serfs to the mercy of their masters in return for unquestioned aristocratic support of her monarchy. Under her rule, Russia expands westward, annexing much of Poland.

1764: **Faced with an intolerably large national debt,** British lawmakers decide to pay off part of the expense of the Seven Years War through taxation of its North American colonies.

CONTEMPORARY PHILOSOPHIES

DEISM

18th-century religious philosophies sought to isolate the essential from the superficial

The sense of secularism and scientific interest that had been gathering strength throughout the 16th and 17th centuries finally achieved its full force in 18th-century Europe. Reflected in part by the intellectual and artistic movement known as the Enlightenment, this larger cultural shift toward scientific reasoning and analysis led to new, creative approaches to religion. One of the most pervasive of these innovative spiritual attitudes was a religious philosophy known as Deism.

Deism is an interpretation of religion as a concept. Skeptics of any established faiths' rituals and ecclesiastical structures, deists looked for principles common to all religions, focusing more on general concepts than specific manifestations. By identifying the moral base inherent in all religions, they sought to establish a code of behavior and faith free from the emotional beliefs of any particular practice. To more extreme deists, the Bible was a collection of metaphoric tales; while the moral message was important, the historical accuracy was irrelevant.

Most deists agreed on several key points from which their individual religious practices evolved. They accepted the existence of God, the belief that the best means to praise this God was to live a moral life, and the certainty that conduct on Earth would be rewarded or punished in an afterlife. Many also believed that God, having created the universe, essentially removed himself from it and allowed it to function according to understandable laws. Embracing Newton's discoveries in physics as proof of their conclusion, they compared the universe to a giant clock, running in a predictable fashion.

Originating in England, Deism spread to Germany and to France, where it influenced Voltaire and the "philosophes." Wherever religious freedom was championed, as in the new United States, the movement exerted influence throughout the early 19th century, shaping the views of American founding fathers such as George Washington and Thomas Jefferson.

Deism made religion a personal issue for many leading thinkers of the 18th century. By negating the importance of specific doctrines, rituals, or dogma, the new system of thought circumvented the need for an organized church. By removing God from a role of direct influence on the world, Deism also eliminated the concern with obeying a tyrannical creator's highly specific mandates. Replacing the faithful member of the church with the rational, moral individual, Deism provided another key step in the Western transition from religious to secular culture.

Since much of the war's cost was expended defending the American colonists, the new policy seems reasonable enough, but the Americans disagree. Parliament will institute several new taxes and duties over the next decade, only to rescind most of them in the face of severe colonial protest. A growing environment of American discontent foreshadows the approach of the American Revolution.

1765: **Patrick Henry, newly elected to the House of Burgesses,** leads Virginia's legislative assembly in denouncing the Stamp Act, one of many abortive attempts by the British government to raise revenue through colonial taxes. During one of his speeches, Henry warns George III that "Caesar had his Brutus, Charles I his Cromwell." Among the most radical of American libertarians, Henry will later oppose the Constitution of the United States, fearing it gives the national government too much power.

1768: **Antoine-Laurent Lavoisier becomes the youngest man ever elected to the prestigious French Academy of Sciences.** During his prolific career, the famous chemist will establish the principle of conservation of mass, assemble the first periodic tables, isolate several of the noble gases, and make significant observations on combustion and respiration.

1769: **Scottish inventor James Watt, improving on the earlier designs of Thomas Savery and Thomas Newcomen,** develops a highly effective steam engine. While the concept of the steam engine belongs to Savery and Newcomen, it is Watt's developments that turn it into a feasible industrial tool. Designed to pump water from mine shafts, the new engine will be modified to a variety of additional uses, literally powering the Industrial Revolution in Great Britain.

1770: **Austrian princess Marie Antoinette is married to the Dauphin of France, the future Louis XVI.** The 14-year-old's Austrian manners, at odds with the customs of Versailles, make her instantly unpopular at all levels of French society. Probably not as contemptible as popular legend will later suggest, the beautiful young woman nonetheless becomes a magnet for antagonism toward the crown as revolutionary tensions build up to the French Revolution. In 1793, she will be accused of treason, and, like her husband, decapitated.

1771: **Richard Arkwright builds the first textile mill in England.** Driven by inventions like James Hargreaves' spinning jenny and Edmund Cartwright's power loom, the textile industry will become one of the chief mainstays of the new economy. Within a decade, Arkwright will have more than 300 employees working in his new facility as the fresh production slowly extinguishes a home-based textile industry.

1772-1782: **The Qing dynasty sponsors the creation of the "Ssu-k'u uh'uan-shu,"** a definitive collection of China's greatest literary works. The selection process demonstrates the growing importance of the empirical school of Chinese scholarship. Influenced by Western science, mathematics, and culture, the new thinkers reject many Confucian models of learning. Conflict between Confucian and anti-Confucian protagonists will contribute to the turmoil that will destabilize China in the 19th century.

1773: **The Boston Tea Party** drives the British government ⑰ to harden its position on American social insurrection. Samuel Adams' stunt, in which he and some friends dressed as Mohawks board a British merchant ship and dump all of its tea overboard, results in the closing of Boston Harbor by British authorities. Within a year, what began as a protest against trade regulations on tea will become a call for open, full-scale American rebellion.

1774: **Robert Burns, the last great Scottish vernacular poet, composes his first verse, "My Handsome Nell."** Of humble origins and forced to work as either a farmer or tax collector throughout his short life, Burns nonetheless took advantage of his father's emphasis on education to become Scotland's most famous modern bard. Known as the "Ploughman Poet," he is intensely popular in his own day:

> ## "Every man who possesses power is impelled to abuse it"
>
> M O N T E S Q U I E U

10,000 spectators will attend his funeral when he dies at 37.

1774: **German author Johann Wolfgang von Goethe cements his growing reputation** with a new novel called "The Sorrows of Young Werther." The central figure of German literature, Goethe is a key voice in the developing Sturm und Drang aesthetic movement in Central Europe. Breaking new ground both in fictive prose and poetry, Goethe's work will mark a transition away from classical, French models of writing and anticipate the Romantic movements of the early 19th century.

1774: **Louis XVI, newly crowned King of France, is driven in** ⑱ **this ornate carriage.** Unmotivated to rule and lacking the discipline to overcome his own indifference, Louis proves a miserable king in a time of extreme political turmoil. As the country moves inevitably toward revolution, the king will

devote most of his time to hunting and practicing the peculiar hobbies of masonry and locksmithing.

1775: **The American Revolution begins with open fighting** ⑲ **between American colonists and British troops in New England.** Attempting to seize caches of powder and weapons that the Americans have stockpiled outside of Boston, British columns are turned back by short, crisp engagements at Lexington and Concord. Although only a third of all Americans will actively support independence from Great Britain throughout the conflict, the actual shedding of blood makes reconciliation increasingly unlikely.

1775: **Virginian colonist George Washington is appointed by the Continental Congress to command the American rebel army besieging British-controlled Boston.** Throughout a military career that spans both the Seven Years War and the American War of Independence, Washington will bring his various commands to the brink of destruction through strategic incompetence, only to save his men from total annihilation through personal courage and force of character. A man of somewhat limited talents, he will win the military victory needed for American independence more through endurance than brilliance.

1775: **American frontiersman Daniel Boone establishes Boonesborough in Kentucky.** After a failed effort in 1769, Boone's second attempt to establish settlements west of the Appalachians is successful. Instrumental in forging a migration route through the Cumberland Gap, Boone also is a key figure in organizing the white invaders to defend against indigenous American counterattacks.

1776: **Thomas Jefferson drafts the Declaration of** ⑳ **Independence,** formally beginning the American Revolution. Before fighting broke out in 1775 and Jefferson's document was written, American colonists already had been in a state of rebellion, demanding the repeal of British laws, taxes, and duties they found unfair. With the Declaration of Independence, however, American leaders formally renounce any hope of reuniting with Great Britain and seek to create an autonomous state.

1776: **Scottish thinker Adam Smith publishes his economic treatise** "Inquiry into the Nature and Cause of the Wealth of Nations." A synthesized expression of economic ideas already latent in European intellectual culture, Smith's text popularizes and defends capitalism. Arguing that the promotion of self-interest is to the common good, that specialization and division of labor increases production and wealth, and that the economy works at its best when government interference is kept to a minimum, Smith is one of raw capitalism's most ardent advocates. However, his consideration of labor as a commodity, and his belief that men are

DAY TO DAY:
IROQUOIS AMERICA

Preserving core values while adapting to external change, Iroquois culture flourished in the face of growing European presence

Throughout much of the 18th century, Iroquois culture and society flourished in the western regions of modern New York. Less damaged by European disease and military aggression than most of their American neighbors, the Iroquois grew in prominence even as much of the continent's indigenous culture was being destroyed.

The matrilineal clan structure of the Iroquois was based around the longhouse. Twenty-five feet wide and as much as 200 feet long, these structures housed all the descendents by blood or marriage of the clan's eldest female. Built with a structural frame of elm wood, the longhouses were clad in the same elm bark used to make eating bowls and canoes.

Each clan claimed an animal as its original ancestor. The image of this animal (a wolf or a turtle, for example) was hung over the door. Since all members of the clan descended from this single progenitor, marriage within the clan was considered incestuous and forbidden. When a couple married, a man moved into his wife's longhouse and became part of her clan.

Each town or village of longhouses, often surrounded by a wooden palisade, was ruled by a council of elder men. The members of this council, however, were selected and, if necessary, excused by the female clan leaders. It was these women who would often figure prominently in the selection of representatives to attend the national meetings of the six Iroquois tribes. Controlling most of upstate New York, these tribes maintained conceptual "longhouses" of land, stretching in north-south strips across the entire length of the future state. Meeting in the middle of this territory, the representatives would decide issues of common concern. Highly organized and usually united in foreign policy, an Iroquois populace of less than 15,000 resisted colonial expansion right up until the American Revolution.

While Iroquois men left on extensive hunting, trapping, and military campaigns, domestic life and agriculture were largely controlled by women. Cultivating corn, beans, and squash, Iroquois females also gathered berries and seeds, producing more than 75 percent of their society's food supply. Excess produce was saved in underground granaries for times of need.

The Iroquois thrived in the 18th century because they were able to integrate themselves into the new Latin-influenced economic and political system without sacrificing their autonomy. While benefiting from European weapons, kettles, and farming implements, they also made themselves an essential component of the extensive fur trade. Adaptive and resourceful, they were able to maintain their autonomy for a century longer than most of their indigenous neighbors.

reproduced according to the economy's demand for them also reveal a darker side of capitalism ultimately explored by thinkers as anti-capitalist as Karl Marx.

1778: **France enters the Anglo-American conflict on the side of the Americans,** accelerating an inevitable American victory while inflicting revenge on the British for the humiliating loss of the Seven Years War. Unfortunately, the expense of the war also hastens economic instability in France, laying the groundwork for the horrors of the French Revolution.

1779: **Attempting to rebalance a growing trade deficit,** the British East India Company authorizes the sale of Indian opium in China. The growing opium market in China will become a source of tremendous international conflict and domestic Chinese ruin during the 19th century.

1781: **The surrender of a British army at Yorktown, Virginia, effectively ends the war in America,** guaranteeing the continued existence of the United States. Although the war will technically continue for several more years, the defeat at Yorktown marks the end of any serious British attempt to regain control of its former American territories.

1781: **German professor Immanuel Kant finishes "The Critique of Pure Reason,"** one of the seminal works of modern philosophy. The first important professional academic of Western philosophy, Kant is infamous for bringing opaque language and excessively complex structures of argument to serious European thought. His model of human consciousness, however, in which the mind extrapolates a subjective reality out of fragmentary impressions supplied by the senses, is a vital moment in the development of Latin philosophy. By combining the empirical observation of Francis Bacon and the abstract reasoning of Descartes into a single theory of human experience, Kant defines the starting point of many subsequent philosophical investigations.

1783: (21) **Benjamin Franklin and four other American representatives sign the Treaty of Paris,** ending hostilities with Britain and acknowledging the United States as an independent nation. More than just a statesman, Franklin is an American personality. Author of "Poor Richard's Almanac," a pioneer in the study of electricity, inventor of the Franklin stove and the glass harmonica, and founder of Philadelphia's first library, fire department, and police force, Franklin is a major force in early American culture.

1789: (22) **The French Revolution begins when Louis XVI is forced to call a gathering of the Estates General.** Louis calls the meeting intending to resolve problems caused by continuing financial crises and bad harvests, but the gathering has its own agendas. Declaring itself a National Assembly, it immediately sets about completely restructuring the national government. Arms are seized from the Bastille to protect the assembly from royal troops, and an armed mob forces the king to leave Versailles and take up a de facto house arrest in Paris. "The Declaration of the Rights of Man and the Citizen," drafted later in the year, defines a series of principles to which all leaders, including the king, are bound.

1789: (23) **The Constitution of the United States is ratified,** and George Washington is elected the first president of the United States. Heavily influenced by the French thinker Montesquieu, the architects of the document wil create a government in which power is carefully distributed among multiple authorities, preventing abuses of power by any one person or office. By first refusing to become king and by later stepping down as president after two terms, Washington will prove instrumental in establishing the government's independence from any cult of personality.

c.1790: (24) **Japanese printmaker Kitagawa Utamaro begins to develop his distinctive okubi-e portrait style.** Focusing on the head and bust alone, Utamaro explores emotive expression in a manner unprecedented in Japanese art.

1791: (25) **Wolfgang Amadeus Mozart writes the popular opera "The Magic Flute"** and begins work on his Requiem shortly before his death in December. The ultimate child prodigy, Mozart began playing the harpsichord at the age of 3 and wrote his first composition at 5. Traveling the courts of Europe as a spectacle, the young genius absorbed the best of German, French, English, and Italian music, skillfully incorporating them into his own work. Brilliant in all the standard forms of music, he is perhaps best as a composer of piano concertos, where his prodigious talents create works of symphonic grandeur and expressive depth.

1793: **Radicals gain control of France's revolutionary government, and the constitutional monarchy is abolished.** The king and queen, accused of treason, are executed. As France struggles against invading foreign armies intent on restoring a Bourbon monarchy, the revolutionary leaders become increasingly hysterical; thousands of people are guillotined during the infamous Reign of Terror. Finally, public sentiment recoils from the endless executions, and the radical leaders are thrown from power and executed.

1795: **A new constitution in France establishes the Directory.** Less progressive than the 1793 government, the new organization concentrates power in the hands of wealthy landowners. Weakened by internal corruption, the Directory will fall in 1799, replaced by a new government effectively run by a military officer named Napoleon Bonaparte. By stabilizing finances and establishing an effective bureaucracy and a comprehensive legal code, Napoleon earns the trust of the people; a plebiscite will declare him hereditary emperor of France in 1804.

1797: (26) **Franz Joseph Haydn composes the national anthem of the Austrian Hapsburg empire.** A famous composer in his day, Haydn will be a great influence on his friend Mozart and a revered teacher of Beethoven. His symphonies, choral masses, and string quartets epitomize Neo-Classical composition.

1799: (27) **French soldiers expanding a fort in Rashíd, Egypt, uncover the Rosetta Stone.** Originally erected in 196 BC, the broken stele proves vital to modern archaeology because it contains the same message both in Egyptian hieroglyphics and Greek. Although the actual message is of limited importance, the translation makes it possible for modern scholars to decode Egyptian hieroglyphs; something they had proven incapable of doing before the stone's discovery.

BIBLIOGRAPHY AND FURTHER READING..

Abrams, M. H., ed. Norton Anthology of English Literature, W.W. Norton & Co., New York, 1975, pp. 914-916, 1120-1125, 1204-1207.

Adams, Laurie Schneider. Art Across Time: Vol. 2, McGraw-Hill College, Chicago, 1999, pp. 675-715, 766-769.

Cahill, James. Japanese Painting, Rizzoli International Publications, Inc., New York, 1990, pp. 165-175.

Joel Colton and R.R. Palmer. A History of the Modern World, 5th ed., Alfred A. Knopf, New York, 1978, pp. 182-188, 238-381.

Creede, Constance. "Jean-Jacques Rousseau," Great Thinkers of the Western World, HarperCollins Publishers, Inc., New York, 1992, pp. 271-274.

Horst de la Croix and Richard Tansey. Gardener's Art Through the Ages, 8th ed., Harcourt Brace Jovanovich, New York, 1986, pp. 480-482, 768-801.

Dugi, Don Thomas. "Adam Smith," Great Thinkers of the Western World, HarperCollins Publishers, Inc., New York, 1992, pp. 275-279.

Fleming, Thomas. Liberty!: The American Revolution, Viking Penguin Group, New York, 1997, pp. 51-52, 93-96, 174.

Goetz, Philip W., ed. The Encyclopedia Britannica 15th ed., Encyclopedia Britannica, Inc., Chicago, 1990. vol. 6 p. 47, vol. 7 p. 502, vol. 9 p. 589, vol. 16 pp. 120-125, vol. 17 pp. 454-456, vol. 22 pp. 320-321, vol.23 pp. 520, 741-742, vol. 29 pp. 716-723.

Chandice L. Goucher, Charles A. LeGuin, and Linda Linda A. Walton. In the Balance: Themes in Global History, Vol. 2, McGraw-Hill, Boston, 1998, pp. 582-588, 652-654, 671-679.

Grun, Bernard. The Timetables of History, Simon and Schuster, New York, 1979, pp. 320-373.

Hanes III, William Travis, editor. World History: Continuity and Change, Holt, Rinehart, and Winston, Austin, TX, 1997, pp. 450-473, 482-496.

Janson, H.W. History of Western Art, 3rd ed., Prentice Hall Abrams, Englewood Cliffs, NJ, 1986, pp. 574-617.

Johnson, Oliver. "David Hume," Great Thinkers of the Western World, HarperCollins Publishers, Inc., New York, 1992, pp. 266-270.

Johnson, Oliver. "Immanuel Kant," Great Thinkers of the Western World, HarperCollins Publishers, Inc., New York, 1992, pp. 281-285

Johnson, Oliver. "Jeremy Bentham," Great Thinkers the Western World, HarperCollins Publishers, Inc., New York, 1992, pp. 306-309.

Leiser, Burton M. "Thomas Jefferson," Great Thinkers of the Western World, HarperCollins Publishers, Inc., New York, 1992, pp. 301-305.

Popkin, Richard H. "Voltaire," Great Thinkers of the Western World, HarperCollins Publishers, Inc., New York, 1992, pp. 257-260.

Riley, Mark T. "Antoine-Laurent Lavoisier," Great Thinkers of the Western World, HarperCollins Publishers, Inc., New York, 1992, pp. 297-300.

Rousseau, Jean-Jacques. The Social Contract, Maurice Cranston, trans., Viking Penguin, New York, 1968.

Smith, Adam. The Wealth of Nations, Andrew Skinner, intro., Viking Penguin, New York, 1979.

ON IROQUOIS AMERICA
Goetz, Philip W., ed. The Encyclopedia Britannica 15th ed., Encyclopedia Britannica, Inc., Chicago, 1990. vol 6 pp. 390-390, vol. 13 pp. 344-348.

ON DEISM
Goetz, Philip W., ed. The Encyclopedia Britannica 15th ed., Encyclopedia Britannica, Inc., Chicago, 1990. vol. 26 pp. 606-608.

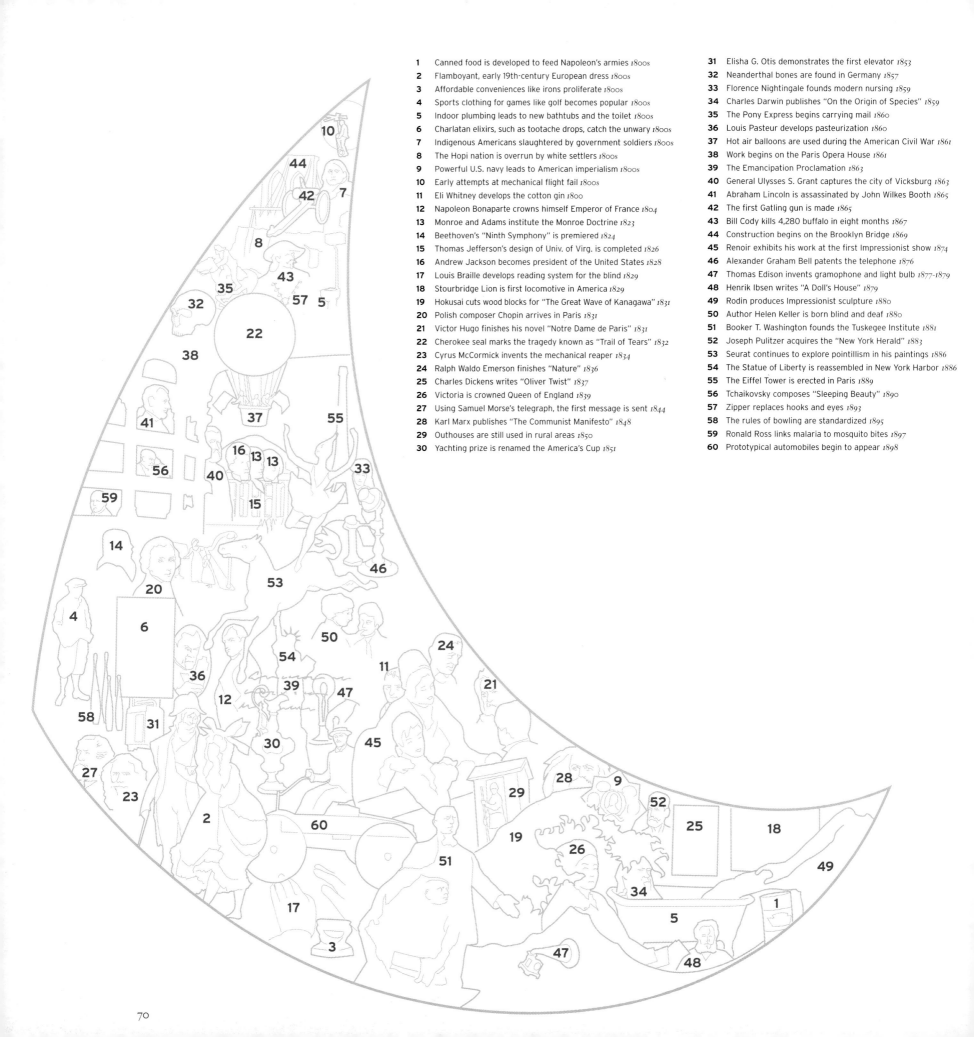

1 Canned food is developed to feed Napoleon's armies *1800s*
2 Flamboyant, early 19th-century European dress *1800s*
3 Affordable conveniences like irons proliferate *1800s*
4 Sports clothing for games like golf becomes popular *1800s*
5 Indoor plumbing leads to new bathtubs and the toilet *1800s*
6 Charlatan elixirs, such as tootache drops, catch the unwary *1800s*
7 Indigenous Americans slaughtered by government soldiers *1800s*
8 The Hopi nation is overrun by white settlers *1800s*
9 Powerful U.S. navy leads to American imperialism *1800s*
10 Early attempts at mechanical flight fail *1800s*
11 Eli Whitney develops the cotton gin *1800*
12 Napoleon Bonaparte crowns himself Emperor of France *1804*
13 Monroe and Adams institute the Monroe Doctrine *1823*
14 Beethoven's "Ninth Symphony" is premiered *1824*
15 Thomas Jefferson's design of Univ. of Virg. is completed *1826*
16 Andrew Jackson becomes president of the United States *1828*
17 Louis Braille develops reading system for the blind *1829*
18 Stourbridge Lion is first locomotive in America *1829*
19 Hokusai cuts wood blocks for "The Great Wave of Kanagawa" *1831*
20 Polish composer Chopin arrives in Paris *1831*
21 Victor Hugo finishes his novel "Notre Dame de Paris" *1831*
22 Cherokee seal marks the tragedy known as "Trail of Tears" *1832*
23 Cyrus McCormick invents the mechanical reaper *1834*
24 Ralph Waldo Emerson finishes "Nature" *1836*
25 Charles Dickens writes "Oliver Twist" *1837*
26 Victoria is crowned Queen of England *1839*
27 Using Samuel Morse's telegraph, the first message is sent *1844*
28 Karl Marx publishes "The Communist Manifesto" *1848*
29 Outhouses are still used in rural areas *1850*
30 Yachting prize is renamed the America's Cup *1851*

31 Elisha G. Otis demonstrates the first elevator *1853*
32 Neanderthal bones are found in Germany *1857*
33 Florence Nightingale founds modern nursing *1859*
34 Charles Darwin publishes "On the Origin of Species" *1859*
35 The Pony Express begins carrying mail *1860*
36 Louis Pasteur develops pasteurization *1860*
37 Hot air balloons are used during the American Civil War *1861*
38 Work begins on the Paris Opera House *1861*
39 The Emancipation Proclamation *1863*
40 General Ulysses S. Grant captures the city of Vicksburg *1863*
41 Abraham Lincoln is assassinated by John Wilkes Booth *1865*
42 The first Gatling gun is made *1865*
43 Bill Cody kills 4,280 buffalo in eight months *1867*
44 Construction begins on the Brooklyn Bridge *1869*
45 Renoir exhibits his work at the first Impressionist show *1874*
46 Alexander Graham Bell patents the telephone *1876*
47 Thomas Edison invents gramophone and light bulb *1877-1879*
48 Henrik Ibsen writes "A Doll's House" *1879*
49 Rodin produces Impressionist sculpture *1880*
50 Author Helen Keller is born blind and deaf *1880*
51 Booker T. Washington founds the Tuskegee Institute *1881*
52 Joseph Pulitzer acquires the "New York Herald" *1883*
53 Seurat continues to explore pointillism in his paintings *1886*
54 The Statue of Liberty is reassembled in New York Harbor *1886*
55 The Eiffel Tower is erected in Paris *1889*
56 Tchaikovsky composes "Sleeping Beauty" *1890*
57 Zipper replaces hooks and eyes *1893*
58 The rules of bowling are standardized *1895*
59 Ronald Ross links malaria to mosquito bites *1897*
60 Prototypical automobiles begin to appear *1898*

TECHNOLOGY
& EMPIRE

19^{th Century}

TECHNOLOGY & EMPIRE

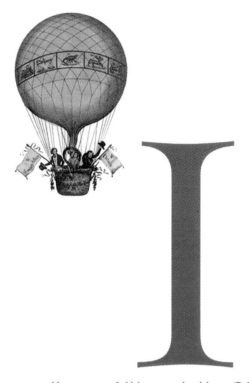

In the 1800s, European culture reached the apex of its influence on the outside world. During the reign of Queen Victoria, from 1839-1901, the Western world's technology, politics, economics, and military strength would forcibly dominate many of the world's other cultures. Although the 20th century would see much of this control thrown off by a world unwilling to submit to European and American control, the decades following 1850 largely belonged to Latin civilization.

This geopolitical imbalance, best exemplified in the economic exploitation of India, China, and Japan and the colonial conquest of Africa, was paired with another growing imbalance between man and the natural world. As Western culture grew more dominant, the European mania for technology and science also grew in importance, and humanity began to redraw the physical environments of the globe in its own image.

To the 19th-century individual, the natural world grew ever more removed and distant. Mechanical trains replaced horses, reapers replaced scythes, factories and mines replaced gardens and fields. As technological conveniences proliferated, an increasing buffer of machines and devices erected itself between people and their natural surroundings. In cities like London, the soil was covered with pavement, the trees largely were replaced by buildings, and even the air was transformed by industrial smog.

For many, this profound and accelerating transition called for reflection. Some, like the English Romantic authors and artists, rebelled against the changes, attempting through their work to revive an image of a mythical natural past now lost. Others, like the philosopher Nietzsche, saw modern changes as an opportunity to frame new values and ideas in place of outmoded ideologies.

In the end, however, the change was beyond the ability of anyone to control. Those who accepted the new order, like the imperial faction of Japan, prospered. Those who attempted to resist, like the Qing Chinese and the indigenous American nations, were crushed.

In this context, English culture reached its full glory. Reflected not only in the vast reaches of the British Empire, upon which the sun literally never set, the global dominance of English values and methods also was demonstrated in the growing power of the United States. Both nations, powered by societies that embraced industrialization, endured great political challenges (the Napoleonic Wars and the American Civil War) to claim the world's center stage. More than anything else, it was Anglo-American creativity and economic might that set the world on its new and uncertain path to a mechanized 20th century.

1800s: **(1)** **Canned food is developed to feed the armies of Napoleon.** Realizing that speed is essential to strategic advantage, Napoleon is unwilling to wait for his armies to gather fresh supplies, thus creating the need for a way to preserve food. French ingenuity responds with vacuum-sealed food in metal cans.

1800s: **Industrialization,** fueled by technological advances in transportation and production, continues to accelerate in the Western world.

1800s: **(2)** **Flamboyant European dress,** as exhibited by this couple, is rapidly replaced in the early 1800s by more somber

fectly legitimate indigenous American herbal remedies, most of the new panaceas are nothing more than over-priced alcohol and sugar water.

1800s: **(7)** **Those indigenous Americans not already killed by European disease** are systematically pushed back or slaughtered by white American settlers and soldiers. Overwhelmed by the sheer numbers of whites, the indigenous Americans will lose most of their traditional territory by 1900.

1800s: **(8)** **The Hopi nation of Arizona struggles to maintain its identity** in the face of Euro-American expansion. By forming a union among their individual towns, the Hopi and their

1793 invention enhances the efficiency and profitability of cotton farming. Revitalizing a flagging cotton industry in the southern United States, Whitney's invention expands the use of slaves in America and polarizes the American economy between an industrial North and an agricultural South.

1800: **The initial version of the Library of Congress is established in Washington, D.C.** Burned by British soldiers during the War of 1812, the collection will be rebuilt around the personal library of Thomas Jefferson. Eventually containing at least one copy of every written work published in the United States, the library will develop into one of the most comprehensive collections in the world, with stack

> ## "We hold these truths to be self-evident: that all men and women are created equal"
>
> ELIZABETH CADY STANTON

attire. English fashion, which dominates European clothing for men, proscribes black trousers, long-tailed coat, and top hat. Women's clothing, still dominated by French styles, will replace elaborate headdresses with simple bonnets, introduce the shawl, and revive the hoop skirt for much of the century.

1800s: **(3)** **In industrialized nations, affordable domestic conveniences such as the iron** become common. As more and more workers move away from farming, new industries must be created to keep them employed. With the advent of a new, modern consumer economy, a host of appliances flood the world's markets, easing everything from washing clothes to cutting grass.

1800s: **(4)** **Late in the century, sports clothing, like knickerbockers worn by golfers,** becomes popular in the West. Throughout the century, men's fashion will become increasingly informal—bowler hats will replace the silk top hat, and shorter jackets will supercede the more formal black morning coat.

1800s: **(5)** **The wide-scale introduction of indoor plumbing** late in the century will lead to the development of the water closet and flush devices.

1800s: **(6)** **Charlatan elixirs,** like these toothache drops, take advantage of unwary American consumers. Inspired by per-

Pueblo cousins had been able to resist Spanish infringement in the 17th century, but the American settlers will prove too formidable. In time, the distinctive agricultural, matrilineal culture of the Hopi, characterized by their unique clustered towns and their dancing arts, will be submerged beneath an endless flow of whites into Arizona.

1800s: **(9)** **American nationalistic pride,** particularly fueled by a powerful U.S. Navy late in the century, is expressed in posters like this one. While individual freedoms and minimal government intervention will remain important domestic issues, American foreign policy and international military presence will grow increasingly aggressive and invasive as the century progresses.

1800s: **With the development of modern plumbing, bathtubs** become an increasingly popular luxury item in the Western world. In the 19th century, both public and private bathing will become an increasingly important social ritual for Europeans and Americans.

1800s: **(10)** **Early attempts at mechanical flight** are completely unsuccessful. Inventions like the bicycle-powered helicopter are singular for their foolish optimism and completely insufficient understanding of aeronautical physics.

1800s: **(11)** **Eli Whitney's cotton gin transforms American agriculture.** Designed to remove the seeds from cotton, the

areas so large that runners sent to retrieve volumes are equipped with roller skates.

1800: **The Qing dynasty of China exhausts its federal treasury while repressing the White Lotus Rebellion.** Burdened by a population that triples between 1636 and 1850 and weakened by a growing trade deficit heightened by the opium trade, the Qing government finds itself increasingly unable to meet the fiscal demands of its many responsibilities. Crippled by financial insolvency, the central government in China will see its authority usurped by aggressive foreign powers and regional governors throughout the 19th century.

1800: **The second edition of William Wordsworth's and Samuel Taylor Coleridge's "Lyrical Ballads" is published.** Together, the two English poets will father the famous Romantic movement of early 19th-century Britain. In works like "Tintern Abbey," Wordsworth will explore the themes of bittersweet nostalgia that characterize much of the new movement's writing.

1802: **African-American rebels under Toussaint-Louverture rise up** against French authority on the Caribbean island of St. Dominque. Despite the capture of the rebel leader, French forces cannot extinguish resistance and find themselves powerless to stop the declaration of the new state of Haiti in 1804.

1803: **A new opiate derivative, morphine,** is developed in Europe as a painkiller.

1803: **The Louisiana Purchase doubles the geographic size of the United States.** Purchased from France by American representatives Lawrence and Monroe, the expanded territory gives birth to the notion of Manifest Destiny. A doctrine proclaiming that the United States has a divine right and mandate to control the continent from coast to coast, Manifest Destiny will be used as the intellectual justification for expelling indigenous Americans from their hereditary homelands.

1804: **Napoleon Bonaparte crowns himself Emperor of France.** In a national referendum, the leader of the French Republic receives public permission to assume the title, and a coronation ceremony quickly follows. Over the next 10 years, Napoleon's armies will spread the revolution by force through all of continental Europe. Ill-advised invasions of Spain and Russia, however, will sap and eventually crush French military strength. Exiled in 1814, the emperor will make a dramatic return to power in 1815, only to be defeated once again by English and Prussian troops at Waterloo. Although his reign spans little more than a decade, Napoleon's military victories spread the ideologies of the French Revolution throughout Europe, changing its political and intellectual composition forever.

c. 1810: **American-born populaces in South America revolt against Spanish colonial rule.** With Spain under the control of a French puppet government, Spanish-Americans see no reason to continue respecting Iberian authority. Chile and modern Argentina declare their independence under the leadership of José de San Martin. To the north, Spanish

Russia, France, England, Prussia, and Austria, under the influence of Austrian foreign minister Prince Metternich, essentially attempt to turn back time. Ousted monarchies are reestablished in France and Italy, and artificial states are established in the Netherlands and southern Germany as "buffers" against future French aggression. Unrealistic in tone and intent, the arrangements agreed to by the congress will last less than 20 years.

1815: **A safe and reliable gas lamp is developed by English inventor Sir Humphry Davy.** Originally designed for use in coal mines, where gas concentrations make lighting a very dangerous business, the new lamps also are used in houses and as street lights. As the century progresses, Davy's invention will take the darkness out of urban European nights, greatly expanding available time for social interaction and making a whole series of new evening entertainments possible.

1817: **The Buttonwood Agreement sets up a constitution and rules of conduct** for the New York Stock and Exchange Board. In effective operation since 1792, the exchange forum will develop into one of the major financial transaction centers in the world.

1818: **Mary Wollstonecraft Shelley wins a writing competition with her short novel "Frankenstein."** One of the earliest protests against the dangers and potential evils of technological progress, the book is an excellent example of early 19th-century Romantic literature.

1818: **Under pressure from the aristocracy, the king of Prussia agrees to lift all tariffs on trade** with other German states. The unilateral action is quickly imitated by the other

> ## "If there is a way to do it better, find it"
> ### T H O M A S   E D I S O N

Americans under Simón Bolívar will overwhelm imperial forces by 1821. Bolívar's dream of a united South America will be quickly dashed, however, as the former Spanish territories break up into multiple states.

1812: **The United States and Britain go to war over the rights of American merchant shipping.** Engaged in a desperate struggle with Napoleonic France, the British have imposed a naval blockade on French-controlled territory that they expect Americans to respect. When American ships are boarded by British sailors to bring the point home, an outraged United States goes to war. Largely indecisive, the war results in the British burning of Washington, D.C., but provides America with a military hero in Andrew Jackson and inspires Francis Scott Key to write the American national anthem. In 1814, with Napoleon defeated and their needs met, the British quickly negotiate a peace with their American cousins.

1814: **The Congress of Vienna, a convention of diplomats from all the major European powers,** attempts to restore Europe to its pre-French Revolution structure. Leaders of

German nations, resulting in the formation of the Zollverein, a free trade zone within the Germanies. The economic cooperation, which includes most German states by 1844, is a crucial precursor of German unification.

1819: **Frenchman René Laënnec invents the stethoscope,** allowing him to listen to female chests without excessively indiscreet contact.

1820: **The Missouri Compromise divides the American territory of the Louisiana Purchase** into regions where slavery is legal and areas where it is not. As an attempt to assuage the fear American Southerners have about whether their political needs will be neglected as the nation grows, the agreement is largely a failure. The agricultural interests of the South lose significance for a federal government that is increasingly dominated by a more populous, industrially focused North. This true political crisis ultimately remains unaffected by the compromise.

1821: **Greek nationalists,** supported by Russia, France, and Great Britain, revolt against Ottoman rule. By 1830, Greek

CHILD LABOR IN INDUSTRIAL ENGLAND

Crowded housing, dangerous conditions, and 17-hour workdays made childhood a sad proposition for England's urban poor

In 1833, an investigation into working conditions in English textile mills resulted in the passing of Lord Althrop's Act, a new law that limited children under the age of 13 to 48 hours of work per week. Before that time, John Birley, who began working at the Cressbrook Mill when he was seven, would typically work from five in the morning to 10 at night six days a week. To combat inevitable fatigue, he and his fellow child workers often were struck with sticks or dunked in buckets of cold water by their foreman.

During the early years of the Industrial Revolution, factory owners exploited young children. Youths like Birley were bought from orphanages and workhouses to become pauper apprentices in the mills. Sought out for their small size, which allowed them to get in and out of difficult places, these children were forced to sign contracts that legally bound them to the factory owner. In return for labor, the children were given rough lodging in an apprentice house and some food. The stone house that Birley lived in, built about 300 yards away from the mill, roomed roughly 150 apprentices—three to a bed. Twice during the day, the workers were fed light meals. According to Birley:

"We went to the mill at five o'clock and worked till about eight or nine when they brought us our breakfast, water-porridge with oatcake in it and onions to flavour it. Dinner consisted of Derbyshire oatcakes cut into four pieces and...milk. We drank the milk and with the oatcake in our hand, we went back to work without sitting down."

Children usually picked up loose cotton from underneath the moving machinery or leaned over the spinning machines to repair broken threads. In either case, accidents were frequent—many workers lost digits or some even entire limbs. The uncomfortable body contortions required to complete these tasks often resulted in painfully sore knees, ankles, elbows, and wrists.

Contemporary medical examiner's reports suggested that mill conditions stunted the growth of men by several inches and reduced their life expectancy by as much as 13 years. Malnutrition often led to weak bones, causing flat feet, bowed legs, and poor spinal alignment. Overworked, underfed, poorly housed, and surrounded by dangerous machinery, child laborers faced difficulties that were only partly eased by the legislation of the 1830s.

independence will be established, and Ottoman presence in Europe will be confined to Constantinople.

1821: **Mexican Agustin de Iturbide leads a successful revolution against Spanish rule of Mexico.** Earlier revolts in Mexico, too radical in their social agendas, failed to gain broad enough popular support and were violently repressed by colonial authorities. Iturbide's more conservative platform, based on resistance to liberal reforms in Spain, is more successful in uniting the various strands of Mexican society in the effort to obtain independence. An ineffectual ruler, Iturbide is ousted in favor of a republican government in 1823.

1823: **American Secretary of State John Quincy Adams**
(13) **and President James Monroe define the strategic foreign policy of the United States with the Monroe Doctrine.** In essence, the new policy attempts to isolate the Americas from Europe, announcing a refusal to tolerate European colonies in the Western Hemisphere and an unwillingness to become embroiled in European controversy. This doctrine of isolated distance will dominate American foreign initiatives for the next 100 years.

1824: **Ludwig van Beethoven's "Ninth Symphony" debuts**
(14) **in Vienna.** Heard by many as a musical picture of the struggle and eventual triumph in writing a symphony, the German composer's crowning masterpiece has been called an epic journey into D major. The stirring vocal finale, set to the poet Friedrich von Schiller's "Ode to Joy," is one of the most memorable and moving in Western music.

1824: **English mason Joseph Aspdin patents Portland Cement.** A mixture of clay and limestone, the new bonding agent is the first since Roman times that will set underwater, opening many new possibilities in bridge foundations. Concrete construction, hardly used in the West since Roman times, once again becomes a prominent building material with Aspdin's invention.

1826: **Construction is completed on Thomas Jefferson's**
(15) **design for the University of Virginia campus.** Anchored at one end by the famous dome of the library, the campus opens at the other end of a central yard to frame a view of nearby mountains. Metaphorically, education is presented as a balance between abstract knowledge (library) and experiences of nature (mountain). The university campus, the great contribution of American urban design to world architecture, finds its prototype in the partially enclosed yard of the school.

1827: **English chemist John Walker** develops the first modern friction match.

1828: **Noah Webster completes his comprehensive dictionary of the English language.** With full definitions of the words included, the new volume is a substantial improvement over the simpler spelling and pronunciation guides of the 1780s.

1828: **American war hero Andrew Jackson wins a mud-**
(16) **slinging contest with John Quincy Adams to become president of the United States.** Victor over the British at the 1814 Battle of New Orleans, largely responsible for the American seizure of Spanish Florida, Jackson is the first mass public icon to enter the White House. The first national political leader in America to build his power base west of the Appalachian Mountains, Jackson represents a shift in the United States' political center of gravity.

1829: **French educator Louis Braille publishes a treatise on**
(17) **his new reading system for the blind.** Blinded at age three, Braille begins working at 15 on the language system of raised dots that bears his name. In time, Braille writing will become the principal non-audio language of the blind throughout the Western world.

1829: **French tailors develop the first genuinely operable sewing machine,** complete with chain stitch. In 1846, Elias Howe will patent the design of a device that really deserves to be called the prototype of the modern sewing machine.

1829: **The "Stourbridge Lion" becomes the first locomo-**
(18) **tive to operate on American soil.** Developed in Great Britain, railroad technology will accelerate industrialization much as canals had in the 18th century. Facilitating the expedient and inexpensive transport of raw materials and finished products over large distances, railroads will help to foster integrated, national economies.

1830: **Revolution in France replaces absolutist King Charles X with a constitutional monarchy under Louis-Phillippe,** Duke of Orleans. Louis-Phillippe will himself be overthrown during the revolutions of 1848. During the 19th century, France will experience constant political change and turmoil as a result of being ruled at various times by two emperors, an absolute king, a constitutional monarch, and a series of different republican governments. Its continuing instability will create repeated international reverberations throughout Europe during most of the 1800s.

1830: **The failure of the Congress of Vienna's reactionary agenda** is revealed in a series of nationalist uprisings throughout Europe. In addition to the overthrow of French King Charles X, Belgium secedes from the Netherlands, and popular uprisings have to be repressed in Poland and Italy. Even those revolts that fail in the short run indicate that the nationalist and liberal sentiment initially ignited by the French Revolution cannot simply be erased. The revolutions of 1830, and those that follow throughout the 1800s, reveal beyond question that the old order of Europe cannot be restored.

1831: **Japanese printmaker Katsushika Hokusai finishes**
(19) **cutting the woodblocks** for "The Great Wave of Kanagawa." Part of a series entitled "Thirty-Six Views of Mount Fuji," the print shows the mastery of form, color, and composition achieved with 19th-century Japanese woodblock printing. When copies of the print filter into Europe, they have enormous aesthetic influence and impact on painters like van Gogh and the French composer Debussy, whose masterpiece "La Mer" is directly inspired by "The Great Wave."

1831: **Polish composer and pianist Frederic-Francois Chopin**
(20) moves to the Romantic intellectual environment of Paris. In France, the musician's composing will mature into a distinctive style that produces an extremely emotional music characterized by complex rhythms and bold use of dissonance.

1831: **English chemist and physicist Michael Faraday publishes his findings on electromagnetic induction.** The observations will have many practical applications, including the electric motor. One of the great experimental scientists of the century, Faraday will be the first to isolate benzene, synthesize chlorocarbons, and develop classical field theory.

1831: **French author and political liberal Victor Hugo fin-**
(21) **ishes his novel "Notre Dame de Paris."** His first major novel, Hugo's new book is much like the later "Les Miserables," serving as a political platform for leftist social agendas.

1832: **The Reform Bill of 1832 largely restructures political power in Great Britain.** Keenly aware of violent revolutions on the European continents, the English ruling aristocracy decides to voluntarily surrender its monopoly on British government. While political districts are redrawn to acknowledge and allow representation of new industrial interests, the voting population is expanded by approximately 50 percent. Through a series of gradual, peaceful transformations, English political authority will be shifted to account for irreversible social and economic change.

1832: **The Cherokee nation sets out on the migration known**
(22) **as "The Trail of Tears,"** moving from Georgia to modern Oklahoma. Almost a quarter of their population will die from causes directly linked to the winter journey, which occurs during some of the worst weather of the century. The Indian Removal Act, signed by Andrew Jackson the previous year, gives the state of Georgia the authority to force the Cherokee off their property. Even though the act is found by the Supreme Court to be an unconstitutional violation of treaties signed with the Cherokee, the white government takes no action when Georgia militia units descend on the indigenous American settlements. The faint Cherokee seal represents this forced removal.

1833: **Slavery is abolished in the British Empire.** Trade of slaves has been outlawed in British territories since 1807, and, with the new law, all remaining slaves are granted their freedom. England, once the greatest beneficiary of a lucrative slave trade, now becomes the chief moral leader in the drive to abolish slavery throughout the Western world. The same year that slavery is outlawed in Britain, the Anti-Slavery Society is established in the United States.

"He only earns his freedom and his life, who takes them by storm"

GOETHE

1834: (23) **American inventor Cyrus McCormick patents a design for a mechanical reaper.** A huge improvement in farming methods, the reaper, like the seed drill before it, will decrease the number of farmers needed to raise crops. Displaced agricultural workers, migrating to cities, will become the urban work force of the American Industrial Revolution. After beating out rival reaper-maker Obed Hussey, McCormick's company will dominate the market,

attempts to block the illegal drug smuggling had been largely unsuccessful. Fearing the loss of their lucrative tea-for-opium trade, the British government intervenes militarily.

1842: **The Treaty of Nanking ends the Opium Wars,** effectively neutering the Chinese Qing government. Unable to defeat British ships and advanced weaponry, the Chinese are forced to capitulate. Forced to open five ports to British

1848: **A National Board of Health is established in England.** Responsible for overseeing the construction of new drainage and sewer systems and the effective disposal of garbage, the new organization largely is created through the efforts of Sir Edwin Chadwick, who believes that sickness brought on by unsanitary conditions is the chief cause of urban poverty.

1848: **German radical thinker Karl Marx publishes "The**

"When dictatorship is a fact, revolution becomes a right"

VICTOR HUGO

eventually evolving into the International Harvester Company.

1836: (24) **American writer and thinker Ralph Waldo Emerson finishes his short book, "Nature."** A manifesto of the Transcendentalist movement that Emerson essentially founded, the book explores man's potential to overcome the predictable and numbing world of Newtonian physics and mechanistic social sciences. Fearing that modern science, with its focus on cause and effect, denies the free will of man, Emerson seeks a personal communion with God or nature that supercedes rationalistic rules and formulas.

1837: **Popular uprisings in Canada encourage the British government to reconsider its colonial political system.** On the advice of the new governor, Lord Durham, Parliament agrees to grant Canada domestic autonomy. In 1867, the multiple British territories in North America are united and given full right to self-government as an independent Dominion of the British Empire. Dominion status is granted to Australia in 1901 and New Zealand in 1907.

1837: (25) **Serial publication begins of Charles Dickens' first novel, "Oliver Twist."** Through his stories, Dickens will raise social awareness of the harsh living conditions endured by the British urban poor. Author of such famous works as "David Copperfield," "A Tale of Two Cities," and "Great Expectations," Dickens will emerge as one of the most popular English writers of the 19th century.

1839: (26) **Queen Victoria ascends to the throne of Great Britain.** Although the political power of English monarchs largely has been curtailed by the time she is crowned, Victoria still exerts enormous social influence. Throughout her long reign, her personal conduct and family life will define the cultural values of European life so completely that the era will come to be known as Victorian.

1839: **The daguerreotype, a precursor of the modern photograph,** is developed by French inventor Louis-Jacques-Mandé Daguerre. A metal plate covered with silver salts and exposed to light through a large wooden camera obscura, the new system is both awkward and expensive. During the 1840s, it will be replaced by the cheaper negative-film system of Henry Fox Talbot.

1839: **Chinese anti-drug commissioner Lin Tse-hsü orders the burning of 20,000 chests of opium in Canton,** sparking the Opium Wars. Until Lin's appointment, Beijing's

trade, surrender Hong Kong to English authority, and pay a $21-million war indemnity, the Chinese emperor is humiliated. With the prestige of its central ruler crushed, China is plagued by numerous devastating rebellions throughout the rest of the century.

1842: **Diethyl ether** is used as an operating room anesthetic for the first time.

1843: **Christian Danish philosopher Søren Kierkegaard writes "Fear and Trembling,"** one of the earliest explorations of existentialism. Believing that Hegel's universal meaning is not to be found, Kierkegaard exhorts his readers to summon the passion and courage to commit to their own reasons and values. In effect, the Dane argues that the absence of a preexisting reason for being constitutes an enormous opportunity for a personal "leap of faith."

1844: (27) **The first telegraph message is sent** over an experimental American line built between Baltimore and Washington, D.C. The concept of the magnetic telegraph, conceived by Samuel Morse in 1832, is made a reality when Congress supplies Ezra Cornell with funding to build the line. An alphabet of electric pulses, developed by Morse and known as Morse code, will remain the standard form of telegraph communication until the technology is replaced by telephones and radios.

1844: **American physician John Gorrie builds the first compressed air refrigerator** for use in a Florida hospital. Mechanical engineer Jacob Perkins laid the groundwork for Gorrie's accomplishment in 1834, when he secured a British patent for his technique of producing cold by expanding volatile liquids in a closed circuit.

1844: **American inventor Charles Goodyear develops vulcanized rubber,** stimulating the growth of a vast rubber-producing industry. Among other things, Goodyear's invention will lead to the development of the automobile tire brand that bears his name.

1848: **American feminists Lucretia Mott and Elizabeth Cady Stanton organize the Seneca Falls Convention.** A national gathering, the convention drafts a Declaration of Sentiments, in which basic legal and political rights are outlined as essential requirements for gender equality. The agenda, constructed in upstate New York, will become the heart of mainstream suffrage and feminist movements that follow in the United States.

Communist Manifesto." In this and his later book "Das Kapital," Marx will provide an economic analysis of social and political thinking that will not only provide inspiration for various Marxist governments, but also will provide a fundamentally different approach to history that will influence pro- and anti-communist scholars alike.

1850: **Rural outhouses** continue to be used. (29)

1851: **The first world exhibition is held in Hyde Park, London.** The feature exhibit and symbol of the fair is the Crystal Palace, a giant glass and iron gallery designed by British engineer Joseph Paxton. Extrapolated from greenhouse designs, the new structure will have enormous impact on the aesthetics and technology of 20th-century Western architecture.

1851: (30) **An American crew wins the Hundred Guinea Cup,** a prestigious British yachting prize. Continuously won by American teams for the next 132 years, the prize will come to be known as the America's Cup.

1851: **The Taiping Rebellion begins in China.** Declaring an independent country centered on their new capital of Nanking, a group of protocommunist, monotheistic religious zealots secede from disintegrating Qing China. Although internal division, the failure of their attempted communist system, and Western support of local Qing armies will eventually suppress the rebellion, the insurrection lasts 13 years and costs more than 30 million lives.

1852: **French merchant Aristide Boucicaut revolutionizes retail sales and service.** By reducing profit margins to expand volume and instituting policies of exchange and refund, Boucicaut finds that he is able to expand both his customer base and overall profit.

1853: (31) **Elisha Graves Otis presents his new invention, the elevator,** at the first World's Fair in New York. Installed with safety catches, the new device will not fall even if the main cable snaps. With the elevator's development, the five-to eight-story de facto height limit on most buildings is removed, paving the way for the development of the skyscraper.

1853: **American ships under Commodore Matthew Perry arrive in Japan,** announcing that the Western world will no longer tolerate Japanese isolation. Unable to overcome the superior force of Perry's armaments and keenly aware of the recent Chinese thrashing by European armies in the Opium

Wars, the shogun has no choice but to sign a trade treaty with the American government. The new agreement puts the United States on par with France, Germany, and England in their exploitation of northern Pacific nations while simultaneously revealing the weakness of the shogunate. In 1868, with its reputation shattered by economic crisis and an inability to contain Western economic aggression, the Japanese government will be overthrown during the Meiji Restoration.

1856: **English inventor Sir Henry Bessemer develops the Bessemer Process for producing steel.** The new production method, combined with later open-hearth technology, will make the wide-scale production of steel possible for the first time. Significantly stronger than pure iron, carbon-strengthened steel will become the chief industrial metal of the Western world.

1856-60: **The loss of a second Opium war** further prostrates the Chinese government to the demands of Russia, France, England, and the United States. European dignitaries take permanent residence in Beijing, railroad right-of-ways and border territories are ceded, and further trade concessions are accepted by the powerless Qing rulers.

1857: **Neanderthal bones are discovered in Germany.** Different from modern human anatomy in several important ways, the Neanderthal skeleton will provide important evidence in support of the theory of evolution.

1859: **American Edwin L. Drake leads the drilling of the first oil well** in Titusville, Pennsylvania. The new oil well will serve as a technological prototype for the modern petroleum industry.

1859: **Expanding out from the Kingdom of Sardinia,** Italian nationalist forces under Giuseppe Garibaldi take control of Lombardy and the Kingdom of the Two Sicilies. The new territories are united with Sardinia under King Victor Emmanuel as the new Kingdom of Italy. In 1866, Italian troops will seize Venetia from a preoccupied Austria; the Papal States will be similarly annexed in 1870 when French protection is withdrawn. With the occupation of Rome, the

1859: **French physicist Gaston Plante develops the electric cell battery.** Used in applications as diverse as starting automobiles and powering submerged submarines, the electric battery will become one of the most pervasive forms of power in the modern world.

1859: **English liberal and utilitarian hedonist John Stuart Mill** publishes his famous essay "On Liberty." The chief inheritor of Jeremy Bentham's philosophy, Mill adds to and transforms it. An extreme advocate of individual rights, he believes in the protection of the minority from the tyranny of majority opinion. Perhaps most provocatively, Mill contends in his "Three Essays on Religion" that, because evil exists, God is either not omnipotent or not good. Defiantly, Mill refuses to call God good if God does not live up to the philosopher's higher sense of goodness.

1859: **English biologist Charles Darwin** develops the first comprehensive theory of evolution in his book "On the Origin of Species." Although transmutation of species has been a topic of conversation for much of the early 19th century, it is Darwin who first shapes it into an organized body of thought, backs it with sufficient evidence, and exposes the ideas to a large audience. Both "On the Origin of Species" and his 1871 book "The Descent of Man," in which he suggests that man and apes descend from a common ancestor or primate, are received with extreme objection by much of European society.

1860: **Celluloid, the precursor of modern plastic**, is used for the first time in the production of dental plates and shirt collars.

1860: **The Pony Express**, carrying mail from Missouri to California, begins its brief one-year existence. Riders on the 1,800-mile route, including a young Bill Cody, change horses hundreds of times on their 10-day gallop. Financially unsuccessful, the enterprise will close in 1861 with the erection of a transcontinental telegraph line.

1860: **French chemist Louis Pasteur identifies the decay of food** and fermentation with airborne microorganisms. His

interests. Fought with tactics that fail to reflect substantial improvements in weapon technology, the five-year war is remarkably expensive in terms of human life; more than 620,000 men will die during the conflict from disease, exposure, malnutrition, and combat wounds.

1861: **Hot-air balloons are used for observation during the American Civil War.** Although the first manned balloon flight had occurred in 1783, its implementation by the warring American armies constitutes the first widespread use of the first truly successful flying machine. Manned balloons will be used for a variety of military, scientific, and recreational uses throughout the next century-and-a-half.

1861: **Construction begins on French architect Charles Garnier's design for the Paris Opera House.** With its multiple entrances for different classes of theatre-goers and its elaborate layers of lobbies and halls, the new opera house is more about the complex theatre of Victorian culture than it is about opera. In an architectural environment perfectly suited to the task, Parisian society acts out its highly stylized and precise interactions, seeing and being seen as expected.

1862: **King William I of Prussia appoints Otto von Bismarck as the head of the Prussian cabinet.** Under his famous policy of Realpolitik, Bismarck will play whatever part is needed to assure Prussian power and the creation of a pan-German state under William's rule. Now the conservative, now the moderate, and now even the socialist when it is useful, Bismarck scorns abstract ideology in favor of concrete gain.

1863: **American President Abraham Lincoln issues the Emancipation Proclamation,** "freeing" all African-American slaves in rebellious Southern states. The executive order quite specifically declines to free slaves in any territories loyal to the federal government. In effect, the presidential order applies only to those regions where Lincoln has no authority, making its immediate de facto importance limited. A private racist himself, Lincoln's primary concern with the new proclamation is to gain the moral support of antislavery

"If all mankind minus one were of one opinion, mankind would be no more justified in silencing that one person than he, if he had the power, would be justified in silencing mankind"

JOHN STUART MILL

entire peninsula is united as a single nation for the first time in more than 1,300 years.

1859: **Florence Nightingale writes "Notes on Nursing,"** a canonical resource of modern nursing practice. As a nurse during the Crimean War, Nightingale established basic principles of sanitation in field hospitals, greatly reducing unnecessary deaths by disease. Her book will greatly raise awareness of just how important cleanliness is to good health.

new process of pasteurization, which kills the organisms by exposing them to heat, will greatly reduce sickness caused by milk, wine, and vinegar.

1861: **The American Civil War begins with the shelling of Ft. Sumter in Charleston, South Carolina.** Frequently oversimplified into a war about slavery, the conflict is initiated by the rebellion of an agricultural southern society that feels the federal government has failed to protect its rights and

European nations in his fight to reunite the country.

1863: **After capturing the key rebel city of Vicksburg,** American Civil War general Ulysses S. Grant is given command of the North's Army of the Potomac. Grant's ruthlessness will help crush the Southern Confederacy. Realizing he has a vast numerical advantage in men and materials over his Southern adversary Robert E. Lee, Grant forces a grueling war of attrition upon the rebels. Throughout the rest of the war, he will accept heavy Union casualties, almost callously sacrificing his men to exhaust limited Southern supplies of bullets, materials, and men. A hero after the war, Grant will serve as an American president of dubious quality, heading an administration largely characterized by corruption.

1865: **The American Civil War ends with the total collapse of the rebel government, economy, and military.** Overwhelmed by the sheer weight of the North's population, wealth, and industrial development, the rebellious Southern states are slowly crushed by a brutal war of attrition. Martial law is later established throughout the subjugated territories.

1865: **American president Abraham Lincoln is assassinated** by Southern sympathizer John Wilkes Booth. A vain gesture after the war is already lost, Booth's murder of the president only reinforces and cements a federal attitude of oppression toward the defeated Southern states.

1865: **Former Confederate general Nathan Bedford Forrest founds the Ku Klux Klan** in Pulaski, Tennessee. Originally conceived as a social order of modern knights committed to protecting Southern whites from oppression at the hands of opportunistic Northern businessmen and immigrants, the order rapidly declines into an ignorant and xenophobic hate group committed to repressing racial and religious minorities.

1865: **French physiologist Claude Bernard writes "An Introduction to the Study of Experimental Medicine."** A leading proponent of observation and vivisection in biolog-

establishes the basis of genetic transfer. Through observation and experiment with pea plants, Mendel develops his Law of Independent Assortment, by which the rules describing the passing on of genetic traits from parent to offspring are correctly outlined.

1866: **Prussian victory in the Seven Weeks War** shatters Austrian influence in central Germany. The powerful Prussian army, relentlessly strengthened under Bismarck's almost autocratic rule, easily crushes Austrian resistance. The German Confederation, of which Austria is the leading member, is dissolved as part of the ensuing peace terms. With Austria effectively cut out of German affairs, the ground is prepared for Prussian dominance of Central Europe.

1867: **Bill Cody earns his nickname "Buffalo Bill"** by killing 4,280 buffalo in an eight-month period to help feed railroad workers in the American plains. A former Pony Express rider and a scout for U.S. cavalry during their campaigns to annihilate indigenous American populations, Cody will become a folk hero renowned for courage and marksmanship. In 1883, he will start a "wild west" show that will help forge the lasting myth of the 19th-century American frontier.

1868: **"Beyond Good and Evil,"** one of the major works of philosopher Friedrich Nietzsche, is published in Germany. Heavily influenced by Darwin, Nietzsche proclaims strength, ambition, individual creativity, and selfishness as virtues. Arguing that the notion of God is conceptually outdated, the German thinker calls for a rejection of traditional Christian values. In an openly competitive environment, free of the

and the Mediterranean Sea. Built across the isthmus between Egypt and Arabia, the new canal makes it unnecessary for vessels to sail around Africa on routes between Europe and the Far East. Jointly owned by British and French interests for the next 80 years, the canal will do little to benefit the Egyptian nation.

1870: **The Franco-Prussian War unites the lesser German states under Prussian leadership.** A war manufactured by Bismarck to ignite German nationalist sentiment, the conflict is swiftly won through superior Prussian leadership. Napoleon III is forced to abdicate as emperor of France. Alsace and sectors of Lorraine are reclaimed by Prussia, and France is forced to pay a large indemnity. More importantly, Prussia and the smaller German states declare their political union, creating the German empire.

c. 1870: **The rickshaw,** a one-seat, two-wheeled carriage pulled by a man, is first used in Japan. Using Western springs and ball-bearing technology, the rickshaw will become a pervasive form of taxi travel in Asian cities.

1872: **The secret ballot and universal manhood suffrage is established in Great Britain** by the Liberal government of William Gladstone. Improving upon the expanded suffrage granted by Benjamin Disraeli's Conservative government in 1867, the new laws extend the voting privilege to all of English male society.

1874: **The first public showing of Impressionist painting** is opened in Paris. Repeatedly declined admittance to the annual salons of the French Academy, progressive painters

"No law can be sacred to me but that of my own nature"

RALPH WALDO EMERSON

ical study, Bernard also makes key discoveries about the functions of the liver and the pancreas.

1865: **American Richard Jordan Gatling perfects his design for the Gatling gun,** the ancestor of the modern machine gun. By rotating a series of barrels past the firing chamber with a hand crank, the weapon's operator is able to fire many rounds quickly without overheating any one barrel.

1866: **Swedish chemist Alfred Nobel develops a stable nitroglycerine-based explosive he calls dynamite.** In addition to the industrial explosive, Nobel also will invent smokeless gunpowder. Establishing a manufacturing empire to produce his new inventions, Nobel will amass a huge fortune that he will dedicate posthumously to establish the Nobel prizes.

1866: **The first transatlantic cable establishes telegraph communication** between England and the United States. Connecting Ireland to Nova Scotia, the new cable can transmit up to eight words per minute and will remain in use for six years.

1866: **Austrian monk and biologist Gregor Johann Mendel**

social limitations of charity, mercy, or meekness, Nietzsche believes the inferior will fade away, allowing the talented survivors to thrive.

1868: **Discontent samurai and nobles,** angered by the shogunate's ineffectiveness in dealing with foreign powers, rally an army around the emperor and overthrow the last Tokugawa shogun. For the first time in centuries, Japanese national power is returned to the imperial court in a revolution known as the Meiji Restoration. Quickly adopting useful Western techniques and technologies, the new Japanese government will successfully strive to make its nation competitive in a geopolitical world it recognizes is dominated by European society.

1869: **Construction begins on the Brooklyn Bridge.** Designed by John Augustus Roebling, the 1,595-foot span across the East River is the first suspension structure to use steel wire for its cables. Completed in 1883, the bridge will remain the longest span in the world until 1890, when the Firth of Forth cantilever bridge is constructed in Scotland.

1869: **The Suez Canal is opened,** linking the Indian Ocean

including Manet, Degas, and Renoir privately fund their own exhibition. Abandoning classical models for more subjective or "impressionistic" representation, the group is linked by new attitudes about light and a tendency to use soft, patchy brushwork. Initially shocking, the new style will rapidly grow in popularity and exert a large influence on later painting.

1876: **German inventor Nikolaus August Otto designs the first reasonably functional internal combustion engine.** In 1885, automobile pioneers Carl Benz and Gottlieb Daimler will use the new engine to power the first car.

1876: **Alexander Graham Bell is issued a patent for his new invention, the telephone.** Along with the television, the phone will become one of the most ubiquitous technological accessories of the Western home, increasing the speed and flexibility of individual communication across large distances.

1876: **The first bicycle factory is opened in the United States.** An enormous fad for the rest of the century, the bicycle will remain primarily a mode of recreation in the United States. In parts of Europe and China, however, the bicycle will remain a popular and economic means of per-

CONTEMPORARY PHILOSOPHIES

SOCIAL DARWINISM

In the hands of less gentle men, Darwin's theories of evolution became a philosophical justification of selfish brutality

In 1858, Charles Darwin's book "Origin of Species" caused an enormous stir in popular European thought. Among the text's many provocative ideas, Darwin's concept of natural selection was to be of particular influence. Originally a biological theory arguing that certain members of a species survived over others in competitive environments because of certain genetic advantages, natural selection became the central principle of a new theory called Social Darwinism.

Originally espoused by Herbert Spencer, Social Darwinism contends that individuals and entire societies both are subject to natural selection. Qualities of assertiveness, aggression, strength, and selfishness allow certain cultures and individuals to prevail over others in a world with resources insufficient to meet everyone's needs. Societies that lack this sense of self-interest and aggressive energy will become extinct, lacking the "genetic traits" required for survival. In its most simple and brutal form, Social Darwinism translates into the axiom "Might is right." The new ideology, crude and over-simplistic in many hands, found its most sophisticated development and expression in the writings of German philosopher Friedrich Nietzsche. In his 1885 classic "Thus Spoke Zarathustra," Nietzsche declares the irrelevance and outdated nature of God as a concept, rejecting the Christian social

and moral values that are predicated upon belief in the existence of a higher being. Any kinds of selfless action, including meekness, charity, and mercy, are forms of Christian behavior that protect the weak at the expense of the strong. In so doing, they limit the creative potential of the strong individual, retarding achievement by restraining self-promotion. A society that promotes these values, by effectively stunting its own growth, condemns itself to mediocrity.

In a 19th-century world that was politically dominated by European nations, Social Darwinism constituted a celebration of long extant Western values. Although Darwin's biological text unintentionally provided a growing vocabulary and awareness to the ideology of self-interest, already at the very heart of European history and culture are intense competition and self-aggrandizement. The powerful individual who transcended social mediocrity, whether Michelangelo, Galileo, or Napoleon, had always enjoyed a cult status in the Western mind. Through constant internal struggle, whether military, economic, scientific, or philosophical, Europe had in fact made itself stronger, often at the later expense of less conflict-driven parts of the world. What Social Darwinism really provided most was an intellectual justification of the European way of life.

sonal transportation, requiring no food, fuel, rest, or housing to remain operable.

1877: **American inventor Thomas Alva Edison invents the gramophone.** Issued more than 1,000 patents in his lifetime, Edison established his famous research laboratory with proceeds from his invention of the stock ticker tape. In addition to launching the gramophone, his facility will produce incandescent lightbulbs, improve microphone and telephone design, and develop the first talking movie.

1879: **"A Doll's House,"** written by Norwegian playwright Henrik Ibsen, is performed for the first time. A pioneer in exploring contemporary social problems, particularly the interactions between men and women in European society, Ibsen serves as a watershed in modern Western drama.

1880: **Herman Holerith, whose Tabulating Machine Company will evolve into IBM,** develops a machine that uses electric currents to punch holes in cards. Used in 1890 to record census information, the new machine is a vital link between Pascal's adding machine and the modern computer.

1880: **French sculptor August-René Rodin completes the casts for his famous "Thinker" sculptures.** In some ways the medium's response to Impressionist painting, Rodin's work eschews natural representation in favor of pure form. Powerfully muscular, carefully modeled to reflect light, and highly interactive with the space that sur-

renamed Annam. Responding to anti-Christian violence on the peninsula, the French occupy it with soldiers. A feeble attempt by China to resist French control of its former tribute state is ended quickly by the complete destruction of a major Chinese fleet in 1884.

1883: **Newspaper man Joseph Pulitzer acquires the New York "Herald."** An immigrant from Hungary, Pulitzer began as a simple reporter in St. Louis, but quickly rose to prominence and wealth, eventually becoming a member of the Missouri state legislature. As his flagship paper, the "Herald" will assure his financial future with its sensationalist stories and questionable ethics. Although Pulitzer and fellow newspaperman Hearst's "yellow journalism" will leave stains on both their names, the Hungarian's posthumous endowment of the Pulitzer prizes for literature, drama, music, and journalism will help redeem his reputation.

1884: **American banker turned inventor George Eastman develops the first roll of film.** As the founder of the Eastman Kodak Company, Eastman will go on to produce the first box camera and collaborate with Thomas Edison on early research into motion pictures. In 1895 Paris, French inventors Auguste and Louis Lumiere will use their recently developed film projector to show the first movie to a paying audience.

1885: **Dutch painter Vincent Van Gogh finishes "The Potato Eaters."** An early work in the artist's brief career, the painting reveals an empathy and concern for the harsh lifestyle

tled version of the drink is released in 1899 and includes extracts from cocoa leaves and kola nuts. The earliest formula also contains a small amount of cocaine, the perceived benefits of which help early growth in the product's sales.

1886: **The Statue of Liberty is rebuilt on Liberty Island** in New York Harbor. Standing 151 feet and weighing 225 tons, the massive building-sculpture is the product of French sculptor Frédéric-Auguste Bartholdi. A symbol of friendly French-American relations, the project is paid for and constructed by France before being disassembled and shipped to the United States.

1889: **The Eiffel Tower is erected at the Paris Exhibition.** Lacking any prosaic function, the tower is a raw celebration of Western technology and iron construction. An inspiration to early 20th-century architects and engineers, the tower will lend cultural legitimacy to modern materials and erection techniques, paving the way for highbrow modern architecture.

1890: **French composer Claude Debussy begins work on "Suite bergamasque,"** one of his most influential pieces. Using unconventional harmonies and instrument voicings, Debussy composes in bold contrasting washes of tone and texture. Often considered analogous to the painting techniques of the French Impressionists, his compositional techniques will have a wide-ranging influence on 20th-century composers like Igor Stravinsky.

1890: **Russian Peter Tchaikovsky composes "Sleeping**

> "... during the constantly recurring struggle for existence, we see a powerful and ever-acting form of selection"

CHARLES DARWIN

rounds and interpenetrates them, Rodin's sculptures are among the most arresting in Western art.

1880: **Future American writer Helen Keller is born blind and deaf.** With the lifelong assistance of Annie Sullivan, Keller miraculously overcomes her disabilities to graduate from Radcliffe with distinction. Through her extensive writing, Keller will champion the concerns and needs of the disabled, greatly expanding public awareness of and interest in the needs of the physically disadvantaged.

1881: **African-American icon Booker T. Washington founds the Tuskegee Institute in Alabama.** One of the first colleges for African-Americans, Tuskegee is transformed from a handful of run-down farm buildings into a respectable academic institution through Washington's energy, intelligence, and dedication. Expanded education opportunities, provided through the effort of former slaves like Washington, will prove instrumental in providing African-Americans with the intellectual and cultural tools needed to demand their full rights and privileges as American citizens in the 20th century.

1883: **Vietnam is annexed as a French protectorate and**

and poverty of European coal miners. Soon after finishing the piece, Van Gogh will move to Paris, where, influenced by the Impressionists and Japanese woodblock prints, he will produce the powerfully colored, flattened compositions that will so profoundly influence 20th-century Western artists.

1886: **French post-Impressionist painter Georges Seurat** continues to demonstrate his new techniques with this circus performer and in paintings like "Sunday Afternoon on the Island of La Grande." Taking earlier Impressionist studies of light and color to the next level, Seurat meticulously constructs his paintings as tiny dots of color in a technique later known as pointillism.

1886: **Burma is annexed by the British Empire.** Recognizing that his Chinese overlords cannot help him, the Burmese king, Thibaw, attempts to stave off British domination through alliance with Italy and France. Learning of his efforts, the British government militarily occupies the country and deposes the king's government.

1886: **The first Coca-Cola®** is served when a new syrup for hangovers is accidentally mixed with soda water. The first bot-

Beauty." The great composer of ballets, Tchaikovsky's most famous works also will include "The Nutcracker" and "Swan Lake." At times over emotional, his pieces gain enormous popularity through their highly accessible melodies, preserving the composer's fame throughout the 20th century.

1893: **The first open-heart surgery** procedure is performed by Chicago physician Daniel Williams.

1893: **Whitcomb L. Judson introduces a prototype of the zipper** at the World Exposition in Chicago. Judson's design, in which a series of hooks and eyes are fastened together by a running clasp, is quickly improved upon by others, taking the modern form of interlocking teeth by the early 20th century.

1893: **Women citizens of New Zealand are granted the right to vote.** New Zealand, the first Western nation to include women in its political franchise, is followed by 13 other states in doing so between 1901 and 1920. Female voting privileges are granted in nations with political systems as diverse as the United States, the Soviet Union, Great Britain, Germany, Finland, Ireland, the Netherlands, and Luxembourg.

"Morality is the herd instinct in the individual"

NIETZSCHE

1895: **The rules of bowling are standardized** by the
(58) American Bowling Confederation. Stemming back to ancient
Egypt, bowling was brought to America by the Dutch in the
17th century largely as a gambling sport. In the late 19th century, however, the game begins to take on its modern recreational role in American society.

1895: **American mariner Joshua Slouch sets out on the
first successful solo voyage around the world.** Supporting
himself by lecturing along the way, Slouch completes the trip
on the sloop Spray in 1898. Setting out to repeat the feat in
1909, he vanishes into the ocean and is never heard from
again.

1896: **The discovery of gold on the border of Alaska and
Canada leads to the Klondike Gold Rush.** For three frenzied
years, hopeful miners will explore the upper tributaries of the
Yukon river for gold. By 1899, however, the craze will end and
the town of Dawson, which appeared out of nothing to
accommodate the miners, will fade into obscurity.

1896: **The first modern Olympic Games** are held in Athens,
Greece. In this modern revival of Greek contests not held
since the year 393, the games, and the athletes who partici-
pate in them, will become, somewhat contradictorily, symbols both of nationalistic pride and world unity.

1897: **English physician Ronald Ross links the transmis-
(59) sion of malaria to mosquito bites.** The first man to identify
a non-bacterial agent in the spreading of an infectious disease, Ross will be knighted by Queen Victoria and awarded
the Nobel Prize in 1902.

1898: **The Spanish-American War** establishes the United
States as a great imperial power. Nominally fought over
Spanish repression of Cuban nationalism, the war really is an
excuse for America to demonstrate its military might. Swift
and total victory over the Spanish results in the American
occupation of Cuba, Puerto Rico, Guam, and the Philippines.

1898: **More than 50 different manufacturers produce
(60) early automobiles like this one invented by Charles Brady
King.** Although the earliest steam-powered car can be traced
back to 1769, it is really in late 19th-century America that the
automobile comes into its own. While most of the early models are powered by steam or electric batteries, these methods of propulsion will be replaced with gasoline-burning
engines in the early 20th century.

BIBLIOGRAPHY AND FURTHER READING:

Abrams, M.H., ed. The Norton
Anthology of English Literature, W. W.
Norton & Co., New York, 1975, pp.
1364-1367.

Adams, Laurie Schneider. Art Across
Time: Vol. 2, McGraw-Hill College,
Chicago, 1999, pp. 739-817.

Appleman, Philip, ed. Darwin. 2nd ed.,
W.W. Norton & Co., New York, 1979.

Ian and Betty Ballantine, ed. The
Native Americans, Turner Publishing,
Inc., Atlanta, 1993, pp. 294-295.

Joel Colton and R.R. Palmer. A History
of the Modern World, 5th ed., Alfred
A. Knopf, New York, 1978, pp. 382-653.

Horst de la Croix and Richard Tansey.
Gardener's Art Through the Ages, 8th
ed., Harcourt Brace Jovanovich, New
York, 1986, pp. 802-885.

Goetz, Philip W., ed. The Encyclopedia
Britannica 15th ed., Encyclopedia
Britannica, Inc., Chicago, 1990, vol. 1
pp. 727-728, 824-843, vol. 2 p. 440,
vol. 3, pp. 722, vol. 6 pp. 52-53, 227-
228, vol. 9 p. 306, vol. 12, p. 923, vol.
22 pp. 324-326.

Chandice L.Goucher, Charles A.
LeGuin, and Linda Linda A. Walton. In
the Balance: Themes in Global History,
Vol. 2, McGraw-Hill, Boston, 1998, pp.
693-783.

Grun, Bernard. The Timetables of
History, Simon and Schuster, New
York, 1979, pp. 374-453.

Hanes III, William Travis, editor. World
History: Continuity and Change, Holt,
Rinehart, and Winston, Austin, TX,
1997, pp. 474-476, 497-585.

Hegel, G.W.F. Reason in History, Robert
S. Hartman, trans., Macmillan
Publishing Co., New York, 1953.

Janson, H.W. History of Western Art,
3rd ed., Prentice Hall Abrams,
Englewood Cliffs, NJ, 1986, pp. 618-
665.

Koolhaas, Rem. Delirious New York,
The Monacelli Press, New York, 1994,
pp. 24-27.

Mill, John Stuart. Three Essays, intro.
by Richard Wollheim, Oxford
University Press, New York, 1975.

Riley, Mark T. "Gregor Johann
Mendel," Great Thinkers of the
Western World, HarperCollins
Publishers, New York, 1992, pp. 388-
389.

Roth, John K. "Friedrich Nietzsche,"
Great Thinkers of the Western World,
HarperCollins Publishers, New York,
1992, pp. 408-413.

Tucker, Robert C., ed. The Marx-Engels
Reader, 2nd ed., W. W. Norton & Co.,
New York, 1978.

ON SOCIAL DARWINISM
Appleman, Philip, ed. Darwin, 2nd ed.,
W.W. Norton & Co., New York, 1979.

Dugi, Don Thomas. "Herbert Spencer,"
Great Thinkers of the Western World,
HarperCollins Publishers, New York,
1992, pp. 382-387.

Hollingdale, R.J., trans. and ed. A
Nietzsche Reader, Viking Penguin, Inc.,
New York, 1977.

Roth, John K. "Friedrich Nietzsche,"
Great Thinkers of the Western World,
HarperCollins Publishers, New York,
1992, pp. 408-413.

**ON CHILD LABOR IN INDUSTRIAL
ENGLAND**
Mitchell, Sally. Daily Life in Victorian
England. Greenwood Press, Westport,
1996.

Scott, F. Johnathan, Alexander Baltzly.
Readings in European History Since
1814. F.S. Crofts and Company, New
York, 1930.

Stephens, R. John. "John Birley," The
Ashton Chronicle 19 May 1849.

Simkin, John. "British History 1700-
1950." Spartacus Internet
Encyclopedia.
http://www.spartacus.schoolnet.co.uk

1 Population explosion places stress on the environment; paper diapers, for example, provide convenience with consequences *1900s*

2 The tiger and the monarch butterfly alike lose habitat but inspire conservation efforts *1900s*

3 Molecular science gradually reveals genetic transference *1900s*

4 Oil fields proliferate across the globe *1900s*

5 Skiing becomes a recreational sport *1900s*

6 Eastern religions and medicine thrive and influence the Western World *1900s*

7 The Olympics foster global unity *1900s*

8 Cowboys fade from the American West *1900*

9 Teddy Roosevelt inspires the first teddy bear *1902*

10 The first plane is flown by the Wright Brothers *1903*

11 Susan B. Anthony founds the International Suffrage Alliance *1904*

12 The Smithsonian Institution provides public enrichment *1911*

13 American Jim Thorpe wins the Olympic pentathlon and decathlon *1912*

14 The Titanic sinks *1912*

15 Russian dancers and composers reinvent classical ballet *c. 1913*

16 American "doughboys" enter World War I *1917*

17 Edwin Armstrong revolutionizes radio design *1918*

18 Baseball becomes a national pastime in the U.S. *1918*

19 Woodrow Wilson designs the League of Nations *1919*

20 "Flappers" arrive on America's social scene *1920s*

21 Freud publishes "Beyond the Pleasure Principle" *1920*

22 Einstein proposes the theory of relativity *1920*

23 James Joyce completes "Ulysses" *1922*

24 King Tut's tomb uncovered by Howard Carter *1922*

25 World-famous escape artist Harry Houdini dies *1926*

26 Work on Mount Rushmore begins *1927*

27 G.W. Carver makes paint from soybeans *1927*

28 The Great Depression begins *1929*

29 "The Wizard of Oz" celebrates color movies *1930s*

30 The Chrysler Building is completed *1930*

31 Hitler becomes chancellor of Germany *1933*

32 FDR is sworn in as president of the United States *1933*

33 The Holocaust *1933-1945*

34 The Golden Gate Bridge opens to traffic *1937*

35 Atomic bomb research begins *1942*

36 Eisenhower leads the Normandy invasion *1944*

37 American Marines capture Iwo Jima *1945*

38 Winston Churchill's "Iron Curtain" speech *1946*

39 Gandhi leads peaceful demonstrations in India *1947*

40 Eleanor Roosevelt begins "Declaration of Human Rights" *1947*

41 Americans adore cars and drive-ins *1950s*

42 Marilyn Monroe is Hollywood's new star *1950s*

43 American jukeboxes play rock-and-roll *1950s*

44 Televisions become common in the U.S. *1950s*

45 The first multiple vendor credit card is introduced *1950*

46 Jonas Salk develops the polio vaccine *1955*

47 Transistors usher in the computer age *1956*

48 Russian-built Sputnik I orbits the Earth *1957*

49 American monkeys are launched into space *1959*

50 The Guggenheim Museum is completed *1959*

51 Polystyrene is used to package "fast food" *1960s*

52 Birth control pills increase sexual freedom *1960s*

53 President John F. Kennedy is assassinated *1963*

54 American troops are sent to Vietnam in increasing numbers *1964*

55 Civil rights leader Martin Luther King Jr. is murdered *1968*

56 Gabriel García Márquez writes "One Hundred Years of Solitude" *1968*

57 Neil Armstrong is the first man to walk on the moon *1969*

58 The AIDS virus begins to infect humans *1970s*

59 Ronald Reagan is elected the 40th U.S. president *1980*

60 Sandra Day O'Connor becomes the first female justice of the U.S. Supreme Court *1981*

61 Mikhail Gorbachev implements perestroika *1985*

62 The Pershing II missile is banned *1987*

63 The Berlin Wall falls *1989*

64 Wireless telecommunications and laptop computers facilitate the portable office *1990s*

65 Mapping of the human genome begins *1990s*

66 Bill Clinton becomes the first Democratic U.S. President to win reelection since FDR *1996*

67 Dolly the sheep is cloned in Scotland *1997*

68 Y2K fear haunts the technology industry *1998*

69 The Euro is introduced as standard currency *1999*

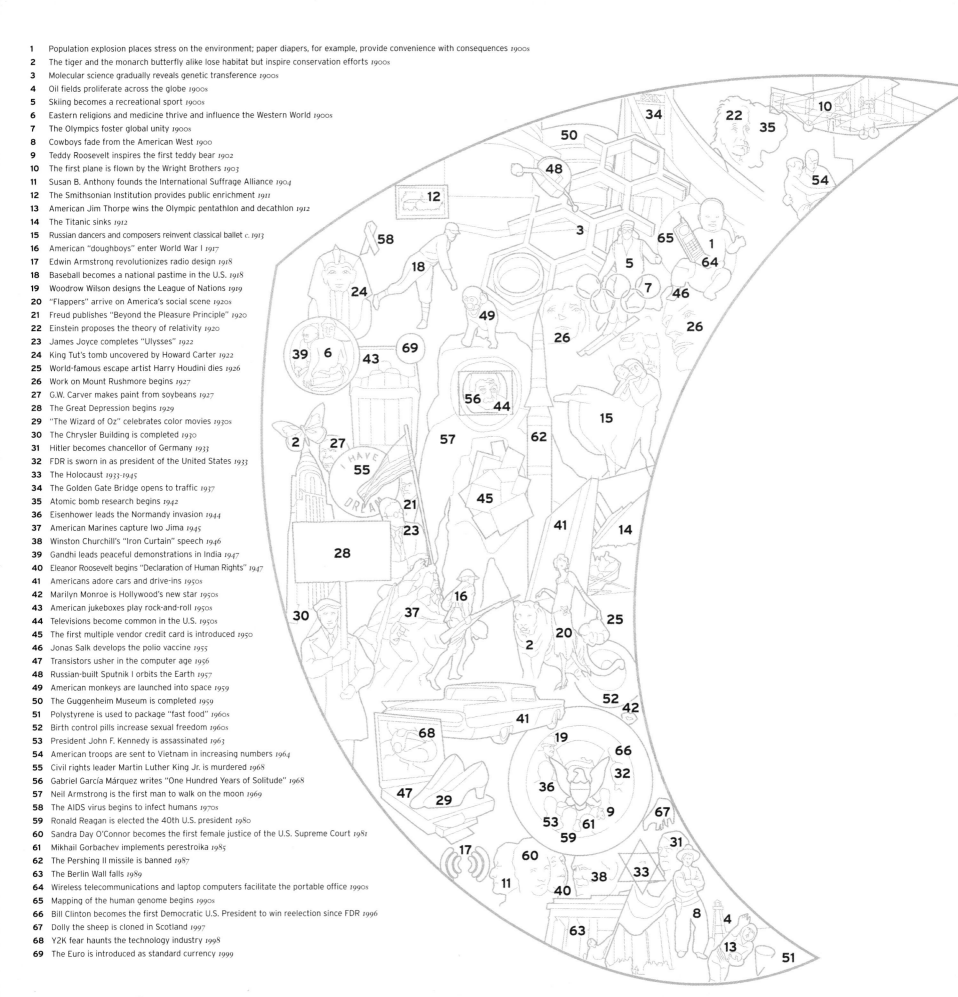

20th Century

WORLD WAR
TO WORLD WIDE WEB

WORLD WAR TO WORLD WIDE WEB

At the end of the 20th century, we see the last 100 years as an epoch that has radically challenged our traditional perceptions of wholeness or totality. Long-distance travel and communication, evolving from 19th-century roots, transformed human understandings of continuous space. In a car or an airplane, one could jump from one locality to another with unprecedented speed. New radios and telephones allowed one's voice to be transmitted instantly hundreds or even thousands of miles away. Movies and TV, the modern computer, and the Internet created temporal-spatial experiences that were independent of physical reality. By century's end, transportation and media technology had completely altered our previous conceptions of time and space.

This sometimes disorienting atmosphere of change was exacerbated by advances in pure science during the early part of the century. The atom, long the indivisible unit of Western science, was split to produce nuclear energy. Universal time, the ultimate expression of 19th-century global continuity, was challenged by Einstein's Theory of Relativity. Through the famous physicist's work, time came to be understood as a subjective, variable experience. Throughout the century, Western art attempted to express the perceived collapse of wholeness and objectivity that these scientific and technological advances suggested. Cubist painters challenged viewing conventions, producing works that showed subjects from multiple perspectives at once. On the canvases of painters like Picasso and Braque, pictorial space and time were bent, fractured, and assembled into a pluralistic collage. In painting, sculpture, architecture, and photography, the holistic, timeless object was supplanted by the fragment and the fleeting moment.

These cultural developments had contemporaneous political parallels. Many of the trans-cultural European empires of the 19th century—Russia, Great Britain, and Austria-Hungary—broke into smaller, ethnically homogenous states. The 19th-century world of large, composite states vanished, replaced by a mosaic of tiny diversities arranged into a global montage.

Even as older bonds of continuity broke down, however, other systems rose to define a new order. If improved communication and transportation dazzled our perceptions of time and space, they also facilitated the development of a highly integrated global economy and culture. In some ways, the world became a smaller, more intimate place, where many cultural and social fragments were reassembled into a highly diverse, but nonetheless closely interconnected global village.

1900S: (1) **Improved medical care and techniques reduce child mortality and increase life expectancy,** resulting in an enormous explosion of human population. While the rate of growth will taper off in heavily industrialized nations as the century progresses, the overall human population still will hover at six billion by century's end. Producing heat, wastes, carbon dioxide, and industrial pollutants on an unprecedented scale, humanity will begin to put overwhelming stress on the global environment. Damage to the atmosphere will increase exposure to solar radiation and increase global temperatures, threatening to redraw coastlines as melting polar icecaps raise the water level of the planet's oceans.

1900S: (2) **The natural rate of animal and plant extinction accelerates** by several orders of magnitude. As expanding human populations transform more and more of the landscape to their needs, natural habitats are destroyed. Species such as tigers, elephants, whales, and seals are reduced to the brink of extinction by human hunters seeking fur, ivory, or adventure.

1900S: (3) **Serious advances in biology greatly enhance the human understanding of life.** Over the course of the cen-

equipment manufacturing, is a typical example of the new, consumption-based economies that are developing in the Western world.

1900S: (6) **Against a background of growing technology and secularism,** ancient religions, ethics, and medicinal practices continue to influence the spiritual life of the world's inhabitants. Despite the growing presence throughout the world of a Western rationalism that opposes them, Eastern religions like Buddhism and Shinto continue to thrive. As European technology infiltrates the Pacific world, Asian religion and medicine (acupuncture, herb remedies, etc.) filter back into the West. These less "rational" or linear systems of practice and thought provide much of the world's population with a spiritual counterbalance to the tactical intellectualism of European science.

1900S: **Ethnic and political conflict continue to devastate the Balkans throughout the century.** Longstanding struggles and feuds among Greeks, Turks, Croats, Serbs, Magyars, and a host of other national and ethnic groups will shock the world with their violence and intensity. In 1914, Serbian nationalism will result in the assassination of Austrian

heroes and events whose significance transcends national boundaries.

1900S: **Nations throughout Africa and Asia throw off the mantle of European colonial control** and revert to self-government. Colonial governments in India, Cambodia, Vietnam, and most of Africa are replaced with indigenous rulers by the 1960s. While most Africans and Asians are united in their happiness to see the Europeans go, they often divide on how their newly freed nations should be governed. Violent civil conflict will kill millions in Cambodia, Vietnam, India, Pakistan, Bangladesh, and African countries such as Rwanda as various factions struggle for control of their own countries.

1900: **The Empress Dowager of China comes out in open support of the Boxer Rebellion.** A violent anti-foreign group founded in 1896, the Boxers are committed to restoring traditional Han culture and recovering Chinese soil controlled by Western governments. In 1901, the uprising is crushed by European troops, shattering the Empress Dowager's already damaged prestige. While anti-Qing sentiments swell domestically, control of China is divided among the various

> " … the true republic: men, their rights and nothing more;
> women, their rights and nothing less"
>
> S U S A N   B .   A N T H O N Y

tury, studies of molecular science will reveal the patterned structures of deoxyribonucleic acids as the primary means of genetic transference. Further investigations will identify genes—nodes on chromosomes—as being responsible for specific inherited traits. Late in the century, combating genetic diseases or engineering certain traits in future offspring will become a very real possibility.

1900S: (4) **As mechanical transportation proliferates** in the form of cars, trains, ships, and airplanes, the production of oil becomes an increasingly important and lucrative world industry. From the coast of Texas to the North Atlantic to the Middle East, oil wells and refineries will spring up across the globe as the demand for power to run the world's engines increases.

1900S: (5) **With increasing wealth and more free time** available to many, recreational sports like skiing gain popularity in industrial nations. Skiing, an entertainment activity that supports an entire industry of vacation/recreation sites and

Archduke Ferdinand, triggering World War I and the collapse of the Austro-Hungarian Empire. During Nazi occupation of the region in the 1940s, Croats and Albanians allied with the Germans will use the opportunity to murder thousands of their traditional enemies. At the end of World War II, the international community will be horrified by the brutality of civil conflict in Greece. While the strength of Yugoslavian leader Tito will bring some stability to the region in the second half of the century, his death and the gradually ensuing collapse of Yugoslavia will throw the region back into chaos at the century's end. In the 1990s, no longer able to tolerate the instability, both the United Nations and NATO will send troops to occupy large sections of the region and isolate the fighting factions from one another.

1900S: (7) **Against a backdrop of continuing violence** and national aggression, the Olympic Games serve as a symbol of global unity throughout the century. Occasionally marred by political conflict, the Olympics still will manage to produce

European powers and Japan, leaving it a sovereign state on paper alone.

1900: (8) **As cowboys begin to vanish from the American West,** their way of life begins to evolve into one of the great myths of American culture. Throughout the course of the century, the cowboy will emerge as the archetypal American hero in countless plays, movies, books, and songs. In part through the myth of the cowboy, the American dream will be transformed from a Puritan vision of religious community to one of rugged individualism and personal freedom.

1901: **Italian inventor Guglielmo Marconi transmits the first transatlantic radio signals.** Marconi's equipment is too large for many applications, but improvements in his designs eventually will make powerful radios small enough to fit on ships. With the new technology, vessels at sea will be able to report their position to others, get weather forecasts, and call for help in times of distress.

Flapper

1902: (9) **A horrified American President Theodore Roosevelt refuses to shoot a trapped bear on a hunting trip.** Famous for his aggressive character and heroic exploits during the Spanish-American War, Roosevelt surprises his fellow hunters with his sudden compassion. When cartoonist Clifford Berryman of "The Washington Post" draws a sketch of the anecdote in the newspaper, it captures the imagination of Brooklyn toy merchant Morris Michtom, who sets about creating the famous stuffed "teddy" bear.

1903: (10) **Americans Orville and Wilbur Wright become the first men to fly a heavier-than-air vehicle successfully.** Although their plane is destroyed in a crash landing after several short flights, the Wrights' design paves the way for future aircraft development. Rapidly developed as a military

non-European art. During the late 19th and early 20th centuries, traditional African and Asian art exert enormous influence on Western artists trying to express growing changes in perception and experience.

1909: **The Robie House, designed by American architect Frank Lloyd Wright,** is built on the outskirts of Chicago. The highpoint of Wright's early career, the house will have an enormous impact on European architecture in the first half of the 20th century. The strong horizontal lines of the design, emphasized by the wide overhangs of the roof, combine with a bold, interlocking geometry to make the house a canonical example of Wright's famous "Prairie Style." After early success, Wright largely is forgotten in his own country until 1936, when his former European stu-

"I am become Death, shatterer of worlds"

J. ROBERT OPPENHEIMER

technology during World War I, motor-driven aircraft will become one of the most pervasive and important modes of global transportation as the 20th century progresses.

1903: **International opera star Enrico Caruso gives his first performance** at the New York Metropolitan Opera. Best known for his performances of Puccini and Verdi, the tenor will become one of the most famous singers in the world during his 18 seasons with the New York company.

1903: **English literary critic George Bernard Shaw** begins to garner notice as a playwright. Shaw's explorations of intellectual elitism, social inequality, and morality in plays like "Pygmalion" will earn him international literary and popular acclaim.

1904: **Convincing land and sea victories during the Russo-Japanese War establish Japan** as an emerging world power. Having successfully adopted European military strategy and technology, the Japanese easily defeat Russian forces to gain control of Manchuria. The first major war fought for the right to exploit a prostrate China, the brief conflict blocks Russian influence in the Far East for 50 years and destabilizes the czarist government, laying some of the foundations for the 1917 Russian Revolution.

1904: (11) **Susan B. Anthony establishes the International Suffrage Alliance.** Since claiming that women are entitled to the same rights offered black males by the 14th and 15th Amendments in 1872, Anthony has been the driving force behind the women's suffrage movement in the United States. Although she will not live to see the vote extended to American women, she will be seen by many as the pivotal figure in the ultimate securing of that right and privilege.

1905: **Pablo Picasso paints "Les Desmoiselles d'Avignon."** Broken into angular, faceted wedges, the painting exhibits both a dynamic composition and depiction of subject matter that make it a critical step in the evolution of Cubist art. The bold forms and colors, combined with obvious references to African masks, also demonstrate an interest in "primitive,"

dents will greatly influence his design for a weekend residence called Fallingwater.

1910: **Ernest Thompson Seton organizes the Boy Scouts of America** on principles established by British scouting founder Lord Baden-Powell. Promoting leadership, self-sufficiency, outdoor skills, and conservative moral values, the Boy Scout organization will influence the development of millions of young Americans throughout the century.

1910: **Spanish architect Antonio Gaudi y Cornet completes his design for Casa Mila,** an apartment block in Barcelona. The most famous of the Art Nouveau architects, Gaudi takes a slightly different stance in his explorations than do his highly individualistic European contemporaries. Rejecting ideal Platonic shapes as unnatural, Gaudi composes his designs in "irrational" parabolic forms that he feels better express the true character and structure of nature. While other Art Nouveau designers seek to express their individuality, Gaudi attempts to bring new formal expression to the idea of universal principle.

1911: (12) **The Smithsonian Institution completes its third building, the National Museum of Natural History,** in Washington, D.C. The necessity of a third building to house the institution's ever increasing collection demonstrates the growing importance and prestige of the educational organization. By the end of the century, the Smithsonian will either directly operate or help fund and direct a host of museums, research facilities, and scientific institutions across the country, promoting both scholarly investigation and general public enrichment and education.

1912: **The Qing dynasty is overthrown by a popular republican uprising.** The emperor is forced to abdicate, and a national parliament is established. For the next 15 years, China will be plagued with domestic chaos as various regional and national strongmen will struggle to rule the country without regard for the new constitution. Until Chiang Kai-shek emerges as a dominant leader in the mid-1920s, political stability will elude the Chinese nation.

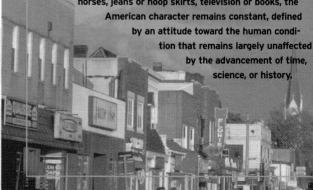

1912: (13) **Jim Thorpe**, one of the greatest American athletes of all time, wins the Olympic pentathlon and decathlon. A professional football player later in life, Thorpe also dabbled in semiprofessional baseball. When it is discovered that he was a paid ballplayer for one summer before the all-amateur Olympics, his gold medals are rescinded and not restored until 1982, 29 years after his death.

1912: (14) **The English luxury-liner Titanic brushes an iceberg** and sinks off the Nova Scotia coast. The largest ship ever put to sea, proclaimed by its owners to be unsinkable, the Titanic is equipped with an insufficient number of lifeboats when it fails to complete its maiden voyage. More than 1,000 people drown or die of hypothermia as Europe is forced to reconsider its unquestioning faith in modern technology.

1912: **Norwegian explorer Roald Amundsen leads the first successful expedition to the South Pole.** Using sled dogs, Amundsen beats by less than a month a rival British team, whose Siberian ponies die along the way. Disheartened to find they have been beaten, the British, under Captain Robert Scott, turn back on foot, but never make it home, dying in their sleep during an extended blizzard.

1913: (15) **Sergei Diaghilev's Ballets Russes premieres Igor Stravinsky's "Rite of Spring" in Paris.** Outraged by the unconventional music, the audience riots after the performance. Touring throughout the West, Diaghilev's company will revitalize the stale art of ballet by combining precise classical technique with bold new music. Stravinsky, in time one of the century's most influential composers, will redirect Western music through his aggressive use of contrast and unusual voicings.

1914: **The assassination of Austrian Archduke Ferdinand triggers World War I.** Europe, continuing to observe balance

1914: **The silent film "Tillie's Punctured Romance" introduces English actor Charlie Chaplin** to American movie audiences. Chaplin's expressive face, comedic timing, and refined body language make him the ideal star for silent cinema. His famous portrayal of the "Little Tramp" will become one of the archetypal characters of Western film.

1917: **Economic strain and continuing military reversals drive Russia to revolution** during World War I. Marxist and communist exile Vladimir Lenin, smuggled back into Russia by the Germans, leads a radical minority in taking control of the country. Under his leadership, Russia immediately withdraws from World War I, signing a peace treaty with Germany and Austria-Hungary. After several years of violent civil war, during which the former czar and his family are executed, the communists will solidify their control and establish the Soviet Union.

1917: (16) **As the United States enters World War I,** with American "doughboys" heading overseas, American propagandist James Montgomery Flagg develops the modern image of Uncle Sam. The original, clown-like depiction stems from the War of 1812, but the new portrait of Uncle Sam, greatly modified to fit Flagg's new recruitment posters, portrays an older, more intense man.

1918: (17) **American inventor and academic Edwin Armstrong** develops the superheterodyne circuit, an essential step forward in developing radio technology. Also responsible for the future development of frequency modulation ("FM") systems, Armstrong, more than any other single individual, deserves much of the credit for the evolution of radio and radio culture in the Western world.

1918: (18) **Baseball legend Babe Ruth is traded** to the New York Yankees by the owner of the Boston Red Sox. While Ruth will

burdened by global economic depression in the late 1920s and early 1930s, the new Wiemar government lacks both vitality and domestic prestige. In 1933, it will become an easy victim for the extremist National Socialist Party that feeds on the desperation of Germany's downtrodden populace.

1919: (19) **The League of Nations, provided for by the Treaty of Versailles, is established in Geneva, Switzerland.** Designed by American President Woodrow Wilson, the new international organization is intended to arrange the peaceful resolution of diplomatic conflict throughout the world. But a general unwillingness on the part of member nations to use military force, a fact exposed by hostile foreign invasions of China and Ethiopia in the following decades, renders the body largely ineffective. Lessons learned from the League's failures and successes, however, will provide a useful blueprint for the later creation of the United Nations.

1919: **The Comintern is established in the Soviet Union.** Dedicated to the support of international communist movements, the Comintern expresses the Soviet ambition to spread Marxist revolution across the globe. The organization will play a vital role in organizing the new Chinese Communist Party, which will hold its first national congress in 1921.

1919: **American rocket science pioneer Robert Goddard publishes "A Method of Reaching Extreme Altitudes."** Through this canonical text, Goddard's development of liquid fuel and engine cooling systems will revolutionize the study of rocket propulsion and flight. A heavy influence on the development of the German V-1 and V-2 rockets during World War II, Goddard's work will serve as an essential precursor both to the ballistic missile and 20th-century space travel.

"Put your hand on a stove for a minute, and it feels like an hour.
Sit with a pretty girl for an hour, and it seems like a minute.
That's relativity."

ALBERT EINSTEIN

---

of power strategies in foreign policy, has divided itself into two large mutual defense alliances. When the assassination results in war between Austria-Hungary and Russia, the French, British, Italian, German, and Ottoman nations all are dragged into the conflict through the treaties they have made. Much like the American Civil War, the conflict will combine highly advanced weapons with outmoded tactics, resulting in the senseless deaths of millions.

1914: **Declaring itself the ally of France and England, Japan occupies all German-controlled regions in China.** Taking advantage of Europe's distraction with the war, Japan opportunistically seizes German holdings and extorts various trade concessions from China's weak government.

go on to become baseball's first superstar, leading the Yankees to a string of World Series victories, the Red Sox will fail to match the success of its division rivals for the rest of the century. Largely popularized by General Abner Doubleday during the American Civil War, baseball will become a true national pastime and passion in great part through Ruth's athletic accomplishments.

1919: **Total German defeat in World War I is reflected by the terms of the Treaty of Versailles.** Forbidden to maintain a respectable army, forced to pay gigantic war indemnities, and subjected to blockade by British ships for months after the war has ended, Germany is left weak, humiliated, and economically impoverished by the harsh peace terms. Further

1920s: (20) **Iconoclastic women's fashions of the decade** reflect a rejection of traditional values in the aftermath of World War I. The shock of the war, and the larger loss of faith in 19th-century values that accompanied it, lead many young women to abandon expected feminine appearances and roles. Cutting their hair short, dressing in men's clothing or short skirts, the "flappers" leave behind old images of femininity that they feel they have outgrown.

1920: (21) **Sigmund Freud publishes "Beyond the Pleasure Principle."** Through work extending back to the 1890s, Freud has become the leading figure of psychoanalysis, a term he coined in 1896. His concepts of ego, id, and superego, combined with his speculations on the powerful subconscious impact of early childhood on adult conduct, will revolutionize study in the behavioral sciences.

1920: **Albert Einstein publishes a paper entitled "Relativity: The Special and General Theory."** An assemblage of groundbreaking observations and conclusions stemming back to 1905, Einstein's scientific paper throws Newtonian physics on its ear. In his essay, the German physicist convincingly demonstrates that time and space, long thought to be both invariable and universal, actually are neither. With conclusions supported by careful observations of the planet Mercury, Einstein contends that space can be deformed by gravitational fields. A further conjecture, proved later in the century by experiments involving high-speed spacecraft, argues that time passes at different rates for different subjects, varying according to their relative velocities to one and another.

1922: **James Joyce completes "Ulysses,"** which is banned and smuggled through international customs to an eagerly

and sense of showmanship will greatly expand jazz's audience while contributing to the evolution of swing from older Dixieland forms.

1926: **Hungarian-born American escape artist Harry Houdini dies.** A master showman, Houdini had thrilled audiences throughout the world with his escapes from seemingly impossible situations. Performing his stunts through a rich blending of skill, extraordinary flexibility, and sleight of hand, the American was one of the great entertainers of the early 20th century. Killed by a punch to the abdomen, his death appears bizarre in the context of his remarkably dangerous stunts.

1927: **Joseph Stalin gains control of the Soviet Union.** Successfully outmaneuvering rival Leon Trotsky after Lenin's death in 1924, Stalin has complete control of the communist government within three years. Prone to paranoia, Stalin will kill or imprison uncounted millions of Russians suspected of not supporting him during the 1930s. While in power, Stalin

peanuts. Through his work, new markets and uses will be developed for economically depressed agrarian communities across the United States.

1928: **American author Eugene O'Neill** produces his first play, "Strange Interlude." As the future writer of "Long Day's Journey Into Night" and "The Iceman Cometh," O'Neill will emerge as one of the great literary explorers of the modern psychological experience.

1928: **British medical researcher Alexander Fleming discovers penicillin.** Fleming will be knighted for his discovery, which will open the door for the development of powerful antibiotics in the 1940s.

1928: **Chinese nationalist leader Chiang Kai-shek declares the Republic of China.** Uniting most of the south and the east of China under his leadership, Chiang Kai-shek announces a new national government from Beijing. Over the next 10 years, the nationalists will extend their control to

"Success is the sole earthly judge of right and wrong"

ADOLF HITLER

anticipating readership. One of the most impressive literary accomplishments of the English language, Joyce's epic is an incredibly dense concentration of symbolic reference and structure. Almost every word is chosen with extreme care to resonate at several levels of meaning. Obscure and opaque to many readers, "Ulysses" is incredibly rewarding and even humorously joyful to those with the time, patience, and educational background to decipher it.

1922: **British archaeologist Howard Carter discovers the tomb of the Egyptian pharaoh Tutankhamen.** Insignificant as a monarch, Tutankhamen is invaluable as an archaeological resource because his tomb had not been discovered and looted by ancient thieves. Giving modern scientists their first experience with the untouched mummy of a pharaoh, the unearthing of the tomb is a major moment for Egyptology.

1925: **In Chicago, American criminal Al Capone** inherits the vast prostitution, bootlegging, gambling, and racketeering empire of Johnny Torrio. One of the pioneers of modern organized crime in the United States, Torrio always managed to keep a quiet, respectable public image. Capone, ultimately incapable of such discretion, will become a central figure of American pop culture through his prominent role in Chicago's gangland violence throughout the 1920s. In 1929, outraged by notorious acts like the St. Valentine's Day Massacre, President Hoover will turn the attention of both the FBI and the IRS to imprisoning Capone. By 1932, the gangster will be in a federal penitentiary and his criminal career effectively at an end.

1926: **Jazz trumpeter Louis Armstrong** and his new band "The Hot Five" record "Heebie Jeebies." Having already played as a sideman with King Oliver, Fletcher Henderson, and Sidney Bechet, Armstrong sets out as a bandleader with "The Hot Five." His technical proficiency, emotive phrasing,

will oversee the establishment of Soviet Russia's complex government-controlled economy and guide his country through World War II. Until his death in 1953, his unpredictable character will contribute to the tense nature of post-world war global politics.

1927: **German philosopher Martin Heidegger** publishes his incomplete study, "Being and Time." A thinker of unusual originality, Heidegger rejects the entire Western philosophical tradition from Plato to Nietzsche. Leaving behind traditional concerns with first causes of the universe and the nature of man, Heidegger explores the nature of being as a universal concept. Although he will have marked influence on various other philosophical movements, including phenomenology and existentialism, Heidegger's chief importance is his position as the first serious ontologist since the pre-Socratic Greeks.

1927: **American pilot Charles Lindbergh becomes the first man to fly solo across the Atlantic Ocean.** In their 33-hour trip from Long Island, NY, to Paris, Lindbergh and his plane, The Spirit of St. Louis, briefly capture the enthusiasm and imagination of the world.

1927: **American sculptor Gutzon Borglum begins work on four presidential portraits,** carving them into the face of Mt. Rushmore. Located in the Black Hills of South Dakota, the 60-foot-tall relief images of George Washington, Thomas Jefferson, Abraham Lincoln, and Theodore Roosevelt will take 14 years and more than $1 million to complete.

1927: **Chemurgist George Washington Carver** develops a process for making paint and stains from soybeans. As a professor and researcher at the Tuskegee Institute of Technology, Carver will come up with hundreds of industrial uses for ordinary agricultural products like soybeans and

the west, expand industry and infrastructure, and stabilize the country's banking system. Largely urban in focus, however, Chiang Kai-shek's policies will allow rival communist power bases to develop gradually in China's rural regions.

1929: **The sudden and dramatic devaluation of American stocks heralds the arrival of the Great Depression.** Unbridled economic growth during the 1920s has encouraged risky investments and dangerous banking policies that all come to a disastrous head in 1929. Affecting markets and economies throughout the world, the ensuing financial collapse leads much of the world into a decade of enormous fiscal recession and poverty.

1929: **American writer William Faulkner** completes his first major novel, "The Sound and the Fury." Heavily influenced by Freud, Darwin, and Einstein, Faulkner gives literary expression to new scientific beliefs and theories. Writing from within the minds of his characters, Faulkner blends experiences of the present, memories of the past, and daydreams or fantasies into a single, flowing stream-of-consciousness narrative. Along with James Joyce, Faulkner is one of the most original and influential Western writers of the 20th century.

1930s: **Color,** celebrated by Dorothy's red slippers in "The Wizard of Oz," appears in movies for the first time. By the late 1950s, color film will begin to replace black-and-white formats as the standard in American film production.

1930: **American inventor Clarence Birdseye** develops a process for packing food in cardboard containers and flash-freezing it under high pressure. Shipped to grocery stores in refrigerated trucks and stored in on-site coolers, the ubiquitous American staple of frozen food is born.

1930: **The Chrysler Building is completed in New York City.**

(30) Designed by the American architect William van Alen, the new office tower is like many skyscrapers in the city: an undifferentiated stack of generic office floors with an ornamental hood stuck on top. The sunburst motif that caps the building, however, finished in stainless steel, glimmers in the sunlight, lending the building some visual distinctiveness. A reference to the metal cars that Chrysler makes, the crown of the tower will become one of the most recognizable corporate icons of the 20th century.

1931: **Japan annexes Manchuria.** Seeking to establish itself as the principal Eastern power, the military government of Japan seizes the territory from a Chinese state too internally weak to resist. An expression of international strength, the occupation of the region also provides a convenient distraction from Japanese domestic woes brought on by the Great Depression.

1931: **American painter Georgia O'Keefe** finishes her work "Cow Skull." O'Keefe's paintings of the American Southwest, with their strong colors, abstracted forms, and powerful symbolic imagery, establish her as the preeminent female American artist of the 20th century.

1933: **Charles B. Darrow invents the game Monopoly.®** In an

World War II, strategically positioning the country to enter the global conflict by the end of 1941.

1933: **Bavarian Bertolt Brecht,** a political exile from Nazi Germany, begins his investigations in experimental theatre. As the author of "Threepenny Opera" and "Galileo," Brecht will earn a reputation as a serious playwright. His unconventional productions, however, characterized by unusual staging, properties, and dramatic presentation, will have an even more significant influence on 20th-century theatrical form.

1933-1945: **Six million Jews living in Nazi-con-**
(33) **trolled territory** are murdered during the Holocaust. Segregated from the main population, first in ghettos and then in concentration camps, the victims are either worked to death, slowly killed by starvation or exposure, or murdered en masse with machine guns and poison gas. The suffering of the Jews, inflicted by the Nazis in an effort to "purify" and "improve" the world's genetic composition, is so horrific that it actually causes many to overlook the millions of political, ideological and religious opponents, Slavs, gypsies, homosexuals, and physically or mentally handicapped also murdered by the Nazi death machine.

and impressive in the world. In time, it will become the visual icon of the city it serves.

1937: **Open warfare between China and Japan** commences with skirmishing outside Beijing. Despite Soviet aid and material, the Chinese slowly are driven back by the superior air power of invading Japanese armies. By 1939, a relative stalemate is achieved, but the eastern half of China, including all of its major industry and ports, remains under Japanese control.

1937: **Theodore Seuss Geisel** begins his career as an author and illustrator of children's books under the penname Dr. Seuss. Geisel's 44 works, including "The Cat in the Hat," "The Grinch Who Stole Christmas," and "Horton, the Elephant Who Hatched an Egg," will set new standards in children's literature and pedagogy with their creative style and content.

1938: **British sculptor Henry Moore completes "Recumbent Figure."** A logical progression from the interest in abstract form and negative space typified by 19th-century sculptors like Rodin, Moore's eroded shapes also capture the sense of "primitivism" still prevalent in Western painting and sculpture. Working in modern materials like concrete, Moore explores how new materials and

> "[The writer must leave] no room in his workshop for anything but the old verities and truths of the heart, the old universal truths lacking which any story is ephemeral and doomed—love and honor and pity and pride and compassion and sacrifice"
>
> WILLIAM FAULKNER

era marked by extreme economic depression, a game involving getting rich and owning property has great appeal to many Americans. In time, the game will grow to be one of the most popular and well-known board games in the world.

1933: **National Socialist Party leader Adolf Hitler becomes**
(31) **chancellor of Germany.** Crippled by global economic depression and vindictive war indemnities imposed at the end of World War I, Germany is left vulnerable to the extremism that Hitler represents. His administration quickly revitalizes the economy, rebuilds the military, and restores national pride and confidence. Given these improvements over previously desperate times, most Germans prove more than willing to embrace the international aggression and minority persecution the new Nazi government also represents.

1933: **Franklin Delano Roosevelt is sworn in as President of**
(32) **the United States.** His famous domestic stimulus policies, known as the "New Deal," will help restore American economic confidence and pull the nation out of the Great Depression. The only American elected president four times, Roosevelt also will guide the United States through most of

1934: **Communist armies are driven across China by Nationalist forces** in what is later known as the Long March. Pushed to the western frontiers of the country, the communist forces are almost destroyed. At the critical moment, however, nationalist leader Chiang Kai-shek is forcibly compelled by his own lieutenants to accept a united front with the communists against growing Japanese aggression.

1935: **Mao Tse-tung becomes chairman of the Chinese Communist Party.** Having vanquished his many rivals for leadership of the party, Mao will remain the dominant figure in Chinese communism for the next 40 years.

1936: **American track and field athlete Jesse Owens** wins four gold medals at the Berlin Olympic Games, with Hitler in the stands. Owens' accomplishment as an African-American refutes many of the racial prejudices prevalent in Nazi Germany and the United States.

1937: **The Golden Gate Bridge is opened in San Francisco.**
(34) Designed by Joseph Baermann Strauss, the 4,200-foot main span of the new suspension bridge is one of the most elegant

techniques transform the art and form of sculpting.

1939: **The Russo-German invasion of Poland commences the European phase of World War II.** Shocked by the attack, France and England declare war on Germany. But France is conquered swiftly by the Germans in 1940, and Britain is subjected to intense Nazi bombing for much of that year. Until the winter of 1941, when Germany's Japanese allies bring the United States into the war and the Nazis' own imprudent invasion of Russia stalls in bad weather, the Central European power will enjoy almost completely unchecked success. By the time German troops cross the Russian border in June 1941, Poland, France, the Balkans, Norway, Denmark, and much of North Africa will be under the control of Germany and its Italian allies.

1939: **Japan attempts to subdue Free China** through intense bombing campaigns. Unable to push Chinese forces any further west on the ground, Japan resorts to an aerial bombardment that will continue for the next four years. During this period of extended hardship, Chinese Nationalist political strength will dwindle as debt and internal corruption increase.

Less susceptible to economic damages, the Chinese Communist Party will grow in power during the same period.

1940s: Women become an integral part of the domestic work force as American men go off to fight in World War II. The impact on American social values and structures will be immense. Encouraged to leave the house and work for the first time, women will develop both a self-confidence and a genuine pleasure in working that they will not want to relinquish when the fighting ends in 1945. Although the labor force initially will return to its largely male composi-

36 Eisenhower invade Nazi-controlled France in a massive amphibious assault. By year's end, the British and American armies will drive the Germans back to their own border. An administrative and political soldier, Eisenhower manages to keep his collection of prima donna generals from bickering as the weight of their forces push the Germans back. In 1952, the general will leave the military and become a two-term president of the United States.

1945: American Marines raise their flag over the island of
37 Iwo Jima. With the American capture of Iwo Jima, the vast

simple blues arrangements like "Billie's Bounce" become dense and sophisticated explorations of musical form.

1946: British Prime Minister Winston Churchill gives his
38 "Iron Curtain" speech, acknowledging the collapse of the Anglo-American alliance with the Soviet Union. By 1955, with the permanent division of Germany, Europe will be divided into two hostile camps—the U.S.-backed NATO and the Soviet-dominated Warsaw Pact. While direct fighting is avoided out of the fear that a large-scale war would destroy all life on the planet, during the next 40 years

"An iron curtain has descended across the continent"

W I N S T O N   C H U R C H I L L

tion in the late 1940s and 1950s, the stage will be set for women to begin demanding equal footing in employment and education during the 1960s and 1970s.

1941: Axis forces attack the United States and the Soviet Union, bringing them into World War II as the allies of Great Britain. Japan's air attack on Pearl Harbor and the German invasion of Russia, while initially successful, will prove to be the undermining of the two attackers. Over the next few years, the apparently endless resources of American industry and Soviet manpower slowly will overwhelm the German and Japanese war efforts, gradually turning the tide of battle against them.

1942: Development of the atomic bomb, led by American
35 scientist J. Robert Oppenheimer, begins n Los Alamos, New Mexico. In less than three years, his research group will produce the most destructive weapon ever created by man. In the summer of 1945, two of the think tank's devices will kill more than 150,000 Japanese, completely destroying the cities of Hiroshima and Nagasaki.

1943: French thinker Jean-Paul Sartre, principal philosopher of modern existentialism, publishes his seminal work, "Being and Nothingness." Building from Kierkegaard, Nietzsche, and his misinterpretations of Heidegger, Sartre brings a philosophical voice to a Western culture that has lost faith in any kind of overarching cause or reason for existence. In a cosmos without objective guiding principles, the French philosopher argues that the only possible meanings are those that we subjectively construct for ourselves.

1944: Swiss psychoanalyst Carl Gustav Jung finishes a new book entitled "Psychology and Alchemy." The greatest of the second-generation psychoanalysts who follow Freud and Adler, Jung adds significant richness and complexity to the rather reductive theories of his predecessors. Expanding beyond the narrow focus and methods of Freud's dream analysis, Jung contends that the subconscious mind, which has certain basic components common to all humans, can be better understood through the careful study of folktale, myth, and legend. His investigations add terms like "archetype," "anima/animus," and "extrovert/introvert" to the common parlance of psychoanalysis.

1944: Allied forces under American General Dwight

Pacific empire that Japan had forged in 1941 and 1942 is completely erased. Totally overmatched by the enormous economic resources and manpower of the United States, Japan has fought tenaciously to hold on to its possessions, surrendering each island only after an enormous loss of life on both sides. By the time Iwo Jima is captured, however, it has become clear that American victory is inevitable.

1945: The detonation of atomic bombs over Hiroshima and Nagasaki convinces Japan to surrender to the Allies, ending World War II. Overrun by Russian, American, and British troops, Nazi Germany had capitulated with the suicide of Hitler several months earlier. The 150,000 deaths inflicted by the two detonations are little more than a coda to a war that has killed nearly 16 million military personnel and uncounted numbers of civilians. The two blasts end a war of brutality and usher in an age of terror in which the possibility of global annihilation is always present.

1945: The United Nations is formally created. Fifty-one sovereign states agree to join the new organization, which replaces the ineffective League of Nations. Evolving from a prototypical structure created in 1942, the United Nations is dedicated to the establishment of international peace, law, and prosperity. In one of its first acts, the U.N. helps establish a war crimes tribunal to investigate Nazi activities during World War II. Of 22 former German leaders tried at the 1946 Nuremberg trials, 12 are sentenced to death. In similar proceedings, seven Japanese leaders also are convicted and executed. No investigation is made into the fate of Germans and Italians who disappeared in Russian prisoner camps, nor is any inquiry conducted into the internment of Japanese-Americans into United States concentration camps between 1942 and 1945.

1945: Civil warfare between Nationalist and Communist forces reemerges in China after Japan's defeat. Underequipped and outnumbered, Communist forces still gain the upper hand. By 1949, Nationalist leader Chiang Kai-shek is exiled to Taiwan, and the Communist victory is complete.

1945: American musicians Charlie Parker and Dizzy Gillespie collaborate for the first time on a series of new recordings. Their quintet, which includes a young trumpeter named Miles Davis, will revolutionize post-war jazz by helping to forge the new be-bop style. In Parker's compositional hands,

smaller wars in Korea, Vietnam, Cambodia, Grenada, Central America, Angola, Afghanistan, and East Africa will be either caused or influenced by strategic jockeying between the two alliances.

1946: The Catholic nun later known as Mother Theresa, believing she has been called to do so by God, leaves her comfortable convent in India to live among the poor. Supported by the Catholic church, her Missions of Charity will be established throughout the world. Dedicated to the extremely poor and the chronically diseased, the missions' work will be significant enough to earn Mother Theresa the Nobel Peace Prize in 1979.

1946: Pediatric specialist Dr. Benjamin Spock releases his book "Baby and Child Care." Fifty million copies of the book are sold in 40 languages, making the new resource second only to the Bible in popularity. Spock's program, emphasizing trust in parents' inner judgment and open affection toward children, will dominate theories of child care in many regions for decades after the book's release.

1946: American scientist Percy Spenser discovers the cooking potential of microwaves. Finding that a chocolate bar in his pocket has melted while working with microwaves, Spenser comprehends the potential applications of the new technology. By the 1980s, microwave ovens will be widely used, cooking a variety of foods in minutes or even seconds.

1947: Ever larger and more frequent peaceful demon-
39 strations in India, led by Mohandas Gandhi, finally result in political independence from Great Britain. With the British gone, Gandhi moves to heal divisions between Muslims and Hindus, but his efforts are cut short when a radical Hindu assassinates him in 1948. The Indian leader's tactics of nonviolent protest will have lasting impact, however, serving in particular as a prototype for the methods of American Civil Rights activists in the 1960s.

1947: Eleanor Roosevelt is appointed chair of the United
40 Nations new Human Rights organ. As the former wife of a president, one-time director of the NAACP, and an effective advocate of human rights interests at the United Nations, Roosevelt will remain one of the most influential and powerful women in the world until her death in 1962.

CONTEMPORARY PHILOSOPHIES

EXISTENTIALISM

In 20th-century Europe, thinkers must create a personal sense of meaning

In the 20th century, Western philosophy finally reached the inevitable conclusions of its cultural heritage. The mechanical view of the universe, which had driven God from the center of Western consciousness, was displaced by the fragmented, subjective physics of Albert Einstein. In this cultural context, the search for universal truth or order, long the focus of Latin philosophy, seemed increasingly irrelevant to European thinkers. Under siege since the time of Descartes, the quest for objective truth and understanding was all but abandoned. In the wake of this gradual collapse, new philosophies concerned themselves with the task of constructing meaning in what was an apparently arbitrary state of being. One of the most characteristic of these new systems of thought was existentialism.

Finding its first voice in the 19th-century Danish philosopher Søren Kierkegaard, existentialism attained wide public attention through the 20th-century writings of men such as France's Jean-Paul Sartre. Typically, existential writers think in relative, rather than absolute, terms. They contend that people are made by the circumstances and conditions in which they find themselves, and that they possess no overall nature or destiny beyond what they construct for themselves. To the existentialist, meaning and value are individual choices, not absolute principles dictated by a higher law or some greater authority.

Both Kierkegaard and Sartre felt that one has the right and the responsibility to choose and create—passionately—one's own subjective values. Since any kind of objective truth is either non-existent or unknowable, one has the freedom to define one's own arbitrary boundaries as best as one can. We must make our own world for ourselves within the context in which we are placed. Both thinkers also felt, however, that most individuals find this enormous opportunity to be an overwhelming responsibility, a duty from which the majority of us balk. Instead, most people defer to arbitrary, outside authorities to avoid the difficult obligation of self-definition. To the existentialist, this need for an external order constitutes a tragic evasion of what may be viewed as a wonderful opportunity to create one's own world.

In a 20th-century environment in which the comforting absolutes of God, space, and time have been vanquished from popular experience and belief, existentialism seeks to generate value out of the subjective reality that remains. Alone in our own experience of reality, each of us must draw our individual limits and values because that is all we have. More excited than afraid, the existentialist takes the place of God, who is no longer present, defining his or her existence as personal creative desire dictates.

1948: **The State of Israel is established by force** as the British withdraw from Palestine. In the 15 years before World War II, more than 300,000 Jews migrated to Palestine, establishing a strong ethnic minority within the predominantly Arab region. In 1947, when British colonial authorities, unable to resolve growing tensions between the Arabs and the Jews, evacuated the region, the United Nations approved partitioning of Palestine into Jewish and Arab states. On May 14, 1948, Israel is proclaimed a state and is immediately attacked by Lebanon, Jordan, Egypt, Syria, and Iraq. The Israelis repulsed poorly organized Arab attacks, and a ceasefire is declared in July 1948.

1948: **The governments of Brazil and China lead the way** in the establishment of the World Health Organization. Modeled on various national agencies extending as far back as 1907, the new international organization will prove instrumental in eradicating diseases such as smallpox through global immunization programs.

1949: **Chinese Communist Party Chairman Mao Tse-tung** declares the founding of the People's Republic of China. Concerned about Western presence in nearby Korea and Japan, the new government will align itself with its longtime supporter, the Soviet Union. Aided by Russian material and money, Mao will consolidate his domestic power and establish a de facto autocracy in China.

1950s: **Drive-in movie theatres combine two American passions: car culture and cinema.** Along with drive-in restaurants, the new theatres suggest that cars are supplanting the need for architecture in American culture. Isolated in their cars while eating or watching a film, Americans are separated from one another more than ever before.

1950s: **Movie stars such as Frank Sinatra and Marilyn**

in American households. With broadcasts sent across the entire nation, television networks will produce a common social experience that will help solidify and homogenize the American national experience. As more and more families acquire televisions, they will be able to see national sporting events and presidential speeches as they happen, without leaving their homes. As the broadcast of these actual events is increasingly mixed with fictional drama and comedy programs or time-delayed footage, television will begin to blur the boundaries between reality and fantasy, presenting both in the same black-and-white screen format.

1950s: **The teenager begins to emerge as a modern social phenomenon.** As more and more American adolescents are allowed to complete high school or even go to college instead of immediately entering the work force, they begin to establish their own culture between childhood and adult maturity. Uncertain of their identities, defined by increasing appetites that are not always checked by increasing responsibilities, teenagers often will construct lifestyles of experimentation, risk-taking, and rebellion against parental authority as they attempt to ground themselves as individuals within a larger context.

1950: **North Korean forces pour over the South Korean** border, igniting the Korean War. A United Nations military coalition, led by the United States, arrives to aid the beleaguered South Koreans just as their complete defeat seems inevitable. Alarmed by the presence of U.N. forces at its borders and the sudden change of fortune for its fellow communists in North Korea, China quickly enters the fray against the U.N. troops. A bloody, inconclusive war ensues for the next three years.

1950: **The first credit card is introduced for use at multiple vendors.** Although retailers had been issuing cards to customers for use at their stores since the 1920s, these

up getting their news from Cronkite; in time he will be called "the most trusted man in America." In some ways a major pop icon, Cronkite will guide Americans through the turbulent political, social, and technological transformations of the 1960s and '70s.

1952: **Swiss architect Le Corbusier's design for the Catholic chapel Notre-Dame du Haut** is constructed in France. An assembly of bulging, curved forms, the biomorphic design is finished in rough, textured concrete. A far cry from Le Corbusier's machine-inspired designs of the 1920s and '30s, the new chapel is designed with an intentionally crude, primitive feel. Deeply impressed by the technological horrors of World War II, many leading post-war architects abandon their enthusiasm for modern industrial progress, choosing instead to explore rougher, more naturalistic forms and symbols.

1953: **Open fighting ends in Korea.** Having satisfied the need to flex military muscle, the United States and China let the conflict expire, essentially restoring the divided Korea to its 1950 status. Strong deployments of U.S. troops will remain in Korea, however, guarding the heavily armed border throughout the rest of the century.

1953: **New Zealand native Edmund Hillary** and Nepalese companion Sherpa Tenzing Norgay lead the first successful expedition to the peak of Mount Everest.

1954: **The first nuclear submarine,** the U.S.S. Nautilus, sets underwater speed records during its first voyage. The sub will become the first vessel to sail beneath the northern polar icecap in 1958. An enormous accomplishment, the Nautilus is one of the first tangible proofs that nuclear technology can be used in nondestructive applications. In 1975, the first nuclear aircraft carrier, the U.S.S. Nimitz, will be launched with the ability to run without refueling for 15 years.

> ## "The hunger for love is much more difficult to remove than the hunger for bread"
>
> MOTHER TERESA

Monroe dominate American pop culture. As Sinatra's domination of American music slips before the new rock-and-roll style of performers like Elvis Presley, he reinvents himself as a film star in pictures such as 1953's "From Here to Eternity." Monroe, unable to handle the stress of her newfound stardom, will die from a drug overdose in the early 1960s.

1950s: **The advent of American rock-and-roll transforms world music.** Growing out of American country and blues idioms, the new music is typified by predictable chord progressions, catchy melodies, and strong, easy rhythms, making it highly accessible to audiences turned off by the complexity of jazz or western classical music. Particularly popular with American youth, the new music will help define the character of America's first post-World War II generation.

1950s: **The television set** becomes increasingly pervasive

new cards are issued by a third party. Throughout the rest of the century, reliance on personal credit, checks, and electronic transfer for financial transactions will begin to reduce the role of hard cash in modern economies throughout the world.

1950: **American painter Jackson Pollock** finishes "One," his first composition rendered without the use of a brush. Dripping paint from cans that he swings over the canvas in arm-length strokes, Pollock eschews representational subject matter for energy and movement. An unrestrained expression of the physical act of painting, "One" momentarily liberates Pollock from the representational and symbolic vocabulary of Western art.

1950: **American newsman Walter Cronkite** joins the CBS television network. America's first TV generation will grow

1954: **English medical student Roger Bannister runs the first sub-four-minute mile** at an Oxford track and field meet. Long thought a physical impossibility, Bannister's time of 3:59.4, achieved despite a strong crosswind, marks a new milestone in human athletic achievement.

1955: **China declares its first five-year plan** for social and economic reform. Heavily supported by Russian aid, the new program is able to stimulate large-scale industrial growth. Government ownership of industry is established, and private farming gradually is abolished in favor of 20- to 30-family agricultural collectives. By 1956, 88 percent of all Chinese farmers work in the new communes.

1955: **American doctor Jonas Salk** completes human trials for his new polio vaccine. Having determined that the vaccine is effective, Salk offers it as a gift to humanity, refusing to take out a patent on his work. Later in life, Salk will do extensive research into a possible vaccination against AIDS until his death in 1995.

1956: **The application of the transistor revolutionizes computer design.** Combined with John von Neumann's 1946 creation of the central processing unit, the transistor makes the development of small, inexpensive, powerful, and flexible computers an increasingly likely reality. Freed from bulky

(47)

1960s: **The ever-expanding importance of automobiles** begins to destroy the vitality of American urban centers. Ironically, cities like Detroit, which prosper economically through a growing automobile industry, simultaneously experience urban decline as their populations move to car-based suburbs and their public spaces are fragmented or destroyed by highways and overpasses. By the late 1970s, Detroit, once one of the most vibrant cities in America, will be a largely abandoned ruin of unprecedented scale.

1963: **American President John F. Kennedy is assassinated in Dallas, Texas.** Kennedy's tragic death lifts a presidency marked by scandalous behavior and uncertain political accomplishments to an almost mythical status. Most Americans will remember Kennedy's handsome face and World War II heroics when they think of the young president, associating his death with the end of a magical period that preceded the social and political chaos of the Vietnam era.

(53)

"I have always thought that each version of a story is better than the one before. How does one know, then, which is the final version?"

GABRIEL GARCÍA MÁRQUEZ

vacuum tubes and storage drums, computer designers quickly will head down the path to the development of the portable computer.

1957: **Soviet scientists and engineers successfully launch Sputnik I,** the first man-made object to orbit the Earth. Immediately grasping the military potential of spy satellites and extraterrestrial weapons platforms, both the United States and the Soviet Union embark on aggressive, expensive space programs. For many years, the Russians will be the leading pioneers, sending the first man into space in the early 1960s.

(48)

1958: **Hula Hoop mania strikes American youth.** More than 100 million of the new toys, made by Wham-O and sold at $1.98 each, are purchased in the first year of production.

1959: **Communist guerillas under Fidel Castro** finally succeed in overthrowing the Cuban government of Fulgencio Batista y Zaldívar. Allied with the Soviet Union, the new Castro regime will actively support Marxist revolutionaries throughout Central America and in Angola at various times throughout the rest of the century. Politically cut off from Europe and the United States, however, Castro-led Cuba will experience enormous economic depression after the collapse of the Soviet Union in the early 1990s.

1959: **Monkeys Abel and Baker become the first astronauts** in the United States space program. Sent into space in the nose of a Jupiter missile, the monkeys provide American engineers with the data they need to send humans safely out of the Earth's atmosphere.

(49)

1959: **The Guggenheim Museum,** designed by American architect Frank Lloyd Wright, is completed in New York City. Described as a "giant washing machine on Fifth Avenue," the circular building exemplifies a continuing boldness in architectural design as well as an alarming willingness to subordinate basic issues of function and program to the formal vision of the architect. The museum exhibits the work of contemporary artists and continues to do so.

(50)

1960s: **Global marketing offers diverse** geographical regions more standardized foods and beverages. By the end of the century, quickly prepared meat and potato products, soft drinks, and bottled waters will influence day-to-day life in various cultures.

1960s: **Disposable products and packaging begin to crowd American landfills.** American consumer culture reaches its height with one-time-use disposable commodities like diapers and food wrappers, allowing shoppers to use a brand-new, never-touched product every single time. Made from inexpensive materials that do not readily decompose, the disposable products rapidly become a major environmental concern.

(51)

1960s: **The introduction of the birth control pill** revolutionizes contraception and interweaves with changing social values, radically altering sexual behavior and practice throughout the Western world. The effectiveness of the pill in preventing pregnancy, combined with wide-scale public awareness of its use, allows women a newfound sexual freedom and greater control over their own lives. Unfortunately, the pill provides no protection against sexually transmitted disease; with the coming of AIDS in the late 1970s, the centuries-old condom will return as a prophylactic of choice.

(52)

1962: **American naval vessels impose a blockade on communist Cuba** when it is discovered that Russian missile platforms are being installed on the island. With tensions already high from the recent erection of the Berlin Wall, the blockade marks the most intense moment of direct confrontation during the Cold War. Initially threatening to run the blockade, the Soviets eventually back down and remove the Cuban installations in return for an American nuclear withdrawal from Turkey.

1962: **Astronaut John Glenn becomes the first American to orbit the Earth.** A combat pilot in World War II and the Korean War before joining NASA, Glenn will go on to a career as a U.S. senator. In 1998, he will return to space on a shuttle as the oldest man ever to leave the Earth's atmosphere.

1963: **Soviet cosmonaut Valentina Tereshkova** becomes the first woman to enter space. Alone on her three-day orbit of the planet, Tereshkova will precede the first American woman in space, Sally Ride, by 20 years.

1964: **American combat advisors are replaced with regular troops** as the United States becomes deeply embroiled in Vietnam. Attempting to uphold a succession of unpopular anti-Marxist governments in South Vietnam, the U.S. government will commit hundreds of thousands of men to fight communist guerillas and North Vietnamese soldiers.

(54)

1964: **Political buttons** endorsing candidates for president are a popular form of election campaigning.

1966: **Mao Tse-tung announces the Cultural Revolution in China.** Fearing the loss of revolutionary zeal in Russia will occur in his own country, Chairman Mao attempts to impart the radical spirit to the next generation of Chinese citizens. Many established Communist Party and government institutions are declared corrupt and are replaced with new structures; high-ranking cultural ministers are removed from office. Physical and mental labor are given equal value—the privileging of intellectual work being declared bourgeois—and scores of intellectuals are legally persecuted, beaten, or killed. The military is granted administrative power over cultural affairs, and even more power is concentrated in Mao's hands. An almost religious cult of the chairman spreads among Chinese youth.

1966: **American doctor Michael De Bakey surgically installs the first functional artificial heart.** Designer of the military mobile hospital system (MASH) during World War II and a future pioneer in heart transplants, Debakey is one of the most successful medical pioneers of the 20th century. With devices like the mechanical heart and sophisticated prosthetic limbs, modern technology begins not only to reshape the human world but humans themselves.

1967: **The Six-Day War reaffirms Israeli strength in the Middle East.** Sensing growing Arab aggression from Egypt,

Syria, and Jordan, Israeli leaders authorize a preemptive strike. Egypt's air force is destroyed, Jordan loses control of the west bank of the Jordan River, and Syria is driven out of the Golan Heights. Syria and Egypt briefly resume hostilities with Israel in 1973, but with largely inconclusive results that persuade Egyptian leaders to seek long-term diplomatic solutions to their conflict with the Jewish state.

1967: **The Beatles,** England's most popular pop-music band, records "Sgt. Pepper's Lonely Hearts Club Band." With the indispensable aid of their technical producer, George Martin, the Liverpool musicians are able to lend musical legitimacy to modern rock through the diverse textures and complex structures of their later albums.

1968: **African-American civil rights leader Martin Luther King Jr. is murdered in Memphis, Tennessee.** A key force in the passage of the 1965 Civil Rights Act, King called for non-violent protest against racial inequality and brought real change to America's social structure. While his assassination by a white supremacist is a great loss to the nation, the impact of his message of racial harmony, characterized by the famous "I Have a Dream" speech, is irreversible.

(55)

1968: **Richard Nixon is elected president of the United States.** With advisor Henry Kissinger, Nixon will form one of the most competent and effective foreign-policy teams in American history, extracting U.S. troops from a losing war in Vietnam and restoring diplomatic relations with China. A man of dubious character, Nixon also will be the

American space program beats its Russian competitors to a major milestone. Of mostly symbolic value, the trip to the moon is a source of immense national pride.

1969: **American alternative culture, 500,000 people strong, descends on the Woodstock Music and Arts Festival in Bethel, New York.** Although plagued by inadequate facilities for food and plumbing, inhospitable weather, and a series of musical acts too stoned to play with competency, Woodstock becomes a symbol of peaceful coexistence and happiness for many Americans. In time, another free concert turns violent in California, and the culture of drug addiction, physical filth, and truncated education that arises in San Francisco will tarnish the image of American counter-culture. In 1969, however, Woodstock serves for many as hope for a better world.

1970s: **Western doctors and researchers begin to identify the AIDS virus.** During the 1980s, the fatal, incurable disease will spread across the globe with alarming speed, infecting as many as one of every 10 people in some African nations. Although growing public awareness and education will help slow the spread of the sexually transmitted disease, and various treatments will help slow the deterioration and suffering of AIDS victims, an actual vaccine or cure for the viral infection will remain elusive throughout the rest of the century.

(58)

1973: **Skylab, the first American space station, is launched into orbit.** Over six years, three consecutive

Egypt signals a break in the united Arab front against Israel. While other neighboring Arab governments gradually come to terms with Israel, little concern is given to the agenda of the Palestinian guerillas displaced from their ancestral home by the Israelis. Continued violence, particularly in Lebanon, will continue throughout the next decade as Israeli forces attempt to exterminate Palestinian nationalist organizations that threaten Jewish security.

1979: **Religious leader Ayatollah Khomeini becomes the de facto ruler of Iran.** Iran's experiment with secular government under the Pahlavi family has ultimately proved unsuccessful, and revolutionary forces under the Ayatollah return Persian culture to its religious fundamentalist past. During his decade of rule, Khomeini continually will denounce Western influence, lead Iran in a bloody, inconclusive war with the secular government of neighboring Iraq, and restore traditional Muslim laws, customs, and mores to Iranian culture.

1980s: **Increasing concern with issues of health and wellness redefine American culture.** As accumulating evidence begins to convince the nation's population that smoking and overeating are cutting substantially into their expected life span, many Americans move to change their lifestyles and habits. The use of tobacco products drops, exercise routines and vitamin regimens become popular, and diets improve as people seek always to appear—if not to actually be—healthy.

1980: **Former film star Ronald Reagan is elected the 40th President of the United States.** "Reaganomics," the policy

(59)

> ## "Liberty means responsibility. That is why most men dread it"
>
> GEORGE BERNARD SHAW

first president forced to resign, driven from office for illegal activities conducted during the 1972 presidential election campaign.

1968: **Colombian author Gabriel García Márquez starts the magic-realism literary movement** with his new book "One Hundred Years of Solitude." Awarded the Nobel Prize for Literature in 1982, Marquez is regarded by many as one of the finest novelists of the 20th century. His ability to make the ordinary strange and the bizarre familiar captures the essence of great fiction writing.

(56)

1969: **Chinese and Soviet forces engage in fierce skirmishing along the Sino-Russian border.** Indecisive in itself, the fighting illustrates a growing rift between the two nations. Under reforms largely initiated by Kruschev, the Soviet Union has adopted a more socialist political system, relaxing the extreme policies typical under Stalin. In contrast, the Cultural Revolution in China attempts to reinforce radical communist doctrine. The 1969 border conflicts largely reflect this increasing ideological separation between the governments of the two nations.

1969: **American astronauts under Neil Armstrong successfully return from a landing on the moon.** An enormous feat, the lunar mission is the first time that the

(57)

three-man crews will overcome various technical problems to prove man can live in space for extended periods. In the meantime, the teams conduct more than 300 scientific experiments. A decaying orbit will force the station to be decommissioned in 1979, and that same year it will disintegrate over the Indian Ocean and western Australia.

1976: **Mao Tse-tung dies, effectively ending the Cultural Revolution in China.** A purging of radical elements within the government and announced reforms officially terminate the program the following year. Under Deng Xiaoping, the new government reopens many coastal regions to international trade and investment, stimulates industry, restores private enterprise and property, and reintroduces wage incentives to increase productivity.

1978: **Polish Archbishop of Krakow Karol Wojtyla is elected Pope John Paul II.** The first non-Italian elected pope since 1523, John Paul II will continue to endorse the strictly conservative brand of Catholicism he promoted as an archbishop. Taking full advantage of modern transportation technology, he will become the most traveled pope in history, visiting hundreds of nations as he leads Catholicism's charge to resist modern social change.

1979: **The Camp David Agreement between Israel and**

of increasing spending while reducing taxes, will drive America to the brink of economic ruin, but it serves as part of a larger foreign policy that is ultimately more successful. Greatly increasing defense spending, Reagan's administration forces the financially less secure Soviet Union to follow suit. When the Warsaw Pact collapses in the early 1990s, it will in part be due to Soviet economic insolvency brought on by efforts to match Reagan's extreme military commitment.

1981: **Sandra Day O'Connor becomes the first woman to be appointed Justice of the United States Supreme Court.** Selected by President Reagan, O'Connor pursues a predictably conservative agenda in her legal interpretations, making her a pivotal figure in the 1980s Republican mission to reverse landmark liberal rulings from the 1960s.

(60)

1981: **Lady Diana Spencer is married to Charles, Prince of Wales.** An instant pop icon, Diana will be a source of great shame to the House of Windsor when incompatibility with her husband and mutual infidelity lead to her divorce from Charles in 1996. Her accidental death in 1997 is mourned by millions throughout the world.

1984: **Future sports legend Michael Jordan** becomes a professional basketball player for the Chicago Bulls. Cut from his high school team one year, Jordan will become one of the most dominant athletes in modern history. Before his retirement from the game in 1998, Jordan will guide his team to six National Basketball Association (NBA) championships, earn five NBA Most Valuable Player awards, and average 31.5 points per game. His almost unbelievable athletic accomplishments will make him an international personality and spread the popularity of basketball around the globe.

1985: (61) **Mikhail Gorbachev, recently named general secretary of the Communist Party** in the Soviet Union, leads his nation in a series of reforms known as "perestroika." Gorbachev's economic policies, based on introducing more capitalism and free-market environments into the Soviet economy, essentially fail in their effort to raise the Russian standard of living. The social turmoil and transformation they produce, however, will prove instrumental in the collapse of the Soviet Union and the restructuring of Russian government.

1987: (62) **The Intermediate-range Nuclear Forces Treaty bans the use of missiles** like the American Pershing II and the Soviet SS-20. Seeking to alleviate the enormous political and economic strain of maintaining vast nuclear arsenals, the two superpowers agree to eliminate all their medium-range nuclear weapons by 1991.

1989: (63) **Anti-communist revolutions in Eastern Europe** and the dismantling of the Berlin Wall signal the collapse of the Soviet system. Financially exhausted by 40 years of military posturing, the Soviet Union has been led through a series of economic, social, and political reforms by Mikhail Gorbachev. When Soviet leadership indicates that part of this new approach involves non-interference in Eastern Europe, unpopular puppet governments are overthrown in Poland, Czechoslovakia, and Romania. Germany is reunited under West Germany's government. In 1991, the Soviet Union itself dissolves into a series of loosely confederated states, and a new republican government is established in Russia under Boris Yeltsin.

1990s: (64) **Powerful, portable electronic technology,** including beepers, wireless phones, and laptop computers, become increasingly popular and affordable across the globe. Much of the world's workforce finds itself permanently in touch, and consequently never away from work. The laptop, no larger than a small briefcase and requiring minimal electrical power, is an incredible advancement over the room-size, vacuum-tube computers that preceded it by less than 50 years. Equally dramatic progress in telecommunications synchronizes hemispheres.

1990s: (65) **The mapping of the human genome nears completion.** As the next century approaches, the possibility of gene therapy, gene testing, and genetic engineering is an ever more likely reality. But as the frontiers of medical technology expand, difficult ethical questions are raised. For many, the excitement of eliminating birth defects or treating genetic diseases is counterbalanced by apprehension about controlling physical appearance or including genetic data in job applications, for example.

1990: **South African political activist Nelson Mandela is released from prison after 27 years in confinement.** A sign that oligarchic control of the nation by a white minority is crumbling, Mandela's release symbolizes the beginning of the end of racial inequality in South Africa. Elected president in 1994, Mandela will surprise many by instituting a policy of forgiveness toward the former apartheid government and a general platform of tolerance among South Africa's many tribal and ethnic populations.

1996: (66) **American President William Jefferson Clinton is reelected to office.** In 1999, he will become the second American president to be impeached by the House of Representatives; but insufficient votes will be gathered in the Senate to remove him from office, and the president's administration will continue to oversee the longest period of steady economic growth in the history of the United States.

1997: (67) **Scottish scientists Ian Wilmut and Alan Coleman** successfully clone a sheep from cells obtained from a mammary gland. The exact replica sheep, Dolly, reveals the growing power of modern biologists and doctors as they begin to master the genetic sciences. A profound scientific achievement, Dolly also provokes serious debate about the potential moral dangers of cloning and genetic engineering.

1997: **With the expiration of its lease, British Hong Kong reverts to Chinese control.** Extorted from the Chinese during their worst period of 19th-century weakness, the island has developed into a vital economic center under British control. Appreciating its financial strength, the communist government of China chooses to minimize its interference with the region's capitalist practices, adopting the policy phrase "one nation, two systems."

1998: (68) **"Y2K" concerns begin to grip many computer users** throughout the industrial world. With the realization that a design flaw may cause many computer systems to fail on January 1, 2000, computer specialists and owners begin to scramble in an attempt to remedy the problem. The fear that everything from toasters to bank accounts to air traffic control may be affected reveals the extent to which computerization has integrated itself into modern life.

1999: (69) **Ten continental European nations and Ireland adopt the Euro** as their common standard currency. Although the actual coins and paper money will not be distributed for three more years, the Euro becomes the benchmark for all electronic transactions in the eleven states. The adoption of a common currency is seen by many as the first crucial step in the establishment of a western European political confederation.

BIBLIOGRAPHY AND FURTHER READING:

Adams, Laurie Schneider. Art Across Time: Vol. 2, McGraw-Hill College, Chicago, 1999, pp. 818-944.

Joel Colton and R.R. Palmer. A History of the Modern World, 5th ed., Alfred A. Knopf, New York, 1978, pp. 654-945.

Horst de la Croix and Richard Tansey. Gardner's Art Through the Ages, 8th ed., Harcourt Brace Jovanovich, New York, 1986, pp. 886-975.

Goetz, Philip W., ed. The Encyclopedia Britannica 5th ed., Encyclopedia Britannica, Inc., Chicago, 1990.

Chandice L. Goucher, Charles A. LeGuin, and Linda A. Walton. In the Balance: Themes in Global History, Vol. 2, McGraw-Hill, Boston, 1998, pp. 784-945.

Grun, Bernard. The Timetables of History, Simon and Schuster, New York, 1979, pp. 453-591.

Hall, Donald E. "Albert Einstein" Great Thinkers of the Western World, HarperCollins Publishers, New York, 1992, pp. 478-482.

Hanes III, William Travis, editor. World History: Continuity and Change, Holt, Rinehart, and Winston, Austin, TX, 1997, pp. 594-851.

Janson, H.W. History of Western Art, 3rd ed., Prentice Hall Abrams, Englewood Cliffs, NJ, 1986, pp. 666-791.

Moss, M.E. "Sigmund Freud," Great Thinkers of the Western World, HarperCollins Publishers, New York, 1992, pp. 414-419.

Roth, John K. "Jean-Paul Sartre," Great Thinkers of the Western World, HarperCollins Publishers, New York, 1992, pp. 541-544.

Sattler, Gary R. "Carl Gustav Jung," Great Thinkers of the Western World, HarperCollins Publishers, New York, 1992, pp. 469-473.

Stiver, Dan R. "Martin Heidegger," Great Thinkers of the Western World, HarperCollins Publishers, New York, 1992, pp. 519-523.

ON EXISTENTIALISM
Roth, John K. "Jean-Paul Sartre," Great Thinkers of the Western World, HarperCollins Publishers, New York, 1992, pp. 541-544.

ACKNOWLEDGMENTS

At the time of the American Bicentennial, Joanne Slater, a New York-based developer of fine giftware and commemoratives, decided that there needed to be a sophisticated art piece to symbolize 10 centuries of human endeavor. The work was not intended to be a contemporary interpretation, but rather one comprised purely of archival art. The authenticity of the visuals would better enable the viewer to imagine the historical milestones that have led up to the conclusion of the 20th century and the second millennium. The work would arouse the curiosity of all who might come in contact with it and bring the images to life as they might have appeared in their own era.

Since early 1997 Patrice Gillespie, a marketing consultant, has been developing a broad spectrum of products incorporating what would become the Millennium Time Tapestry.™ Mimi Van Swall, an educator and artist, has managed the archival research and curated an extensive collection of images. Artist and sculptor Liz Bailey created the digital artwork from the images selected. She also designed the entire product collection and created the illustrations for this book. Fortunately, computer technology made a timely leap forward, allowing her better to manipulate, layer and compose the work. Thus the Millennium Time Tapestry™ came to be.

It was soon apparent that the digital tapestry was in fact an educational tool that deserved a matching book. Matthew Hurff, a lifelong scholar of history and an accomplished architect, wrote the thought-provoking text. The Millennium Time Tapestry™ image itself, Matthew Hurff's worthy book, and other companion products provide an inviting set of keys that open doors to the past and to a more enlightened future.

We heartily thank Joseph "Jay" Vissers and Joe Gschwind for their steady guidance and exceptional talents. We are grateful to publisher Harvey Rubin and his fine staff at Pindar Press, especially Izabella A. Jaskierny, Joe Guise, Cathy Sylvis, and Geoff Graser.

The following persons and organizations were essential in producing the Time Tapestry collection: Donald Bailey; Benjamin Barnes; Chris Berry; Leigh Berry; Melissa Bliven; Everett Bootzin; Martha Phillips Bootzin; Cowan, DeBaets, Abrahams & Sheppard, LLP, New York; Audrey and F. Michael Donohue, Jr.; Nancy Doyle; Fitz and Floyd, Lewisville, TX; Adair Garis; Tim Gelling; Cliff Giles; Dick Gillespie; The Great American Puzzle Factory, Norwalk, CT; Diane Hibbert; Betty Hodas; Tom Iampietro; Image Works, Westport, CT; Robyn Inserillo; Kathleen Kennedy; Lady Clare Limited, Lutterworth, England; Dave Link; Cathy Manning; Mantero, NYC and Como, Italy; Lauren McGee; Miller Johnson, Meridan, CT; Val Monasterio; Ray Nelson; The New York Public Library; Guy Ortoleva; Perman & Green, LLP, Fairfield, CT; Sharon Pleasant; Tod Pleasant; Projects Viscom, Wilton, CT; Karen Ronald and the Wilton Library, Wilton, CT; Mary Saccary; Saddle River Day School, Saddle River, NJ; Irma Serafini; Joe Simeone; Stoneleigh-Burnham School, Greenfield, MA; Three Wishes, Westport, CT; Kevan Vanek; Dan Verdery; Janice Weeks; Maurice E. Williams.

TIME TAPESTRIES, LLC
Wilton, Connecticut

For more information about Time Tapestry designs, call 888-324-3623, or visit our website at www.timetapestries.com

CREDITS

The authors wish to thank the many individuals and organizations that have provided images from their libraries and media resources. Every effort has been made to trace and credit the copyright owners of the images depicted here. If it is brought to our attention that any rights have been inadvertently infringed upon or an image was improperly credited, we apologize and promise to include the correct attribution in the next edition. In particular, the authors wish to acknowledge or credit the following sources:

20TH CENTURY

20-1   Courtesy of Anna Foster
20-5   Courtesy of Kristin & John Foster
20-7   Olympics logo is a registered trademark of the I.O.C.
20-15   Courtesy of Victoria Charlton
20-23   Emile Blanche, Courtesy of the National Portrait Gallery, London
20-24   Courtesy of Lee Boltin, Boltin Picture Library
20-26   Courtesy of Anne & Jim Kellett
20-28   Milton Brooks, Courtesy of The Detroit News Archives
20-32   Courtesy of FDR Library
20-33   Courtesy of United States Holocaust Memorial Museum
20-36   Courtesy of Eisenhower Library
20-37   Courtesy of Jenny Koella
20-38   Courtesy of H. Armstrong Roberts, Inc.
20-40   Courtesy of FDR Library
20-41   Courtesy Ford Motor Company; Courtesy of H. Armstrong Roberts, Inc.
20-43   Courtesy of H. Armstrong Roberts, Inc.
20-49   Courtesy of U.S. Space & Rocket Center
20-56   Courtesy of H.W. Wilson
20-59   Courtesy of Ronald Reagan Library
20-60   Courtesy of The Stoneleigh-Burnham School
20-65   Courtesy of P.E. Biosystems and J. Glickman Designs

19TH CENTURY

19-19   Courtesy of Mastergraph
19-30   Logo of America's Cup
19-50   Courtesy of H. Armstrong Roberts, Inc.
19-59   Courtesy of Illustrated London News
19-60   Courtesy of Robert O. King

18TH CENTURY

18-8   From the collection of the Geography and Map Division, Library of Congress
18-24   Courtesy of Editions D'Art, Geneva

17TH CENTURY

17-2   Courtesy of Illustrated London News
17-5   Courtesy of Illustrated London News
17-7   Courtesy of Illustrated London News
17-24   Courtesy of Gayle Agee

14TH CENTURY

14-1   Courtesy of Hungarian National Tourist Office
14-9   Courtesy of Giovanni et Muriel DAGLI ORTI
14-10   Courtesy of Illustrated London News
14-12   Courtesy of Christie's Images, LTD. 1999

The Estate of Dr. Martin Luther King Jr.

Image of early chronometer, Courtesy of Ed Radlauer

Images of Costumes Through The Ages, Courtesy of Dover Publications, Inc.

Navigation and Wind Forces by R. Ottens, from the collection of the Geography and Map Division, Library of Congress